Urban
Dreams

Rural
Realities

Urban Dreams

Rural Realities

*One couple's pursuit
of the Good Life*

Daniel Butler & Bel Crewe

POCKET
B O O K S

LONDON · SYDNEY · NEW YORK · TOKYO · SINGAPORE · TORONTO

First published in Great Britain by Simon & Schuster UK
Ltd,1998
This edition first published by Pocket Books, 1999
An imprint of Simon & Schuster UK Ltd
A Viacom Company

3 5 7 9 10 8 6 4 2

Simon & Schuster UK Ltd
Africa House
64-78 Kingsway
London WC2B 6AH

Simon & Schuster Australia
Sydney

A CIP catalogue record for this book is available from the
British Library

ISBN 0-671-01580-X

Printed and bound in Great Britain by
Omnia Books Ltd, Glasgow

To Jack and Molly

Introduction:
Dan

It was raining the day we moved in and the farmyard was ankle-deep with icy sludge, but nothing could daunt my spirits. Although city-reared, I had drooled at the thought of a wild and windswept life for as long as I could remember. Now, after years of stifled urban life, my dreams of pastoral bliss were becoming a reality.

I suppose I was born with the yearning, but it began to take concrete form on my eleventh birthday when I was given two books which were to revolutionise my world: T. H. White's *The Goshawk* and *Self-Sufficiency* by John Seymour. For the next seven years they were to work on me like the intellectual equivalent of Creutzfeld-Jacob Disease, eating away at thoughts of conventional lifestyles and employment. I became obsessed with the idea of providing all my own food, surrounded by nature and removed from the noise and pollution of modern life.

In practice, of course, I found myself slipping down the very paths I longed to leave behind: exams were followed by more exams, then university, a job and a small Islington flat. This last was as far removed from the open fields as it is possible to get and my thoughts continually strayed to the countryside. They became more focused when the magazine on which I worked unexpectedly 'rationalised' me and I found myself propelled suddenly into the world of freelancing. In possession of a large redundancy cheque, I decided to celebrate by treating myself to a few luxuries.

These came in living form. I already shared my flat with a nondescript black mongrel, Dill, but now I had time for another pet. The flat being too small for a second dog, my thoughts turned quite naturally to ferrets, which I had once owned as a boy. Small and playful, a pair would make an interesting addition to my life. A few weeks later, when I visited my parents in Oxford, I noticed a litter being advertised in the local paper and thus acquired two jills: Mrs Peel and Purdy.

It was at this point too that I noticed my battered copy of *The Goshawk* and decided this would be the perfect opportunity to investigate falconry seriously. So, within a few weeks of taking on ferrets, I had added a large male red-tailed buzzard to the household.

Then I met Bel at a party. Tall, witty, with a job in public relations, unlike every other publicist I knew, she was disparaging about the value of everything she did. More importantly, she had an amazing ability to knock back a tequila slammer without so much as blinking. I was most impressed by this, but positively struck dumb by her encyclopaedic knowledge of the Lowland distilleries. We talked about gastronomy generally and got very drunk, and as we left the party, I must have invited her around for dinner – although the viciousness of the following day's hangover erased all memory of this.

Thus I was extremely surprised to find her standing on my doorstep the following week, bottle of malt in hand. My initial embarrassment was wiped out as Bel caught sight of Mrs Peel bouncing down the stairs. I had omitted to mention my menagerie during our first meeting, but far from expressing fear or disgust, Bel actually squeaked with excitement. She seemed positively intrigued by my household and this had a far more profound impact on me than almost anything else she could have done or said: I knew that at last I had found my soul-mate.

For the next six months we saw each other frequently, usually at my flat. This was because, much as I loved cooking and entertaining, virtually no one I knew was prepared to visit any more, thanks mainly to the ferrets' habit of scaling trouser legs without warning. At weekends we would frequently head for my parents' holiday cottage near Oxford where we spent the time eating, drinking, walking and reading.

It was during one of these breaks that I spotted a horse-drawn caravan parked on the roadside with a large sign advertising lurcher puppies. My flat had become distinctly crowded, but I had always wanted one of these and it occurred to me that Bel lived on her own. I convinced myself that she would welcome the gift of such a sweet creature – after all she seemed to have a natural affinity for my pets. So on the spur of the moment I reached into my pocket and handed over ten pounds: Bracken was now mine – or Bel's to be precise. I had reckoned without the leasehold system, however: after two weeks, Bel's neighbours complained and I found my household swollen by a second dog after all.

I could see the situation was getting slightly out of hand, but the last straw came when I noticed that Dill's waistline appeared to be growing rapidly. Though I had thought she was under constant supervision, something had clearly got where it shouldn't – and soon afterwards she produced seven wriggling little black balls beneath the stairs. My initial reaction was delight, but reality quickly sank in as Bel began making increasingly frequent remarks about hygiene and smells.

Soon, even I found life fairly unpleasant until inspiration struck. I decided to borrow my parents' cottage again

– this time for a fortnight – intending to return to London once the worst was over. It was a gloriously hot July and it didn't take much to persuade Bel to spend time idling in the Cotswolds.

For once holiday plans worked as they do only in dreams and travel agents' brochures. Perhaps if it had rained, if the wind had swept in and the temperature dropped, things would have worked out very differently, but luck was on our side. Not a cloud marred the sky, the temperatures stayed constantly high and the leaves hung limp on the trees for the whole fortnight. Given the generally idyllic conditions, it was not surprising that romance swirled around the house.

We would get up late, stagger outside on to the lawn to sip freshly pressed orange juice and stay there for the rest of the day, drowsily reading the papers or a book, or playing with the puppies or Mrs Peel and Purdy. Towards midday I would stagger to my feet, throw a handful of twigs on the barbecue and in no time a couple of chops would be charring away, while I knocked up a watercress and orange salad in the kitchen. We would eat it slowly, mopping up the bloody juices and sweet dressing with hunks of bread torn from a granary cob, as we gazed through the heat haze lifting off the hay meadows and corn fields which spread out in front of us.

Cold beer, chilled glasses of crisp Orvieto and strawberries marked out the passing of time in the afternoon and as the sun began to dip towards the horizon I would stir the embers of the fire into action again. The evening meal would be a slightly more formal affair than lunch – if only because we would sit at the table to eat – but was still conducted in the open air, while bats flitted back and forth above our heads and owls called across the pollen-laden dusk. In that heady, lazy atmosphere it was natural our conversation should dwell, time and again, on how wonderful it would be to live permanently in the country. I found myself painting word pictures out of the last two decades of slowly fermenting daydreams.

In spite of the glorious weather which enveloped us as I talked, the romantic in me composed a different scene. I had visions of tracking rabbits, hawk on fist, across snow-covered fields, and after long hours spent out in the open, of returning to the comfort of a farm kitchen, with its huge wooden table, to prepare a hearty stew with the results of the day's hunt. This would be consumed in front of a roaring pile of oak logs, before we curled up with a good novel in the armchairs in the study, glasses of whisky in hand and exhausted dogs sleeping on the hearthrug.

Bel joined in with gusto, but in her paradise it was always summer and she gently corrected my omission of the climbing rose and the flower beds thick with the purples, reds and blues of lush bedding plants. Indeed, in many ways she was more enthusiastic than myself, being particularly struck by the thought of ducks waddling around the house: "I like ducks," she would say as we lay back on our garden loungers, staring up at the stars and moon. "I like the way they waddle. I would like a dozen of them. I'd call them all Jemima." I smiled indulgently, adding them to my growing mental check list.

At the end of our blissful fortnight, I found I could not face the thought of returning to London. As Bel packed I announced suddenly that I needed to stay in Oxfordshire for another couple of weeks to find homes for the puppies. This proved to be a serious miscalculation as getting rid of them proved stubbornly difficult, but given the surroundings, it was no major hardship. The weeks rolled by and the puppies found homes – all but one which I decided to keep. She followed her mother's habits and I named her Havoc.

If I did not have total control over my domestic

arrangements, it was countered, to my surprise, by the discovery that finding work and writing articles was easier in the countryside than in the hustle and bustle of London and thus I inevitably began to think seriously of turning my daydreams into reality. My plans received an unexpected shunt forward when Bel arrived out of the blue at the front door. It appeared that the romance of our summer holiday was bearing fruit: she was, in her own words, well and truly 'up the duff'. Although this state of affairs was not entirely accidental, the process had certainly taken less time than we had anticipated and Bel was in a mild state of shock.

If she was unsure how to adjust to her condition, my reaction was total delight. Here was the last element to add to my daydreams of long hunts crunching through fresh snow after rabbits. I would be the perfect father and teach my son (I was immediately convinced it was a boy) how to live off the land. I would give him his first ferret when he was five and his first dog when he was eight. For the time being I could not decide when he would get his first hawk, but that could wait.

For now the most important thing was to be as supportive as possible. That night we stayed up for hours, talking through the options, but I could see there was only one sensible course of action. When Bel started talking about setting up home back in London, I pointed out the cost of housing, the dangers of traffic and paedophiles and the problems of inner city schools.

Bel took my point and we began making a few tentative inquiries about property in the surrounding villages. Prices were way beyond our limited means, but by this stage my imagination was galloping off. The Cotswolds were all very well, I thought, but they were a little . . . well, tame really. I wanted something wilder and more romantic – a place where I could rely on at least a couple of decent snowfalls each winter. I wanted a view where peregrines circled over cliffs and waterfalls, where goshawks flitted through oak forests and merlins cavorted across heather moors. Within a couple of days my sights became firmly set on Wales.

All the same, I anticipated a degree of resistance from Bel, so I introduced my idea gently by taking her on day trips westwards. We began with Gloucestershire and watched prices slide slowly downwards with every mile we put between ourselves and London. By the time we got to the Forest of Dean, attractive cottages were actually within our grasp, but I was mentally committed to the idea of a smallholding – although I had yet to tell Bel just how committed. Fortunately for me, her normally sharp instincts were dulled by approaching motherhood and she didn't really seem to notice any significance in our expeditions straying across the border into South Wales.

Once we were in the Principality, finding affordable property proved remarkably easy. This was the early nineties and estate agents across Britain were reeling from five years of the worst recession they'd known. Wales was awash with smallholdings fitting our requirements. If that wasn't enough, the delight on the faces of the local estate agents as we walked through their doors was telling.

"How can I help you? You want to *buy*? Please, please, take a seat – can I get you a coffee? A biscuit? Cake?" Then came the note of suspicion – what sort of work was I in? Ah! I wasn't hoping to find anything locally, was I? From the worried expressions it was clear they were all too familiar with enchanted holiday-makers toying with the idea of a country cottage and indulging their fantasies by exploring their dream properties and wasting the agents' time. We became adept at slipping in my line of work and confirming subtly that yes, I could, and was, prepared to bring it with me.

Even here property prices were tied directly to distance from London. As a result, we found ourselves driving further north and west, to discover increasingly remote and romantic properties. By now Bel was increasingly car- and morning-sick, but just as she was beginning to panic, we spotted a large farmhouse way beyond our original reconnaissance area. It was four hours from London, but now the situation was becoming urgent and in spite of a price tag significantly beyond our budget, we thought it worth a look.

We fell in love with Allt-y-Gwalch from the moment we drew into the farmyard. The white-washed 16th-century building sits on the 1,000 foot contour nestling on the eastern flank of the Cambrian Mountains, cradled from the elements by two huge traditional barns. Better still, as a smallholding which until recently had been the core of a larger working farm, it came complete with pigsty, duck pond and thirteen acres clinging to the hill behind. A thin belt of pines provided a shelter belt from the prevailing west wind and – much to my delight – a huge and clearly well-occupied badger set was tucked into the corner of one field.

More than anything it was the view which clinched it. The house, which faced south-east, nestled in a little valley running down to the Wye and had panoramic views across virtually the whole of South Wales. To the east lay the uplands of Radnor Forest and Offa's Dyke, south was the hazy shadow of Hay Bluff, while the rolling Cambrian mountains framed our view to the west. Later we were to discover that on a clear day one could even glimpse the foothills of Snowdonia from the top of the hill.

The owners, a middle-aged couple, were desperate to move. They had bought the place five years before with dreams of a comfortable semi-retirement amid the fresh air and scenery. Unfortunately, they had not realised just how little work there is in the area and running a smallholding turned out to be more expensive than they had bargained for. Worse, arthritis struck the wife and soon she could no longer take the steep gradients. Caught out by the property recession, they were now stranded and desperate.

"We love the place, but it's really a young person's home," said the chair-bound wife. "It needs youth, love, money and energy – and we're running short of all of those."

I was captivated by the possibilities of the place and asked if they were ever snowed in?

"Oh no, never," the wife replied, just a little too quickly. For a second I was crestfallen, but quickly realised that given the altitude this couldn't be true. I explained that I was actually keen on the idea and was she really sure? Her tune changed abruptly – now she came to think of it, she did think there had been the odd occasion when it was difficult to get in and out.

I was satisfied by this response and by now Bel's main preoccupation was less where we went, but more whether we could get in and settled before 'Junior' made his appearance. So we offered as much as we could afford and, rather to our surprise, it was snapped up.

Thus, after twenty years, I was at last facing the realisation of all my dreams.

Introduction: Bel

I feel like one of those innocent, but slightly gullible young men in the eighteenth century who would go for a quiet drink in their local, only to end up in a merchant ship headed for the South Pacific. I can imagine them swaggering into the Slaughtered Pig, minding their own business, just fulfilling the daily routine. Then one knock on the head and they wake up to find themselves in a bunk with a cracking headache, surrounded by the smell of scurvy, gangrene and salt water. In much the same way, one day I was living a contented existence in West London and the next I was waking up in Wales surrounded by acres upon acres of wet mud with a splitting headache, a sense of nausea and the distinct smell of unwashed animals.

I have had no experience of wet muddy fields. For me the countryside was somewhere you were dragged to stay with people who fed you endless meals, had faces flushed with alcohol and talked loudly.

The city was my whole life. I lived in a small flat. Every morning I walked to the station and bought my paper and take away tea, always at the same kiosk. The same tube, the same stops, change once and the same walk to the office.

I worked in Central London for a public relations

company specialising in art exhibitions. I had a lovely office desk, a computer, a phone and a large pay packet every month. The position was not excessively taxing, I just had to interest the media in minor exhibitions in London's smaller galleries. Occasionally these would be of Fabergé eggs or Constable prints, but usually they would be collages of dyed wool by some unknown Scottish crofter or a twisted metal construction on a bed of polystyrene.

It was certainly true that I was not overly enamoured with this career. I was exhibiting very little talent in the public relations world and it was not going unnoticed. Even the habitual journey on the tube had become irritating and frustrating, particularly as I invariably slept in and it was always a mad rush. First night parties had started to seem inconvenient and tedious, the exhibitions themselves were losing even their artistic appeal.

In the evenings I had dinner parties. The meals were easy to organise as I lived next door to the best delicatessen the world has ever known. They baked perhaps thirty different types of their own bread, cakes and pies. There was the softest Parma ham and the largest collection of fresh pasta, pâtés and cheeses I had ever seen.

Dan and I met at about this time through a mutual friend from university. His lifestyle was refreshingly different from most of my friends. He worked from his Islington flat as a freelance journalist and had a host of peculiar animals living with him. He was interested in falconry, which struck me as so unusual as to be intriguing. His back garden was partly obscured by a home made aviary with a sulky red tail hawk in residence. Next to the aviary was a hutch, but the two ferrets which were supposed to live there actually spent most of the time running around inside the house closely investigating people's legs. The first time I saw one of his ferrets bounding down the stairs I thought it was a rat and yelped with shock.

He also had a dog which presented more of a problem. I don't like dogs. I never have, ever since I was forced to share my childhood with a decrepit smelly poodle. Dan's animal was obviously important to him and as I liked the owner, I pretended to like the pet too. I would make myself reach down and scratch behind her ears as if it were an unconscious instinct. Every time she licked me in gratification I had to suppress a desperate urge to pick her up by the back legs and swing her out of the door. Dan would comment on how fond Dill had become of me – which secretly made me want to go and bath in disinfectant for a week.

My relationship with Dan was fairly part time; a couple of evenings a week we would go out, but more often he would cook me delicious meals at his little North London zoo. On odd weekends we would travel down to his parents' cottage in Oxfordshire with a selection of house guests and cheeses from my deli. These breaks would involve sporadic walks of a maximum of two miles, usually involving a public house, but mostly we just sat around reading the papers and eating lengthy meals.

On these weekends I would occasionally offer to take Dill for walks on my own hoping she might run away never to be found again, but Dan interpreted this as affection. A few months into the relationship he responded to my false devotion for Dill by buying me a surprise lurcher puppy which he named Bracken. The new arrival was sweet – as all little furry things are – and for a while even I thought I might be persuaded. But not for long: after a few weeks of vomit and poo I understood the RSPCA slogan about puppies and Christmas. I explained that there were complications in the conditions of my lease and Dan was forced to take Bracken to live with him.

Generally, Dan and his menagerie did not make too much of a drastic impact on my life. I still had most of my evenings to devote to restaurants, dinner parties, bars and other social nocturnal comings and goings. Perhaps this would still be the case today if Dan and I hadn't decided to spend a two-week holiday alone at the cottage. This break was necessitated by the dreaded fact that Dill had given birth to a multitude of more bloody dogs. I pretended I thought this was the sweetest thing that had ever happened.

It was July and extremely balmy at the cottage. Every night we were able have dinner outside, cooking on a stove that Dan had made: a simple construction of a grill, bricks and a small fire. We ate dinner with delicious crisp white wines and the sound of cooing wood pigeons rolled up from the willows lining the stream at the bottom of the slope. During the day we would follow the stream till it turned into a river and have a picnic in total solitude, followed by an invigorating dip in the pools. Meanwhile the puppies all slept outside in the old summer house and during the day we would let them out and watch them scamper about play fighting.

Early on into the holiday Dan showed me his battered copy of *Self-Sufficiency*. He spoke in reverential tones about the mysterious John Seymour – who of course I'd never heard of – explaining every chapter and drawing endless diagrams of his own far-fetched schemes. He told me of his dream to live in the countryside and fly birds of prey from his fist on horseback. None of this really appealed to me, but I did start my own dream of what it might be like to live in the country.

I imagined a beautiful little cottage with a slightly untidy thatched roof, the faded redbrick front smothered with a climbing white rose or possibly a wisteria, the garden a beautiful array of flowers. An outdoor loggia running the length of the house, over a cobbled floor decked with a long oak table.

Inside my dream house, the kitchen would be furnished with a dark blue Aga, a double Belfast sink and elm draining board. An old milk churn full of unpasteurised milk from the local dairy would stand in the larder with a freshly baked pastry pie on the sill.

The sitting room should have a large soft sofa with a faded William Morris cover, dark velvet curtains, an open fire surrounded by a fender with a dark red leather padded seat. Somewhere there might be a large grandfather clock and a 19th-century barometer. Upstairs the bedrooms with lace curtains, wrought-iron beds (or maybe four posters), cloaked with crisp linen monogrammed sheets. The bathroom would have an old cast-iron bath with lions' feet and the wooden walls would be stained with a faded lapis lazuli colour.

This was a place where the sun always shone and there was a constant smell of new-mown grass in the air. Alongside the house would be an old lane flanked by the most perfect low hedgerows and opposite there would be a meadow with Jersey cows munching on cowslips and buttercups. Perhaps I would be lying in the hammock in the orchard listening to the sound of laughing children dancing around a maypole, with a trio of domesticated plump-breasted ducks waddling around the garden gently quacking.

It was all too magical for words, but it was definitely a daydream. In spite of the fact that this two-week holiday was one of the best I had ever had, I never seriously considered leaving London. Dan, however, was more captured by his dreams of rural living and extended his holiday further.

Back at work I felt even more unsettled at the office routine, thinking of Dan still having evening picnics. I went down to see him every weekend and with every successive visit I noticed he had moved more and more of his personal belongings to the cottage. He had managed to free himself of all but one of the puppies and there was no practical reason not to return to the capital. It was then that he admitted for the first time that he was not entirely sure he would go back to the city. He had realised that his work could be conducted from anywhere provided he had a phone and a fax and he told me that he was thinking of putting his flat on the market.

At first I thought this state of affairs was going to be awkward, but actually it was rather nice coming for the weekends. The cottage was a very comfortable driving distance from London and my misgivings were unfounded.

Then I discovered I was six weeks pregnant.

This was not a total surprise, but for some reason I had always assumed I was probably infertile or lacked something essential, like a womb. I felt, naturally, overwhelmed with the discovery and took the day off work and drove to the cottage to tell Dan. The thought of paternity obviously thrilled him to the core. He spoke with giddy excitement of all the things he wanted to show our child. He would make his baby a beautiful cot, he would read stories every night, take him/her on long walks in a back pack and pass on his vast knowledge of falconry knots. I was more concerned about where we were going to live.

We talked over the various options for days. My first thoughts were of London. It was, after all, where I had been brought up and it had the added advantage of being close to family and friends. Dan said he would be prepared to move back there if that was what I really wanted, but had I thought about the advantages of moving in the opposite direction? To be fair, he did try hard to discover where I wanted to live, but morning sickness had turned into all-day sickness and most of the time my overriding concern was to avoid throwing up on the table. Through my intense nausea I could see straight enough to admit both that I was not exactly committed to my career and how much I had enjoyed our two-week holiday.

I remembered my dream thatched cottage. Why not make it a reality? Obviously year round sunshine wasn't a likelihood, but somehow I managed to reason that bad weather probably did not matter so much in the country.

I could grow vegetables and tend flourishing borders of flowers: that might be fun. We could have a few animals, I could press flowers and make bread, cakes and chutney. Maybe I could take up watercolouring? The baby could sleep safely in a pram outside in the orchard, free from lead emissions. Later as a child he/she could run around playing with small fluffy animals, away from traffic and murderers.

Whatever the decision, I was going to have to sell my flat, so we could start looking for houses in our price range. Whether in town or country could be decided later. When the flats were valued, however, we found we had less than we had hoped for. The result was that in London we would have to move a long way out to buy a reasonably-sized flat and our enquiries around Oxfordshire revealed that even three-bedroomed houses were a long way beyond our resources. By now I was two months pregnant and feeling as sick as it is possible to feel. Nausea penetrated every bone in my body, even my fingers wilted with queasiness.

I was taking more and more time off work as we went on long weekends further and further west. Gloucestershire was still too highly priced, so we carried on through the Forest of Dean and eventually into South Wales. Somehow it had become evident that we were definitely not going to live in London and in my distracted state I never really questioned this premise. I handed in my notice and we began to tour Wales in earnest.

It is difficult to imagine a concept more alien to my childhood dreams. Tuscan Villas, Parisian apartments and Colombian Haciendas – they all figured in my grand scheme of things, but not once did I picture a Welsh farmhouse. Until then I had always thought of Wales as that lump tacked on to the left of Britain – like an afterthought. It had places like Swansea and Bangor in it: that did not sound promising. I turned to another page of the atlas to discover the average rainfall was much higher than almost anywhere else in Britain, but then again, it was an old map. All the same I felt strangely uncomfortable at the idea. I had a vague feeling I was not supposed to like Wales – something to do with close harmony singing and torched holiday cottages.

We toured the Brecon Beacons, staying in B&Bs while we viewed a dozen properties a day. Internally my hormones felt like they had entered the Latin open freestyle finals at *Come Dancing*. Almost every time we stopped to inspect a property, I would burst into tears hugging the steering wheel or have to find an obscure corner in which to be sick. One farm we saw had an adjoining barn with upside-down red crucifixes painted all over the inside. Dan said they were markers for livestock, but I was sure they weren't. Another had a decapitated doll on the window sill – its separated head lying the other side of the window and every farm was decorated in the same type of garish flock wallpaper. It seemed they were all the former homes of Devil worshippers.

The worst of them was a small shack with a corrugated-iron roof. It was on a mountain road ten miles from the nearest shop. The place lay deep in a dark valley and had no electricity or telephone. Dan kept telling me to imagine the potential, but all I could picture was a large wrecking crane. It was horrible.

While we were there I felt weak and had to lean against

the wall for support. My hand reached out and I felt a moist slippery surface. There was some kind of green organism slithering down the inside of one of the dark small rooms that the estate agent called 'a living room with commanding views and many original features'. Even today I am haunted by the thought of the kitchen with a hole in the ground beneath the sink for drainage. Dan started to talk about the endless opportunities. I explained, calmly, that he would have to kill me before I would enter that house again.

We saw Allt-y-Gwalch on the last day. It was in an open position with panoramic views. Compared to the previous shack it was a palace. Inside there was an oak staircase, every window had a built-in wooden seat and the enormous inglenook fireplace had a little stone seat next to it. But what really helped was the weather – for once the sun was glaring down. Then a red kite flew over the house and Dan positively twitched with excitement. It was not exactly the dream cottage that I had pictured only months earlier, but the current owner had filled the house with bunches of dried flowers and there was a comforting smell of lavender around the rooms. We sat outside and drank some home-made lemonade while our host described the amazing wildlife and exceptional weather conditions we could expect.

After that I am not sure what happened. I remember agreeing that I liked it, which I said partly so we didn't have to do any more driving. The rest is all a blur of solicitors and surveyors, although I do vaguely recall trouble with the survey and Dan talking about pulling out and starting a fresh search. That was an unacceptable prospect so I explained forcefully that this house would be all right and convinced myself that we really could mould it to fit my dream. We quickly came to a deal with the owners.

By the time I was six months down the line to motherhood all my belongings in the world were in a large lorry which I was following westwards along winding country roads. Needless to say, I was sick three times.

As I stepped out of the car my black suede shoes sank beneath a foot of mud. It was December, the skies were grey and it was raining hard. The place looked awful. I stood frozen in shock.

The men moving the furniture were just finishing dumping everything in a large pile by the door. One slapped me on the back. "Rather you than me," he said cheerfully. "I could never live in a place like this. It's all very nice to visit, but to live here, well that's a very different matter." I felt very sick again.

"I have to say coming from London to here ... well ... two more different places would be hard to imagine, if you know what I mean," he carried on remorselessly as he looked around, eyeing the sea of mud and the dark grey sky.

Dan arrived a few minutes later covered in blood. Apparently he had had a bit of a fight trying to get his hawk into his carrying box. He bounced out of the car and breathed in deeply. An enormous smile of pure contentment shone all over his face. This was everything he had ever wished for.

As I watched the furniture lorry trundle away down the bumpy lane, the man's words were still ringing in my head: 'I could never live in a place like this.' Tears started to trickle down my face. Dan tried to comfort me, but was really too preoccupied with the excitement of it all to concentrate on my life crisis. I couldn't understand how I had ended up here. I walked around the barns kicking fertiliser bags, muttering through stifled sobs. A mangy chicken flew out of a dark corner missing me by inches. The rain had now penetrated my clothes and the mud had reached my socks. I realised neither of us had wellies and became positively inconsolable. How could we have come to this mud bath with no waterproof footwear? How could I live in this mire of sodden earth and drizzling rain? What the bloody hell was I doing here? I couldn't live here. It was all a dreadful mistake.

The dogs were running around in a frenzy of excitement. Since the first pregnant hormone had hit my system, any pretence of dog-loving was dropped like a large rock. The problem had escalated for me, as soon as the three dogs started to live together they started to act as wild pack animals. Far from three brains being better than two, their combined grey matter seemed to de-evolve collectively. Together they had the mentality of the most primitive of swamp creatures, tearing off at the slightest whiff of a rabbit and going berserk at strangers. They clearly loved their new home. This made me hate them even more and fuelled my growing unhappiness.

Dan found me splattered with mud sitting by a pile of rusty chicken wire and a six-foot mountain of cow shit.

"We haven't got any bloody wellies," I yelled at him before he could say anything. "How could we come to this place with no wellies? Oh God! What have we done? And look at all this shit."

Dan began to register the depth of my despair. Desperate to placate my hysteria, he drove me to the local agricultural suppliers and purchased a pair of the best wellies money can buy. Holding on tightly to two reassuringly solid industrial-strength boots, I felt slightly better. All the same, as we drove back through the gloom to our cold wet home, I clutched them to my chest, sniffing and letting out the odd moan for effect.

By the time we returned it was nearly dark. With the end of day the temperature dropped and it began to freeze. It was only now that the ultimate horror of the situation dawned on me: there was no central heating. The only heat was supposed to come from a wood- burning stove – but we had no wood. The previous owners had not even left a twig. How could they do that to a pregnant woman? How could Dan let this happen? I began to feel a rising sense of panic again, but stifled my urge to scream. Believing this was life or death before hypothermia took us to the great gas showroom in the sky, I shouted at Dan to do something. He tried burning some wet pallets but they gave off no heat at all. Luckily I had brought a paraffin heater which I had stolen from a cousin. Wearing two overcoats and three hats, we rummaged maniacally, trying to find it among the vast piles of boxes and packing cases clogging up our new living room.

My other great concern was hunger: I needed hot food. Dan, now desperate to soothe my obvious horror and despondency, snapped into action by trying first to find and then wire up the cooker. He managed this, but couldn't locate the utensils: they were too deeply buried and instead we had to make do with cheese sandwiches. I was still preoccupied by the lost heater which I eventually found behind the sofa in a large brown cardboard box. The real difficulty came when I tried to light this strange mushroom-shaped metal object which might be the only thing separating us from frostbite. It had all sorts of knobs and buttons – none of which seemed to do anything. I groped for the instruction manual, but all I could see were Japanese characters.

Dan's Japanese was non-existent, but my increasing panic forced him into a virtually bilingual state. As luck would have it there was a gallon of paraffin in the garage and it only took him a few minutes to work out where it should go. After that came an agonising wait as he tried to light it. Outside the rain had turned to sleet and from my reflection in the heater's shiny metal I could swear that my lips were going blue. Dan continued to fumble with the knobs and levers.

I was flapping my arms to keep the circulation going. We had to burn something. With the constant steam of tears running down my cheeks I told Dan he had to sacrifice his IKEA dining-room chairs. Very reluctantly he smashed an ugly black chair and shoved it on top of the pallet embers with as much newspaper as he could find. As the flames flickered around the newsprint and the smoke billowed out into the room through the open doors, I gobbled up the merest suggestion of heat by hogging the prime position in front of the cast-iron lump which dominated the room.

Dan, keen to save the rest of the dining chairs, decided to concentrate on the heater again and this time fared better. By now I was totally exhausted and curled up on the sofa with all the bedclothes piled on top and our pathetic little fan heater blowing warm air straight at me at full whack. I had abandoned the idea of the upstairs bedroom not just because of the cold, but also thanks to the discovery of a soiled pair of red underpants in a yellow bucket in the middle of the room. I was not going in there without a necklace of garlic or a wooden crucifix.

Dan sat in the armchair leafing through *Self-Sufficiency*, I could see he was trying to disguise his triumphal joy at achieving his lifelong ambition. He passed me a glass of champagne. "Happy New Year!" he cheered. I looked at him in disbelief and turned over to go to sleep and dream of my thatched redbrick cottage.

January: Dan

'Where is the olive oil? I can't find any olive oil! My God! Are we in a culinary time warp?" Bel's face was a picture of disbelief as she came to terms with the first implications of the shift to village retail culture. It was the first shopping trip following our arrival and the visit to the local store came as a serious shock. When it came to food, it seemed this part of Wales was twenty-five years behind London. Ciabatta? Fresh pasta? Chillies, ginger or okra? Forget it – they simply didn't exist this side of Offa's Dyke – and we soon discovered that even peppercorns would require a twenty-mile round trip.

For a card-carrying 'foody' like Bel, the discovery came as a body blow, but as she reeled in horror, I found myself surprisingly undaunted. Instead I chose to point to the adventurous wine range which, I observed brightly, was impressive for so small a town. Just then nothing could dent my sense of optimism: who cared that the nearest Sainsbury, Oddbins and Tesco were an hour's drive away? It was true that until now they had provided the backbone of my weekly shopping trips, but their abrupt disappearance didn't shake my composure in the slightest. I was quite prepared to adapt to new ways (or, more precisely, to regress to 1960s retailing). After all, the hills were clearly alive with rabbits and the local river was the Wye, famous for its salmon and brown trout. What need had we of comfort food when we were surrounded by such natural bounty?

"Better still," I thought as I stared at the extremely limited range of late winter carrots, parsnips and potatoes, "if this is the competition, our own produce is going to taste all the better." So while Bel looked gloomily at the shelves of baked beans and tinned spaghetti, I remained doggedly optimistic, locked in my inner paradise.

To cheer her up, I pointed out that it gave our new lifestyle an extra spur and that she should see it as a challenge. Far from being buoyed by this, she glowered and announced that a pregnant woman has special dietary needs which didn't appear likely to be met locally and threatened that she would return immediately to London unless I made dramatic improvements in our food supply. Grabbing a pound of onions and two tins of tomatoes, I said it was remarkable what you could produce with basic ingredients, but she was far from convinced.

In spite of the poorly stocked shelves, we really did have very little to complain about. In general, everything had gone more smoothly than we could have dared hope. I spent three days between Christmas and the New Year in London, cramming the contents of our two flats into boxes and trunks while the six-month-pregnant Bel sat in armchairs conducting my efforts with a walking stick. Life is a process of acquisition and when we had completed our packing, it was evident that our possessions would take a considerable amount of ferrying.

Consequently, on New Year's Eve – the actual day of our move – a convoy of four vehicles set off for the Welsh mountains. In the lead were two removal vans, Bel followed in her Renault a few minutes behind, while I brought up the rear in my ancient Fiat, accompanied by three dogs, two ferrets and the hawk.

Not everything continued quite according to plan. After the others had departed, I encountered a minor problem as I was trying to put Gwen, a large and powerful red-tailed buzzard, into her carrying box. She had never liked travelling and her mood was not improved by having been given less attention than she deserved over the fortnight leading up to the move. Consequently her weight had crept up and she was less 'manned' (tame) than she ought to have been. So, when she saw the travelling box, she bated violently, hurling herself off her perch and in the process catching the side of my face with her foot. I subdued her and, pumped full of adrenaline, leaped into the car without checking for damage.

I had travelled four miles before I glanced in the rear-view mirror and noticed that blood was pouring down my cheek. Having no tissues in the car (naturally), I had to stop at a garage to tidy up the problem. The cashier looked deeply perturbed by my appearance and I noticed her jotting down my registration number, with a quivering hand, as I left the kiosk. I had visions of her sitting hunched on the edge of a sofa watching the next edition of *Crimewatch*, her hand hovering over the phone as she waited to match my face with some violent assault in the South Midlands.

There was another minor hitch between Evesham and Pershore when the motorist following me started to flash his lights and toot. I assumed he was annoyed with my steady pace and, in the absence of passing places, wanted me to speed up. Being heavily laden and with a ferret cage tied precariously on to the roof, I was reluctant to speed up and anyway, I was irritated by what I took to be a display of 'road rage'. So instead I slowed down to make it easier to pass, but the flashing and tooting continued over the next five miles in spite of numerous opportunities to overtake and I began to suspect he had a message to convey.

I stopped and after a brief explanation of my facial wound, the driver showed me a large lump on the side of my rear tyre which had caught his attention several miles back. In spite of my elated mood, I realised this was a serious cause for concern, so was forced to crawl along for a further ten minutes until I found a suitable lay-by, where I could change the wheel in safety.

Of course the spare tyre was buried beneath the floor of the boot and I had to unpack the car to get to it. In the meantime, I had the opportunity to watch passing cars swerving across the road at the sight of a blood-soaked man surrounded by luggage, various strange items of falconry paraphernalia and a ferret cage.

The tyre operation added half an hour to the journey and by the time I arrived at our new home, it was to find that the removal men had dumped everything in the two ground-floor rooms and were preparing to leave, anxious to get home in daylight and grimly determined to ignore Bel's appeals for further help. I couldn't blame them – they were unpaid, and looking at the huge pile of possessions, even I had little enthusiasm for the laborious task of unpacking which lay ahead.

The house was bitterly cold and Bel was looking deeply unhappy, but as I glanced around, I felt my spirits soar. Nothing could daunt me and I found the demands for heat a welcome excuse to look around the outbuildings of our new property.

I was taken aback, however, when I walked into the woodshed. Our predecessors, not unreasonably, had run down their stocks and the wood-pile was non-existent. Even this couldn't dent my enthusiasm for long and instead of any sense of concern, I was filled with the romance of the situation and determined to muddle through. In the corner of one of the outhouses I found a few broken pallets and a handful of sodden chips which I bundled up in my arms, returning to the house in triumph.

Lighting the fire proved yet more awkward. Some people have a natural flair for such things and have only to wave a match at a pile of damp logs for it to burst into flame. Another group – and this includes myself – has a distinct inability, so I spent much of the next four hours lying in front of the stove, trying to coax a flame out of the pathetic pile of kindling. It was an uphill task, but eventually I succeeded and announced triumphantly that the room temperature was nearing acceptable level.

Bel evidently didn't agree. In fact she seemed to be on the verge of tears, thanks to the combination of cold, fatigue and pregnancy. At this point she remembered a paraffin stove that she had acquired somewhere along the way and luckily I stumbled across a gallon of fuel which the previous owners had left behind. After a little difficulty with the instructions, it was soon sitting in the middle of the room, kicking out a perfectly respectable warm glow. Bel didn't agree with this either and eventually I found myself having to sacrifice a rather ugly chair to the fire to keep her mollified. Bel still claimed it was too cold and declared that moving from the one room with a heat source was out of the question. She opted to sleep on the sofa rather than risk the sub-Arctic climate of the upstairs bedroom.

I was too excited for rest, but fortunately I had carefully packed my beloved John Seymour in my hand luggage and so instead of retiring to sleep, I settled myself in the armchair to browse through his words of wisdom and encouragement.

Next morning, I bounced up as soon as it was light and negotiated my way past the cardboard boxes jumbled all over the floor and cluttering the corridor. Rather than tackle the unpacking, I turned into the room earmarked for my study and stood in front of the window as dawn broke over the valley. Before my eyes a magnificent panorama was opening up: sunlight bathed the valley through a break in the clouds, glistening on the damp grass while in the distance the mountains along the Marches were dusted with thick hoar frost. There was only one drawback to the room: no bookshelves.

This was a serious departure from my childhood dreams of a book-lined study with a spectacular view and, glancing cursorily at the piles of unpacking waiting beyond, I decided it required an immediate solution. Without delay and while Bel still slumbered in the next room, I picked my way to the front door and drove to the nearest village in search of a builders' merchants.

Like most men, I find that the mere act of buying the materials for a DIY project gives a sense of immense achievement – greater perhaps than actually doing or certainly than finishing the job. Soon the car was full of planks and screws and brackets and hammers and varnish. By the time I got home I felt as if I had been hard at work all morning and was therefore a little hurt that Bel's only observation was that the fire had gone out during the night. She seemed irritated that far from reducing the clutter in our living space, I appeared to have added to it.

I am an inveterate ditherer when it comes to DIY, and I rested on my laurels when it came to putting up the shelves. After a couple of weeks, the wood was still piled high in the library-to-be, so I decided to give matters a boost by buying a cordless drill, convinced some good electrical hardware would provide the impetus I desperately needed. Of course, in practice this remained largely unused – particularly in the construction of shelves – but I found it useful when trying to envisage future construction projects. I would carry it with me as I wandered around the house, and as I contemplated blank walls and jobs which needed attention, I would draw it and 'whirr' at future tasks.

Whatever the condition of the interior of the house, outside life was just as cluttered. With the house we had inherited seventeen bantams. Although we had agreed to take them over, it came as a slight surprise to find that so many had survived the depredation of the local foxes during the two weeks the farm was unoccupied.

In fact I soon discovered to my private delight that there was no shortage of wild food to distract our vulpine neighbours. Late-night sweeps across the grass with a torch revealed gleaming pairs of pink dots as their owners stood to attention in the beam and every morning dozens of rabbits lolloped across our thirteen acres dotting the lawn with thousands of currant-like droppings. The dogs were just as excited as I was, no doubt believing themselves in canine heaven.

I was brought down from my cloud, however, by Bel's firm ruling that from now on the ferrets were to live outside. She said this was because she had once heard of a baby being killed by a pair of ferrets and she was not going to take the risk when our baby arrived in April. Although this was still three months away, she thought it was better to start out as one meant to continue. In addition, she surprised me by announcing that we should use this opportunity to establish some new ground rules for the dogs. In future they would not be allowed on the furniture and upstairs would be out of bounds.

This new regime seemed Draconian – and I said as much, but Bel was adamant, and deaf to my pleas on their behalf. It would be an exaggeration to say we rowed on the issue, but I felt sulky about her high-handed approach. Fortunately such a mood could not last long when surrounded by the glorious scenery of mid-Wales and a brief excursion up the hill with the dogs and ferrets did wonders for my mood. We wandered a hundred yards from the house to the nearest bury, I netted up the exits, popped one of my pets down the hole and sat down to wait. The inexperienced animal took an eternity to work its way through the bury, but I was in paradise. For once there was a lull in the showers and the wind had dropped enough to hear the birds singing as I squatted on the ground outside the highest exit with a sense of contentment.

Half an hour later, I was in proud possession of two fine healthy bucks. These were duly casseroled in cider and, if I say so myself, tasted excellent. Even the generally sombre Bel seemed mollified by my demonstration of fieldcraft.

The effects lasted into the next morning, when I realised that building a ferret run would give me a chance to use my cordless drill properly for the first time and so I set to work with enthusiasm hoping to have it ready in a couple of hours. Unfortunately the process took longer than anticipated. I kept finding I lacked materials and had to go back to the builders' merchant for the requisite items. Inevitably, one visit was not enough, and as the day wore on I found myself making a total of three return trips to buy more nails, screws, hinges, bolts, wire netting – and a top-up supply of wood.

When I proudly showed my efforts to Bel, she was unimpressed, contrasting my energy on the wildlife and livestock fronts with my apathy when it came to unpacking and decorating. She also pointed to the pile of planks in my study awaiting metamorphosis into bookshelves and asked if I could now be expected to put as much attention into our living conditions as I lavished on the ferrets.

Still nothing seriously knocked my elated spirits. There was just so much to see, and although the rain continued to preclude falconry, which by now was dominating much of my thoughts, I was consoled by the plethora of wild buzzards wheeling above the hillside. I spotted a sparrowhawk in the lane leading to the farm the day after we arrived, and later we both sighted a pair of red kites wheeling around the house, one of which returned an hour later. There were a few kestrels, although I soon noticed these Welsh hunters were unlike their English cousins in that they seemed less inclined to hover and were generally much more active, flying faster and with more powerful wing beats. I couldn't quite decide why this should be the case, but concluded it was probably due to a shortage of prey which was forcing the birds into greater activity.

I pointed out the impressive numbers of hawks to Bel and though at first she appeared relatively uninterested, gradually she too became enthused. Her ability to identify raptors came on in leaps and bounds and she was soon able to spot suspected goshawks and even a peregrine, from the passenger seat of the car. Unfortunately, I was just too late to be able to confirm her suspicions, but having great faith in her ornithological skills, I was sure it was only a matter of time before I could add these two to my list of confirmed sightings of British raptors.

Although the weather remained unremittingly wet and there was no hint of hope from the evening forecasts, I continued to bounce to the window each morning. As far as I was concerned, the valley might as well have been bathed in glorious sunshine. This was clearly a paradise for birds and I was particularly excited to glimpse a woodcock flashing into the conifers behind the house. I ran back into the house to relay this exciting news to Bel, to find her reading a birthing book, engrossed in the chapter on coping with labour pains.

She told me that fascinating as our ornithological treasures might be, perhaps with parenthood rapidly

approaching, we might do some useful research on travelling times to each of the nearest hospitals. I made some
wistful observation about how romantic it would be for
me to deliver our first baby at home. With the benefit of
hindsight this was not the best thing to have said. She
turned tearful and in the end we only resolved the situation by driving to the nearest big hospital – 40 miles, and
an hour and a quarter, away. Having made the trip and
stopped the stopwatch, there seemed no point in returning empty-handed so we decided to pop into a supermarket on the outskirts of the town.

The sight of a trolley laden with the sort of choice deli-
cacies we hadn't seen in a month cheered her up considerably, particularly when I grandly said we could splash out
on some smoked salmon. As she curled up in the armchair
by the fire and began to nibble at a pink sliver of fish
draped across a generous slice of rye bread, I caught a rare
glimpse of pure contentment on her face.

Another attraction, stumbled across fairly soon after
our arrival, was the plentiful opportunities for fishing.
According to the newsagent who sold the yearly passes,
come the spring, the trout and salmon fishing was some of
the best in the country. Although I was no angler, I
regarded Bel as something of an expert, having heard
descriptions of her blissful holidays in Norfolk. I saw fishing as the natural complement to my rabbiting activities
and immediately started picturing her triumphant home-
comings, rod sloped over her shoulder and half a dozen
brown trout threaded on a string tied to her belt.

So I encouraged her to follow up an advertisement in
the local newsagent for fishing tackle. It transpired that an
ageing angler with dicky knees was hanging up his landing
net for good and Bel instantly bought the old man's entire
armoury of rods, reels and hundreds of flies, not to
mention a wealth of advice on the best places to go locally.

The daydream of rural harmony did not last long. I was jerked back to reality by the recurring problem of finding a supply of dry wood which by now was beginning to dominate our waking hours. To remain even close to warm in the evenings, I was having to spend hours searching for fallen branches in the fields and hedgerows around the house. The stove was like a growing cuckoo, demanding a never-ending stream of fuel to give out even a modicum of heat. Every day it gobbled up vast amounts of not only wood, but also my precious time.

Barely half-way through one of the wettest winters on record, we were without any fuel at all. Our only piece of good fortune was to stumble across the name of our predecessors' supplier. At first I was reluctant to compromise my notions of self-sufficiency when there was fuel for free in our hedges and from the hundreds of spindly conifers behind the house, but Bel was in no mood or condition to compromise. Also, after a while I had to admit our living conditions were less than ideal. So, armed with my new knowledge, I rang up to request seasoned hardwood logs.

Mike, the forester, readily announced that yes he had some dry hardwood for us – £40 a tonne as opposed to £30 for softwood. He promised to come the next day with a load, but in the end it was a week before he turned up to unload his van in the dark.

"They're pine planks," he announced cheerfully as I helped him with the unloading. "They're bit damp, but with all that surface area, they should dry out in a month or two if you let the wind get at them."

"I thought we agreed on hardwood?" I said as the inevitable squall sent a stream of raindrops running down the back of my neck.

"Look, we've just had the wettest autumn on record, to be honest you're lucky to get these," he countered as he hauled at the rapidly dwindling pile on the back of his pickup. "That'll be £80 for the two tonnes."

My mouth dropped at the price, which also seemed to have changed since our initial conversation, but by now Bel was standing next to me, almost moaning with delight at the sight of all that wood-piled in our barn, so any scope for haggling was fatally undermined.

"You'll need to cut them up as you go along," Mike continued. "Have you got a saw?"

I motioned to the black pruning saw I had bought in Islington to tame a neighbour's overhanging sycamore.

"No, I mean a real saw," he said, waving at his two-stroke chainsaw sitting in the back of the pick-up.

I remembered that we had agreed to buy our predecessors' chainsaw and rushed to fetch it from the garage. As he peered at the huge beast, I had to admit that I found the very thought of waving around a noisy, 30lb, electric carving knife a terrifying prospect. This was a machine that could slice mature oak trees in two with one smooth stroke – I could only imagine what it might do to the limbs of an inexperienced operator like myself.

"Christ! This is a bit of a brute, isn't it?" Mike clearly shared my feelings.

"What do you mean?"

"Well, put it this way, I'm a professional and this is what I use." He pulled out his own saw and shone the torch on it: it was barely half the size of my beast.

"Yours would be good on a giant redwood, but it's a bit of a handful in a Welsh hedge," he said. "I really think you ought to have a bit of training before you start cutting up logs, let alone felling trees."

He then assured me earnestly that a five-day course was a minimum requirement. These, he warned, could be difficult to find and very expensive. Luckily for me, however, he had diversified his firewood business and ran courses for YTS trainees. Even more fortunately, his next session started on Monday and owing to a late cancellation he thought he could just about squeeze me in – at £200 for the week.

It was my turn to look horrified, so in the end we settled on one day's instruction. This, he promised, would leave me competent to maintain the saw and chop wood (but not to fell trees). He insisted, however, that I buy safety leggings before turning up.

"The Health & Safety says you have to wear them and I don't have a spare pair," he explained. "They're a bit pricey, though – £70."

Again I balked at the cost, but any lingering desire to hang on to my money crumbled as Mike cheerfully reeled out a few horror stories about the profusion of local amputees. By the time he had started to climb back behind the wheel of his battered four-wheel-drive truck, I was practically begging him to squeeze me on to his course.

Perhaps predictably, when I rolled up the following Monday, I found it a mixed experience. Instruction involved the repetition of blatantly self-evident safety advice. We learned, for example, that it is inadvisable to use what Mike preferred to call a 'power saw' after drinking heavily. It was also foolish to fell trees while tripping on psychedelic drugs and testing a moving blade for sharpness with one's forefinger was a 'no-no'. Likewise, he urged caution when allowing small children or invalids to use one's machine.

As he rambled on, I couldn't help feeling that even a novice such as myself would be unlikely to fail to spot such blindingly obvious snippets of common sense. Meanwhile Mike rambled on listing all the permutations of possible dangers. All-in-all, he was so enthused by the need to pass on this vital forestry lore that it wasn't until half an hour before dark that we finally fired up our machines. I got in three cuts before it was too black to see anything. This was hardly calculated to inspire confidence, but at least it gave me a modicum of security – enough at least to don my safety trousers the next morning and jerk on the starter cord. It surged into life with a throaty roar and as I stroked the huge pile of sodden planks, I was gratified to see a cloud of shavings and a minor avalanche of tumbling firewood. I even began to feel fairly comfortable.

Fortunately our sole source of income, journalism, had just taken a turn for the good (although it was still far from sufficient to cover the never-ending bills which accompany any move). Far from finding myself isolated from commissioning editors by distance, after only a few days I found I qualified as a genuine countryman and was invited to write a piece on garden birds for one of the nationals. I agreed willingly enough, only to discover the piece was needed by early the next morning. Worse, I had just twenty minutes to think of all the species I would be mentioning so they could do the necessary picture research.

Now, I knew very little about any birds other than those with hooked beaks, but I was still far more knowledgeable than either my editor or the idiot who had written the first draft which I was to re-work. Equally fortunate was the fact that our predecessors had been amateur ornithologists and although the bird table had not been stocked for almost a month, scroungers were still paying regular hopeful visits to the table just outside the window. Thus, armed with a second-hand *AA Guide to British Birds*, and in spite of the adverse conditions, I managed to produce a satisfactory article, finishing by midnight.

Better still, the next morning the editor phoned to say he loved the article. The piece appeared as written – my first wildlife article! In spite of this minor bonanza, our finances were still unhealthy and so, welcome as it was, I greeted the next commission with a mixture of feelings. It came in the form of an invitation to go to Croatia to write a piece on investment opportunities in Zagreb in February. Normally I would be interested by such a potentially lucrative and interesting commission, but now I had little desire to travel. The trip would involve abandoning the farm for a whole week – not to mention leaving Bel on her own to struggle with the mess, mud and perennial fuel problems of our new home. Money considerations won the day, however, and I felt obliged to accept the job.

Bel, at least, appeared to be acclimatising after some initial hiccups. As a mother-to-be, halfway through her first pregnancy, one of her first expeditions had to be to the local surgery. Here the five-minute appointment turned into an hour-long chat as our new GP, Dr McBain, launched into a really good gossip on every subject under the sun. The result was the decision to have Junior in Hereford, with me driving Bel there when the contractions commenced. ("Isn't an hour a bit of a distance to travel?" queried our none-too-confident heroine. "Well, as a doctor I can tell you it's fine," he replied. "But as a father who's done it three times, I can only say it's sheer hell.")

The doctor's friendliness soon turned out to be nothing out of the ordinary. In contrast to the reputation that the Welsh have for being surly, it seemed almost impossible to buy anything without launching into a long conversation. News of our arrival had spread quickly and everyone was fascinated to find out why we had moved here and what line of work I was in.

Our 'next-door' neighbour (he lived half a mile away) was typical. Three days after our arrival and while Bel was out shopping, there was a sharp 'rat-a-tat-tat' on the front door. I opened it to find myself facing a man wearing a green military sweater. The epaulettes were buttoned down and bare, but darker green squares on each showed where pips had once been attached. Clearly its owner had once been an officer and this was confirmed when be began to speak in the precise, clipped sentences of a Sandhurst graduate of the old school.

"John Hartwood, Hafod Neuadd," he barked out. "Saw you arrive Monday afternoon. Bit worried by the van, but spotted your wife in the red Renault and worked out what was going on – although started to think a whole commune was moving in when your 'A' reg Fiat went past."

"Daniel Butler," I stuttered, rather taken aback by his powers of observation and short, staccato speech. He obviously noticed my surprise.

"Live down the hill – Hafod Neuadd – big white farm on the left. Been there yonks. Saw your predecessors come and go. Hope you last longer. Here's a cake – made it myself, so can't promise it's edible, what!"

He handed over a cake, beautifully wrapped in cling film. It was a perfect rectangle of dried fruit and brown sponge so perfect you had to cut it with a bread knife. The corners would have graced any hospital bed and somehow he had managed to cook it to a total uniform colour throughout. It was the most tightly baked cake I had ever seen.

I thanked him profusely and invited him in for a cup of tea. He nodded his head in courteous acceptance and bent down to remove his spotless boots. I found myself wondering quite how he had managed to negotiate the muddy yard without coating the brilliant black shine with a layer of thin grey mud.

As he tugged on the laces, I glanced around the sea of mud trodden into the faded shag pile that we were about to throw out and said he really needn't bother, but it was too late. With a grunt of satisfaction he stood up and wriggled his shoulders to slip off a rucksack. In an instant he was sliding his feet into a pair of immaculate check carpet slippers. I ushered him into the living room and together we carefully stepped around the boxes and debris still scattering the floor.

After seeing the perfectly presented cake, I felt obliged to excuse our haphazard domestic arrangements. "Sorry about the mess, we're a bit disorganised, I'm afraid," I said rather lamely.

"Not a bit of it, not a bit of it," he said. "Saw the wife was expecting: quite understand. Don't worry, won't stay long: things to do myself."

I was still disconcerted by his clipped, no-nonsense speech, but as I made the tea the feeling evaporated. Major Hartwood was a fairly short man, his white hair neatly parted and combed down flat against his head underneath his flat tweed cap. He was a retired army officer who had spent his life in Africa before retiring to Wales about twenty years previously. As he talked I decided he must be at least seventy-five but he certainly didn't look it. His face was tanned and wrinkled by a lifetime spent outdoors, but the flesh underneath still seemed firm and taut with none of the flabbiness of old age.

"Do a bit of farming – not much – but just can't bear the idea of retirement. Fellow's got to do something, you know."

In spite of his evident dislike of superfluous speech, by the time he had finished his tea, I had gleaned a few more snippets of information about our nearest neighbour. It transpired that his idea of 'a bit of farming' was fairly significant as he managed his 50-acre smallholding and three hundred ewes single-handed. He also said he grew almost all his own vegetables and as he stood at the door, carefully tucking his carpet slippers into the rucksack, he issued a reciprocal invitation.

"Thanks for the tea: good brew. Sure you're too busy for socialising now, but come round for a snifter when you're settled in. No hurry – whenever you're ready."

And with that he wheeled around sharply with the precision of a man who has spent a lifetime in the military and strode off down the lane. As he did so he gave a curt whistle, whereupon two border collies rose silently to their feet and loped quickly to his side. I realised with a shock that they must have been waiting in the incessant drizzle for their master with a patient obedience which put our three to shame.

A few days later we had a visit from another neighbour who chugged up to our door in his battered Landrover. He introduced himself as Fred Hir-Rhiw, and said that although he knew there was no right of way, he wondered whether we would mind if he used our lane to get to his lambing shed?

"It would only be once a day, like, until Easter-time," he said with the throaty growl of a heavy smoker.

I agreed instantly to the request and he gave a toothless smile as he pulled a cigarette from a packet. Obviously the ice was melting.

"Got to check the lambs daily, like," he explained. "Got terrible problems with foxes, see. Go out hunting three times a week." He was still smiling, but his eyes were fixed on me, scouring my face for any reaction. I simply smiled back.

I learned afterwards that this was a secret local initiation rite for outsiders. It was considered a guaranteed way of sorting out undesirable do-gooding townies from welcome injections of fresh blood. Vegetarians could be tolerated – just – but any hint of friendliness towards foxes was a sure-fire way of spotting a potential social sore. I had just passed with flying colours.

At the time, however, I was completely blind to the implications. Instead, I was desperate to keep him friendly, anxious for the safety of my three excitable dogs. Before we left Oxfordshire I had had nightmares of trigger-happy Welsh farmers only too ready to shoot first and ask questions later. Instead, as I blethered out assurances about their steadiness with stock (my fingers definitely crossed behind my back), he smiled and drew heavily on his cigarette.

"Never you mind about that," he said. "Any trouble and we'll shut them up with my old tup – that'll sort 'em."

I thanked him profusely, repeated once again that he was welcome to use our lane and as soon as he was out of sight, rushed to consult reference material. It transpired that a tup was a ram and, apparently, shutting any mutt smaller than a Rottweiler in a small shed with a large old ram results in copious canine bruises and is a guaranteed cure for sheep worrying.

More interestingly, however, his name prompted me to reach for a Welsh dictionary. Although this was not a Welsh-speaking area, it was clear from both Fred and the Major that with so many Williamses and Lewises in the area, everyone was known by their holding. It transpired that a 'Hir Rhiw' meant 'long ridge' and a glance at the map showed a farm of that name was located on the other side of the hill from us. I thumbed to 'Hafod Neuadd' to find it meant 'Hall in the Summer Pasture', which seemed appropriate enough for the Major's large white farm sited on a slight plateau high on the side of one of the larger local hills.

It was only when I turned to our own Allt-y-Gwalch that I became really excited. The meaning, it transpired, was 'hillside of the hawk'. I was ecstatic at the discovery and yelled the news up the stairs to Bel before rushing out into the farmyard with the binoculars. Sure enough, there in the stiff breeze and light drizzle were a pair of buzzards, hanging motionless, their heads down-turned, scouring the dead bracken and gorse for movement. I couldn't believe our luck and talked excitedly about fate and coincidence for most of the evening, first to Bel and then on the phone to friends, relatives – anyone who would listen in fact.

Of course with so much to learn about our new lifestyle and surroundings, the novelty of this one discovery soon wore off, but all the same, it continued to be a favourite dinner party topic for some months to come. Meanwhile, I was itching to get farming. I longed to be out there tilling the soil, sowing seeds and watching our animals fatten, but was reluctantly aware of the need to curb my enthusiasm. For one thing the rain was still coming down in sheets and although the mercury was still hovering a few degrees above zero, winter was far from over.

Instead, I had to content myself with my battered copy of 'the Great John' and I quickly latched on to one of his central themes – the worthiness of the pig. As he explained so eloquently, these creatures form the backbone of the genuine smallholding. They live on your kitchen and garden waste, ploughing the land in search of food and at the same time they fertilise the soil. But most important of all, at the end of the year they provide all the top-quality organic meat you could possibly want. Flicking through the Seymour bible, there seemed no end to what a pig could provide: the pork, bacon and ham were obvious, but my mouth watered as the list grew. What could be nicer than home-made bangers? How about turning my hand to continental sausages? And of course there would be more lard than we could ever hope to use.

Bel was at first unenthusiastic, remaining obsessively interested in the heat output of the stove, travelling times to local hospitals and the problems of finding sufficient dietary variety. I tried to cheer her up by reading out the relevant chapters of the Great John in bed each evening, as we huddled together for warmth, but she remained unmoved by the exercise.

I got a better reaction from Fred, who I began to flag down regularly as he chugged past on his way to check up on the sheep: "We used to make bacon when I was a boy," he murmured, his eyes moistening as he lit yet another cigarette. "We had real pigs then, corn-fed in the farmyard – and by God the hams were good, better than anything you can get now." Suddenly the normally taciturn man wouldn't shut up as he poured out his memories of the meat of his youth. The taste, texture and smell were superlative, he claimed. No butcher today could match them.

After he had departed, still licking my lips like the big bad wolf, I turned to the farming manuals. If this was for us to eat, then only the best would do. I wanted no namby-pamby modern pig, designed to grow fast with lean meat. No, I needed an ancient breed, one with flavoursome fat rippling through its flesh, the sort of beast portrayed by those 18th-century primitivist painters, a positively cuboid baconer which fed the men and women who put the Great into Britain – above all one of which the rural radical William Cobbett would be proud:

"The cottager's pig should be bought in spring, or late in winter; and being then four months old, he will be a year old before killing time; for it should always be borne in mind, that this age is required in order to ensure the greatest quantity of meat from a given quantity of food . . . Make him fat by all means. The last bushel, even if he sit as he eat, is the most profitable. If he can walk two hundred yards at a time, he is not well fatted. Lean bacon is the most wasteful thing that any family can use. In short it is uneatable, except by drunkards, who want something to stimulate their sickly appetite."

This passage acted on my imagination like petrol poured on a bonfire. We must have pigs . . . but which type? Even ignoring foreign breeds like Yucatans and Vietnamese Pot Bellied, the choice was bewildering. There were Gloucester Old Spots, Middle Whites, Wessex Saddlebacks, Oxford Sandies, Berkshires, British Lops, Large Blacks, Welsh, Essex and Long Whites. As I studied the pictures in the glossy coffee table guide I had picked up for a song in Hay-on-Wye, there was no question of the winner. I had eyes only for one – the Tamworth. These would be the stunners at any piggy beauty parade. Long-bodied and with a rich ginger hue, to me they were everything a pig ought to be. Better still, one evening long after Bel had gone to bed, I discovered from another battered textbook that they were supposed to be one of our oldest breed, closest relative of the wild boar which used to roam the woods of mediaeval Britain. The idea was too romantic for words.

Better still, a nearby farmer's wife turned out to be a breeder, clinging on to the old-fashioned ways of her childhood. At twenty pounds a throw, we could easily afford two as recommended by the Great John (they are social animals which are much happier when kept together). When I talked to the breeder on the phone, she warned me that they were livelier than your average pig. This only added to their charm and she confirmed she had two eight-week-old boars which were ready to leave their mother. Carried away with the excitement of it all, I asked if I could pick them up immediately.

"Wait a minute!" she cried as I suggested meeting her in a couple of hours' time. "You can't just come and take them away – you need a pig movement licence first!"

"A pig movement what?"

"Licence," she said, explaining that before her piglets could go anywhere, she had to obtain the correct piece of paper from the local Trading Standards office. "It's illegal to move pigs without a licence," she said. This would take a few days. Devastated by the idea of delaying pig acquisition for what seemed an eternity, I suggested maybe we could dispense with the formalities. To me the whole idea of licences sounded suspiciously like something from the film *A Private Function*. It smacked of ancient bureaucracy and the state planning brought in by wartime austerity. This was the 1990s and for over a decade we had had a Government dedicated to slashing away needless red tape and bureaucracy – surely pig movement licences were not really necessary? The woman was horrified by the suggestion and remained adamant that no pig of hers would leave the farm without the proper paperwork. For the next week, I found myself like a child before Christmas, working myself up into a frenzy of excitement at the idea of the new arrivals. I had to release my frustrations by visiting the local farming suppliers to stock up on unwanted pallets. Pulling out my trusty cordless drill, I managed to create a carrying box capable of holding two of the feistiest Labrador-sized piglets.

Not a moment too soon, the licence came through. With pounding heart I managed to squeeze the crate into the rear of my battered old Fiat and sped south to the Black Mountains, where a grinning family of Welsh farmers helped me squeeze the two squealing piglets into the crate.

"Have you ever kept pigs before?" asked one twenty-five-year-old son, the corners of his mouth slightly upturned.

I confessed my lack of experience and his grin widened.

"Got an electric fence?" he continued, a distinct twinkle in his eye.

I began to feel he was quietly laughing at me. I felt slightly irritated and uncomfortable, but armed with years of scouring the Great John, I was confident in my ability to master pig-ownership. I was all too well aware, however, that this might not impress someone born and bred next to a sty, so to speak, and I decided the best option was to leave the scene. I reached for the car door as I answered, "No. No electric fence."

His twinkle became a positive torch beam of delight.

"Well, good luck," he said as I started the car. "You'll need it!"

WELSH RAREBIT

2 ozs butter
1 tbsp flour
1 tsp mustard powder
4 fl ozs bitter
4 ozs grated extra-
mature cheddar cheese
Generous pinch of cayenne pepper
Worcestershire sauce
Salt and pepper

Fresh granary bread

Melt the butter and stir in the flour and mustard
powder. When smooth, slowly whisk in the bitter
and allow to thicken. Add the cheese, a dash of
Worcestershire sauce and salt and pepper, stirring
continuously. The mix should become doughlike.
Remove from heat and when cool, place in the
freezer for half an hour to firm up. Turn on to a
floured board and roll out to a thickness of ¼inch.
Cut to fit bread and then grill until top begins to
turn brown.

February : Bel

After our arrival in our new unheated home it rained
every single day. The locals said it was an unusual winter,
but I wondered if they were just being kind. What if it was
always like this? As I watched the dark clouds hanging
above the valleys anyone could see that this was Nirvana
to a rain cloud. They just hovered there waiting for a
suggestion of wind to bounce them off the valley walls so
they could release many tons of seeping Welsh rain. I
noticed they always seemed to pick our house to rain on,
the farms across the way always seem to miss the really
heavy showers. Perhaps they were anti-English clouds?
Dan thought that was the most paranoid statement he had
ever heard anyone make.

I began to experience a recurring nightmare. In it I was
a private in the First World War, trudging through a
constant sea of mud in my brown-stained khaki, the rain
thumping down on my shoulders. All I could see for miles
around was an endless bog. Then, tired and exhausted, I
would fall into the trench with wet soil up to my gun belt.
By morning my dream had turned into reality as I looked
out of the bedroom window to see sheets of horizontal
rain drifting along the valley over a vast sea of water-
logged earth.

Those poor sodden soldiers. I felt I could imagine what they had gone through. Maybe we didn't have the 'beastly Hun' shooting at us, but every moment we were being watched by armies of voles and rabbits lurking like scouts among the rocks and marsh grass. It might not be exactly the same as active service in the trenches, but after decades of comfortable city life it felt pretty rough to me.

This all passed Dan by. He wandered around in an ecstatic dream endlessly pointing to black dots in the sky and shouting: "I think it's a peregrine . . . or it could be a goshawk!"

When the bird came into closer view it was invariably a buzzard. To alleviate the boredom of pregnancy and the trials of living on the Somme revisited, I took to pointing to the sky and shouting, "There's a peregrine stooping." Then, as Dan rushed to my side I would sigh: "Oh dear, you've just missed it."

As the weeks slowly passed, the thought of ten-foot snow drifts began to prey on my mind. This area was a meteorological hotchpotch of extreme conditions and anything could happen. Back in London I used to have foolish fantasies of being marooned by blizzards in log cabins while large moose quietly strolled across the hills outside. When this promised to become a reality (apart from the moose), any thoughts of the romance disappeared in a flash. All I could picture was the image of me giving birth on the kitchen floor with Dan holding hot towels and a pair of scissors. When I told him of my fears, he reassured me Powys must have a helicopter for just this kind of emergency. "Anyway there is always the duck pond if we want a birthing pool," he added with a sudden laugh.

I remained stony-faced and reminded him there were still two months of pregnancy left and I could feel my hormones surging in prelude to another bout of violent mood swings. He looked suitably frightened and I grabbed the opportunity to make him visit the local town to get some supplies. In particular I stressed the need to stock up on anything that could generate heat.

I had been used to efficient central heating all my life. Twenty-eight years of gas-, oil- and electrically fuelled heat take their toll and I was not sure such a body could adjust to a Welsh winter. As I huddled and shivered around the gently hissing wood-burning stove, I wondered if such harsh conditions could do potential harm to the unborn baby – perhaps we should inform the social services of our situation? Surely the government could help, there must be funds available to help a pregnant woman in such dire emergency. Dan was behaving with an infuriating optimism as if everything was routine, but what was normal about living 1000 feet up a wet Welsh hill with no way to keep the house at the temperatures the human body needs? What would happen if the temperature fell to below minus ten? We would freeze in our beds and no one would discover us for months, perhaps years.

Heat had become one of the most important issues in my life. I had taken to wearing a Rupert the Bear duvet wrapped around me at all times. The softwood that Dan had bought from the forester was as wet as a haddock and burned like mouldy old carpet. I began to eye up Dan's furniture again, doing quick mental calculations about its potential calorific value. He announced he was going to cut down a tree instead. This struck me as an act of immense danger, I argued that his skills with the chainsaw were in their infancy and we needed a professional. But with total confidence Dan reminded me of his extensive chainsaw course and dismissed the chore as a relatively simple operation. He picked a large sycamore whose trunk had already been half cut through by our predecessors and which was now looking particularly treacherous.

He dressed up for the job in his chainsaw safety gear:

thick green leg pads, special reinforced wellies, large black gloves, a helmet and plastic eye protectors. He looked and walked like a cheap extra from *Star Trek*. I watched from a safe distance as he pulled the starter cord: nothing happened. Five minutes later, after much jerking on the cord and scratching of his head, he wobbled back towards the house only to return a few minutes later with a red petrol can. He waved at me on the way back as if everything was going exactly as planned.

This time the saw started first time and he began to cut into the tree. It was a slow process – he had to stop twice to consult the pictures in his *Illustrated Guide to Self-Sufficiency*. Wrapped up in two overcoats and my trusty duvet, I still felt half-frozen and watched the process in a strangely hypnotic state. First he cut a big 'V' shape into the side of the tree. This took some time and when he had finished, he excitedly waved the wedge of wood in my direction as if he had finished the task in hand.

He looked momentarily crestfallen when I pointed out the tree was still upright, but then shrugged and picked up the saw again, disappearing in a cloud of sawdust as the blade bit into the wood. Five minutes later the saw fell silent again – he had managed to lodge it irredeemably in the trunk – and there it stayed for a week, Excalibur-like. Fortunately at this point Mike turned up with a fresh supply of wood and this time it burned without hissing too much. My gratitude was so immense I almost asked him to be a godfather to my unborn child. For the first time in six weeks, the stove began to roar and I could feel the initial flickers of warmth beginning to flow through my icy veins.

Socially, it had to be said we were not making much of an impact on the local community. Apart from the woodsman, our main contact with the indigenous population was the odd chat with the local farmer on his way to feed his sheep and with our nearest neighbour Major Hartwood. He had introduced himself to us and issued an invitation for early evening drinks as soon as we were settled. So one frost-filled night we walked the third of a mile to his farmhouse. I might have insisted on driving the distance except my father had sent me a welcome parcel of fur-lined wellies and thermal gloves to go with a Christmas present of a Russian rabbit fur hat which had flaps over the ears. With these and the monstrously large fur-lined coat I had bought from the local agricultural suppliers I felt sufficiently protected to brave the journey on foot. Actually the coat was genuine Swedish armed forces regulation wear, used mainly on manoeuvres or so the shopkeeper told me.

The Major welcomed us into his parlour. "Good! Good!" he said. "You made it then. Come in and take the weight off your feet. 'Fraid I don't have many visitors. Have to take me as you find me."

He showed us through the hallway and in to a smallish sitting room. My overriding impression of his interior decoration was of numerous African souvenirs lining his walls. There were heads of big game animals, skins, tribal weapons and art. The house was tidy to a precision – not a dog hair in sight. (Come to think of it why *were* Dan's dogs in a continual state of moult?) Anyway, the Major's house was strangely cosy and neatly cluttered with books and all kinds of interesting objects. The sitting room had a large red velvet armchair which the Major insisted I sit in and showed Dan to a deep sofa opposite. He himself took a hard wooden chair which he explained he preferred anyway. On the dark oak side-table was a display of spirits and cocktail accessories. The Major had already prepared a tall jug bobbing with ice.

"Gin man myself. Back in Kenya, pink gin at sundown was a must with all us ex-pats. Came back years ago, but still can't break the habit."

I went for a very small malt and Dan dived into the gin while the Major handed round a saucer of cheese biscuits and twiglets. There was a large stuffed lion's head above the fireplace. Our host saw me looking at its snarling teeth.

"Tricky chap that," he observed cheerfully. "Gave us all a bit of a problem. Man-eater, you know. Got into the stockade one night. Leapt on one chap while he was sitting by the campfire. Seized him by the buttocks. Course the fellow yelled his head off and the cat let go. Bad luck for the chap next to him though – grabbed him by the throat. Killed him instantly, then carried him off into the bush. Too dark to follow, so I could only rub carbolic into the first fellow's behind.

"Started tracking the lion next day. Took a few days to get the right shot. Nice-looking beast, though: rather pleased with him. If you're interested, I have some slides of the hunt."

I said I would be fascinated. He removed a picture from the wall and placed a old metal slide projector on the table by his chair. He spent some time leafing through boxes which were all labelled and indexed on shelves to the right of the fireplace. I got the impression that this was a regular event for the Major.

"Right. Here we go. Everyone all right for drinks? Splendid."

The first slide was a large colonial house with the Major forty years younger and a small woman with her hair in a bun and holding a long stick. He swept his white hair to the correct parting and told us this was his late wife, Susan. The next few slides were of the house. There were a few of his camp in the bush and then various slides of deer-like animals that the Major explained were hartebeest, impala and orbi.

At last he gave a satisfied snort. "Ah yes, here we are – the man-eater." In front of us was a picture of a serious-looking young man in a pristine safari jacket and shorts with a rifle and five black men behind him.

"Took my five best Kikuyu. Excellent men in the bush. That's the trail. See the bits of cloth and blood? Not too difficult to track the beast, but he went quite a way. Found the remains of the poor victim behind this bush. Looked like others had joined in the feast."

I was beginning to find the imagery a tad gory, but he really brought the story alive, particularly as the now subdued perpetrator grimaced at us from his plaque above our heads. Eventually we came to the slide with the dead lion lying at the Major's feet and the slide show ended. The Major refreshed the drinks as I asked him to tell us more about Africa and his adventures, but he changed the subject.

"So have you got any plans for the land?"

Dan explained that we were probably going to rent out the fields as we had decided that with the new baby it was not the time to try small-scale sheep farming for the first time. Actually it had taken me two days to convince Dan not to take on hundreds of marauding sheep all susceptible to foot, mouth and leg diseases. I explained that we were interested in vegetable gardening and asked if he could offer any advice. He looked pleased that I had asked him for a favour.

"You can come here any time for advice. I would suggest that you take a soil test, you may need to lime, particularly for your brassicas. Look here, I have a book that may help you."

He handed me a battered copy of the Reader's Digest *Encyclopaedia of Vegetable Gardening*. As we left we promised we would call on him for any advice or help. He shouted from his front door, "Mind your way, there are potholes on the lane!"

I felt reassured by the Major living next door, there was something about his presence that made it impossible to imagine anything really dreadful happening under his watchful eye.

Apart from this successful liaison with a neighbour, we were left pretty much in solitude. Although we were visited by a few friends from London, most were put off by the drive or the thought of the Welsh weather, but a loyal handful did venture out. Mostly when they finally arrived, after hours spent counting the exits on the M4, they tended to spend most of their time shivering in the corner. They would giggle a lot and punctuate their embarrassment by pointing out the window and observing: 'I bet when you can see the view it's worth it!" Throughout their stay they would look at me with a mixture of anxiety and pity. Generally their visits would be cut short as they suddenly remembered some work that needed completion for Monday, requiring an early morning Sunday departure.

These weekends were not eased by Dan, who invariably got tipsy on Saturday night and brought out his flea-ridden smelly hawk. He would then proudly wander into the living room with the tatty brown bird on his fist, explaining the finer principles of falconry to a lot of glazed expressions. The more he talked, the more involved in details he would get until eventually his audience ceased to matter. On one occasion, for example, he forced a sensitively natured vegan to feed the mangy animal. That was bad enough, but the food was a day-old chick and it still contained the remains of its yolk sack. When the hawk bit into the cute limp fluffy body, there was an explosion of yellow syrup which squirted in all directions like particularly unpleasant lemon juice. The poor girl went white and staggered away holding on to her boyfriend for support.

The problem was that once started, Dan was practically unstoppable – only firm language could interrupt his verbal torrent and this was not really the best answer in company. Loud cries of 'For God's sake! Shut up!' only led to long silences which were even more embarrassing. But the incident with the vegan and the chick was the last straw, so for the sake of humanity and our future social life I felt the need to take action.

I devised a list of topics that were banned from conversation. This was a smidgen authoritarian, but I was heavily pregnant and the usual niceties were blown away by hormonally charged impulses. The list had to be foolproof – I knew Dan would be the first to spot any loopholes. So although I put a lot of time and effort into making the language water tight, I also added a 'catch-all' clause as an insurance policy.

The list was as follows:

SUBJECTS FOR DAN TO AVOID

1. Falconry: This is to include all past and future publications on the subject written by you or anybody else. It also covers any aspect of the training of any bird of prey, living or extinct. It applies particularly to the teething problems you are experiencing with your red tail female, 'Gwen'. You are not allowed to bring birds of prey into the house unless you are requested to by a guest, who must be completely unprompted. There are to be no accounts of peregrines which have flown low over our house and no discussion about the television programme *The Cook Report* (broadcast in 1993) about the same species. It *is* permissible to mention the habitats of birds of prey in the wild, but conversation must be kept to a minimum and at no time are you allowed

to talk uninterrupted for more than 90 seconds. I shall act as time-keeper in such circumstances and my verdict is final. All conversations on the breeding habits of the red kite must be kept to a polite minimum. Any discussion on the import and export of kangaroo leather is also covered by this section and prohibited.

2.   Transport: This includes all subjects related to British Rail and regional railways, particularly the North London Link and its relationship with the Channel Tunnel. It also covers all major and minor roads in the British Isles and the Republic of Ireland. Any examination of the various routes from London to mid-Wales are particularly to be avoided except when guests are determined to leave and are already consulting a map.

3. Agricultural Polices: The CAP is forbidden, as are local farming methods and particularly those subsidies which result in sheep overgrazing. Ecology issues are allowed, but any discussion of wind farms is to be timed and carefully supervised. Coppicing as an alternative energy source is permitted, but the discussion may not exceed 10 minutes and the audience must be heard to speak at least 3 times during the said period of time.

4.   Vegetarianism: This includes all discussion about the virtues of eating meat and specifically outlaws the argument that we are all part of some big food chain and being a veggie is a waste of time. This is doubly banned when the other party is a vegetarian.

5. Favourite Anecdotes: Just to be on the safe side I will briefly list some old favourites so there is no confusion. Any repetition of the following is totally forbidden: the interview with Islington's Chief of

Police; how your bicycle was confiscated as a suspect bomb in Parliament Square; mortgages; computers; what inspired you to become a journalist; the history of the rabbit; how a school teacher persuaded you to read the classics of English literature; anything that relates directly or indirectly to St Paul's Road, Islington.

6. Miscellaneous: This covers subjects that don't fit into a neat category. I will have to add to this list as subjects occur. In particular you may not mention how you failed to chop down the sycamore tree – or indeed anything to do with the chainsaw – nor the joys of cordless drills and your claims of DIY proficiency. It also covers Welsh place names – particularly the amazing coincidence that our farm means Hillside of the Hawk.

At first the list seemed a service to mankind. In fact I suspect most people would really love to create such a blacklist for their own partners, but are stopped by some misplaced kindness. In practice it backfired. Deprived of conversational topics, Dan turned to the list itself for dinner party relief. Along with the main course he would produce a copy to show guests. As a result, most visitors decided I was either mad or Goebbels re-incarnated and they even began to look pityingly at the man who had dragged me out to this rain-soaked mud bath. In the end I had to withdraw it, but was still secretly convinced it was a fair way to behave when you live in solitude on a Welsh mountain with no one else to talk to.

By the middle of February, we discovered we had a greater problem than subjects of conversation: we were seriously broke. The costs of moving in had sucked all life out of our bank accounts and things had reached the point where the discovery of a few pennies at the bottom of my bag was cause for major celebration. So when a magazine rang to ask Dan to go to Croatia for a week, he had to accept. I agreed without contemplating the full consequences of his absence: the constant feeding of the all-important stove, the greedy pigs, the neurotic bantams and worse, the dreaded dogs.

Dan promised me they would soon settle down after our arrival, but he obviously hadn't told the dogs – either that or they weren't listening. Instead they hung around the living room, taking all the space on the sofa, barking at imaginary visitors and being downright thoughtless. They took to ambushing me from dark corners, yapping and leaping up at my swollen tummy.

Things were bad enough when Dan was around, but now I was to be left alone with them for a whole week. The idea filled me with dread and I became very irritable. Dan did his best to make me feel better by spending a whole day chopping wood, stacking a week's supply of split logs next to the stove. He also brought in sack loads of food for the bantams and pigs.

Then the day came and I was alone. It didn't take long for the full horror of the situation to set in. I was heavily pregnant, 1000 feet up a Welsh hill in a drafty farmhouse, with seventeen anxious chickens, three wild dogs, two escapologist pigs, two smelly ferrets and an aggressive hawk. I felt panicky.

On my first night alone a tremendous storm broke out. I have never liked thunder or lightning ever since a near frazzling experience on a Norfolk golf course. I remembered that it was a good idea to insulate yourself so I wore my wellies and curled into the armchair. Wind the speed of a formula one race tore around the farmyard, throwing objects in all directions with huge crashes which made me jump. The television reception was too scrambled to make viewing possible and the lights began to flicker. Every now and again the flap at the back of the wood-burning stove was blown open and smoke puffed into the living room.

I sat very still in the armchair trying to suppress the urge to call my mother. I might have given in had I not remembered that in *Tintin and the Calculus Affair* Captain Haddock was blown into the chandelier by telephoning during a storm – so instead I practised my labour breathing exercises and tried to take my mind off things by reading a birthing book. It proved a foolish choice of literature for a seven-month-pregnant first-time mother – it was full of graphic images of women covered in blood and in obvious agony.

It seemed the only thing to do was go to bed and hide under the covers until morning. This was a timely decision as the lights went out while I was climbing the oak stairs. Fortunately I had a paraffin lamp. It gave off a horrid smell, but at least it relieved the pitch black of a storm-lashed Welsh farmhouse. Ever since childhood I have hated the dark, so it was an uphill battle picturing comforting thoughts. All that came to mind was Fred the farmer's story about a mad woman who had once lived in our house and died falling down the stairs I had just climbed.

I lay semi-rigid with fear still wearing my wellies, hyperventilating under the covers. The wind was beating against the house and the rain was lashing horizontally against the windows and downstairs came the sound of the dogs charging around in panicky circles. Eventually I managed to drift off to sleep by thinking about central heating and convenience shopping, but was woken less than a couple of hours later by the bloody dogs. Normally they slept downstairs by the fire, but with Dan away they lost all interest in their normal beds and invaded my room to howl at the window.

The thunder and lightning had been replaced by a forceful gale and between the fast-moving clouds a full moon was sporadically glaring down. Havoc, the youngest, was the noisiest of the three hounds, as she stood on the window sill, scratching at the glass and letting out dreadful wails. The other two circled the bed like patrolling sharks, intermittently accompanying her misery with whiney backing vocals.

The hefty weight of pregnancy destroyed my sleep patterns and, denied rest, I became hysterical. I covered my head with pillows and attempted to ignore the penetrating howls of the banshees wandering around the room, but it was no use. After an hour of this torture I was seriously considering fetching the air rifle to begin shooting indiscriminately.

I got up and shut them in another bedroom, desperate to submerge myself in deep sleep, but it only made things worse. Now they were clawing at the closed door and the volume of their doggy moans had gone up even further. It was too much. I released them from the bedroom to find they had eaten a pillow and excreted all over the lamb's-wool rug. There were also little spots of blood all over the bed that they had unmade.

By now tears were streaming down my cheeks and there was a well of hopelessness in my tummy – even my unborn baby seemed despondent. I dragged the dogs downstairs and out of the front door and put Bracken and Dill in my Renault 5.

I went back for the aptly named Havoc, but she slipped past my outstretched hand into the stormy black. My last glimpse of her was of a rear end bouncing away down the lane towards the shelter of a nearby wood. I shouted in vain: but my voice was carried away by the wind. My cries turned to sobs of fatigue and exasperation. I stood in the gale for an age, unable to decide what to do. What would Dan say about the loss of one of his beloved dogs? I couldn't do anything in the dark – I certainly couldn't go after her – so in the end I returned to bed and fell into a fretful sleep.

By the morning the wind had died. I got up late and staggered downstairs to stoke the fire, feed the pigs, release the dogs and look for the missing Havoc. In spite of the few hours' rest, I still felt my nerve ends tingling with an anxious sense of dread and fatigue bearing down on me. There was no sign of Havoc as I approached the Renault to release Bracken and Dill, but any concern was swept away by the sight of my poor car. As the two beasts leaped enthusiastically out of the driver's door, they revealed a scene of carnage. They had eaten every scrap of upholstery and the car's interior was reduced to a mess of foam and torn cloth. As I looked at the dogs, they seemed to sneer and laugh at me, tossing bits of car seat in the air with their teeth.

I really, really hated them.

Tears welled up in my eyes. I wanted to go home: proper home; home with wall to wall comfort, heat, no animals and ease at the flick of the switch. Home with no adverse elements. I wanted to be in the city where things like this could not possibly happen.

I fed the pigs who at least seemed calm and contented, but when I arrived at the chicken hut I found the door lying in splinters on the ground. There was no sign of any poultry. In just twenty-four hours, I had lost a dog and seventeen chickens. Surely this was proof enough that I was not cut out for this rural idyll. Not even Dan could discount the evidence of my second day alone in the farm.

The rest of the day was spent looking for the lost elements of our menagerie. Fortunately I discovered the chickens fairly quickly – they were roosting in the conifers behind the house, but then I took on the trial of finding Havoc. She was nowhere to be seen. In the end I took some cushions from the house and tried to make the

Renault comfortable and drove around all the local farms asking anybody if they had seen a small black dog. They all said "no" and were clearly much more interested in what had happened to my car. There were a lot of jokes like, "Have cravings for upholstery, then?" followed by roars of laughter. I managed to grimace. I called in to see Major Hartwood, who looked appalled at my misfortunes. He said he would go and look for Havoc and come up to the house and see to the chicken hut later that day.

I went home alone. On the way back I remembered I had forgotten to feed the hawk and ferrets. I hadn't even defrosted any food for them. They eat these disgusting day-old male chicks killed by battery farmers and then sold for a pittance to falconers. I tried to speed up the defrosting process by leaving them on top of the stove. This was probably playing Russian roulette with botulism, but by this stage I didn't care.

Once they were vaguely soft I tossed a couple at the hawk tethered in the garage. My initial interest in Dan's peculiar hobby had long since vanished and had been replaced by an idle boredom with the whole subject, which I suspect resulted from overexposure caused by Dan's keenness to share information with me. It was not that I didn't like his hawk, I just didn't particularly want to be that close to her. I managed to get rather adept at tossing the chicks from a safe distance. After the bird came the dreaded ferrets and when I opened the cage they seized a golden opportunity to leap out of their cage and disappear under the hut. As I crawled on all fours around the barn calling to them, I couldn't help remembering a friend who has a scar because, as a child, a ferret latched on to his top lip. It refused to be parted from his flesh until someone lit a cigarette and pressed it into the pads of the animal's feet.

After some thought, I grabbed the fire tongs and tried to

tease them out, but they were too slippery to get a grip. Finally I tried bribery – dangling chicks in front of the hole and coaxing them out that way, but that didn't work either. It was at this point that Major Hartwood arrived. In no time he had grabbed the escapees and locked them safely away. He gave me a report on his efforts to find Havoc.

"Followed her down to the cattle-grid," he said. "Got a bit difficult after that. Heavy rain washed away tracks, you know: makes the job almost impossible. Best thing to do is put out the word and wait. Now let's see to those chickens."

This God-like man fixed the chicken hut and explained that if I spinkled some corn in there they would probably come back. He also chopped more wood and stacked it neatly in the house. I thanked him again and again.

Two days passed and there was still no sign of Havoc. I was near breaking point. I rang my mother in a pathetic simpering voice and within a few hours of my call she was unpacking bags of expensive luxury foods from her car and I was feeling slightly better about life. It did not take a genius to realise that all was not well at Cold Uncomfortable Farm.

Fortunately for my sanity, although my mother was a confirmed dog-lover, even she was none too keen on Dan's beasts and we secretly began to agree that perhaps Havoc's disappearance was a bit of a godsend. Naturally I didn't want anything horrible to happen to her, but what could I do? Reduced to two dogs, I was beginning to see the optimistic side of this mini-tragedy. But celebrations were horribly premature – Havoc returned at two a.m. on the fourth night, barking and scratching at the back door. Too tired to be relieved or sorry, I let her in and went straight back to bed.

My head had hardly scraped the pillow when the sound of dogs killing each other could be heard through the incredibly thin floorboards. I would have gladly let them continue had it not been quite so loud. My mother was woken as well and we both went downstairs. In my exhaustion earlier, I had not noticed Havoc was covered in cuts and filth, but this was not the main problem. The real difficulty, as mother diagnosed, was that she was obviously on heat – at least it was a strong possibility, for Bracken was desperately trying to get to know her better. Understandably the invalid dog was not really in the romantic mood and it was her squeals of protest which had drawn us downstairs.

Now we were left with the dilemma of how to keep the two apart. After the incident with the upholstery, I was none too keen on putting her in what was left of my Renault, but couldn't think of anything else. My mother resolved the situation by offering to let Havoc sleep with her. I leapt at the offer and spent the remainder of the night restfully. My mother, however, did not. Havoc whimpered incessantly till daybreak and limped around her bedroom scratching at the door.

My first priority in the morning was to get Havoc to a vet. A brief – extremely unpleasant – examination of her downstairs business showed she was very definitely in season. Almost certainly she had spent the past three days being shagged senseless by every sheepdog in Radnorshire. The thought was horrific: if that dog had puppies I swore to myself that I would book into a hotel for the rest of my natural life. The understanding vet gave her an injection to deal with the consequences. Not for the first time, I found myself cursing Dan for leaving me in this predicament, so just to make sure Havoc remained puppyless, I jailed Bracken in the local kennels until his return.

My mother had to return to London the next day and the final two days of Dan's absence seemed like a year. Finally my sentence was up and Dan returned to find me looking white and shaky. With moist eyes I told him I couldn't live with three dogs. He assured me that something would be done, but I doubted his sincerity. He had a shifty expression and wouldn't meet my pleading look. All the same I could tell he felt guilty because he readily agreed to a comfort shopping trip to our nearest decent-sized supermarket. This was an hour's drive away and would inevitably mean spending yet more of the money we didn't have.

On the way to 'nibble heaven' we stopped at a garage to fill up with petrol. While Dan was dealing with the pump I wandered in to the large garden centre around the back of the forecourt, it was full of accessories. I could see this was a shop we needed to visit. Dan joined me and we were both blinded by the horticultural possibilities: there was so much we didn't realise we needed. We shopped with a ruthless hunger – or at least I did to make up for the past traumatic week. I have always found indulging in mindless consumerism snaps you back on to an even keel. The results of our expenditure included a heated propagator, two dozen asparagus crowns, French seed potatoes, masses of garden tools, packets of vegetable seeds and all manner of vital accessories. I read the back of the seed packets, which gave sketchy insights into when and how to plant. I couldn't quite believe it would really work.

These purchases marked a turning point in my life. As we did our laps round the aisles of Safeway, I began to eye the vegetable shelves in a new light. I now thought of tomatoes actually coming from a live plant and I imagined potatoes being unearthed from real soil. It was an extraordinary idea – I had never thought about the origins of food before. The whole concept began to make me very excited.

As soon as we got home I started to read the instructions for propagation and loaded the machine with compost-filled trays. The next day, when the soil had warmed up, I pricked small holes in the trays. First I opened the packet of tomato seeds. These turned out to be yellowy and slightly hairy. How could anything come from these? It is a truly amazing concept: what on earth happens? I was amazed at the idea that I could be twenty-nine years old and never have given the miracle a second thought.

I filled the trays with cherry and beefsteak tomatoes, sweet peas, globe artichokes, aubergines, cucumbers, mini-sweetcorn, jalapeno chillies and sweet peppers. I put the whole contraption on our bedroom window and swore to keep a vigil until the first green shoot emerged.

I sprayed them daily with the mister, but for ages nothing appeared. After a week I became impatient and dug up a sweet pea. A tiny little shoot was just popping out of the seed. It was incredible, really incredible. It was the most miraculous thing I had ever seen. I popped it carefully back in the soil and delicately covered it up again.

On reflection maybe I was particularly carried away because I was pregnant, but whatever the cause, by the end of the next week I had masses of little seedlings and was happy for the first time since we had arrived in our sodden new home. Ignoring the ever-present rain outside, I watched them grow on the hour every hour, taking copious notes and even photographing their progress.

When they seemed large enough, I transplanted them into some of the hundreds of terracotta pots I found in the barn. I performed the operation with such care that my hands began to shake. Naturally Dan was anxious to feed any interest I showed in anything so he built a lean-to cold frame next to an outhouse. Soon all my budding plants were in neat rows in my mini-greenhouse. I found them deeply inspirational.

One morning as I was checking them I saw a little vole scampering away. He had been munching on a sweet pea.

This was unacceptable, so I set a trap and twenty-four hours later he was dead. That was the first animal that I had ever killed.

After the success of the plant propagation I felt a little more at home in this soggy countryside. I had been shocked at my lack of knowledge about plants, but in fact I was ignorant in most aspects of nature. I gave myself a task to learn a new fact every week. My first snippet of information was that a collection of rhinos is called a crash.

THICK VEGETABLE SOUP

1 large onion/leek
1 large potato
1 large carrot
2 sticks celery
1 small turnip or parsnip
2 ozs pearl barley
15 oz tin of tomatoes
2 spts home-made stock
Knob of butter
Salt and pepper

Dice the vegetables. Sweat the onion or leek for a couple of minutes in the butter, before adding the remaining vegetables. Add the pearl barley, a good pinch of salt and pepper, the stock and tinned tomatoes. Simmer for 15 minutes. Remove a cupful of mixed vegetables for use as a garnish and liquidise the remainder. Ladle into bowls, adding the reserved vegetables and serve piping hot with hunks of fresh bread and butter.

March: Dan

Bel was sceptical about my relationship with our pair of Tamworths from the moment I had returned in triumph from Crickhowell.

"You'll get too fond of them," she had warned as she watched me lovingly scratching behind their ears. She pointed to the flock of bantams pawing the ground in one of the flower beds. "You can't even bring yourself to kill a hen for Sunday lunch, so what hope are you going to have with a pig?" she asked.

I wasn't listening: I was watching the two ginger-coated piglets burying their snouts in the trough, making their enjoyment clear with greedy snorts and smacking of lips as they tucked into our kitchen scraps. Like a child stationed in front of an educational museum exhibit, I was discovering first hand what omnivore means. Rotten potatoes, stale bread and curdled milk were all wolfed down by our two latest acquisitions. Vegetable trimmings and leftovers were tucked into with gusto and every morning the bucket of wine, beer and tea dregs disappeared in a trice.

In my enthusiasm, I found myself following the Great John's prescribed method of washing up. Warm water is trickled across every dirty dish, vessel and saucepan as you scrub vigorously with a brush. The resulting liquid is carefully collected and tipped into the bucket – the dishes which emerge from this treatment may still be covered with grease smears and bits of caked food, but they can then be washed properly and the waste water is positively brimming with nutritious goodness.

At any rate, our two piglets certainly seemed to enjoy this soup, particularly when it was mixed to a thick porridge with barley meal. They would squeal with greed and excitement as they heard the front door open, dashing to stand on their hind legs at the gate in eager anticipation. Then, as they snorted through their favourites – tea bags and banana skins – I would scratch their backs. For ten minutes each morning, all three of us were in our respective heavens.

Although Bel was less of a fan than myself, I soon discovered I was not alone. It seems the world is full of closet pig-lovers. For example, when we were invited to a dinner party by a friend in Shropshire, (she lived an hour's drive away, but to two social outcasts like ourselves, she felt like a next-door neighbour), I found myself talking to a middle-aged bank manager called Geoff. By the end of the main course I'd finished outlining the principles of falconry, had given him a quick guide to the mysterious variations in moulting sequences between the raptor groups and was beginning to give him a glimpse of the exciting self-sufficient world we were embarking on. Up to this point, he had appeared fairly subdued and I was beginning to think him a little boring until the mention of pigs produced an electric effect. Suddenly his eyes lit up and he sat upright.

Apparently, he and his wife Mary had once owned a Tamworth sow called Gloria. The runt of a litter, she had grown up in their garden and had become the apple of Geoff's eye. He had sneaked out to her sty each morning with a carrot or apple, furtively slipping it into the side of her mouth and tickling her behind the ears. Pigs are affectionate animals and in return, she had developed a crush on him. Indeed, things soon got out of hand as she became insanely jealous of Geoff's relationship with his wife. It rapidly reached the point where Gloria would fly into a fury whenever Mary got near her sty and she would attempt to head butt and bite her rival.

"They've such lovely temperaments," sighed Geoff as he recalled his adoring pet.

Next to him, Mary was less positive. In fact she sounded suspiciously like Bel: "Watch out you don't get too attached," she warned. "Gloria almost ended our marriage – we had a terrible row when she had to go to the slaughterhouse – oh, and whatever you do, don't give them names."

The next morning as I scratched their ears I reflected on Mary's words. My two friends were so sweet I couldn't possibly leave them nameless, but remembering the warning I tried to steer clear of sentimentality. In the end I opted for Pork and Bacon – it would never do to forget their destiny.

I was fascinated. This was incredible! Surely it was what self-sufficiency was all about: we were defying the laws of modern society and getting something for nothing! Well nourished on our waste, my little piglets grew even as I watched. One moment they were Spaniel-sized, the next they were Labradors, then Alsatians. After two months they weighed as much as me and I decided they were old enough to meet the world. I opened the gate into the small paddock next to the sty. It was wonderful to see them literally skipping with joy across the grass.

By now I had fallen for them hook, line and sinker, much to the outright fury of the dogs. They had always been suspicious of the two new arrivals, but as I grew increasingly absorbed by the two rapidly growing piglets, this turned to hostility and now they were downright aggressive. Whenever I picked up the swill bucket, they would begin to growl. As I moved to the door, this would turn to outright barks, snarls and bared teeth. Open it, and the pack would fly across the yard towards the pen, howling with rage. Their fury would only increase as I poured the greasy liquid into the trough and Havoc, the most outraged of the three, would hurl herself at the fence if I scratched either pig. She was passionately jealous.

It was also at about this point that the first great lesson about Tamworths was drummed home – pretty they may be, but containable they are not. No sooner were they in their new paddock than they began to nuzzle against the wire fence. In no time, they were in the enclosure next door and soon they had tunnelled into the field beyond.

My days were punctuated by cries from the increasingly horticulturally excited Bel. "The bloody pigs are out again!" Then, regardless of deadlines and workload, I'd have to drop everything to round up the miscreants. Sometimes I'd get there as they wriggled clear of the barbed wire, rounding them up like the POW camp guard in a war film and frog-marching them back to the sty gate. Other times I was not so lucky and would find myself haring out of the house and down the lane or across the fields in pursuit of their bumping orange backsides as they charged for the sheep troughs at the bottom of Fred's field.

This was when I learned the second great rule of pig husbandry – you cannot drive them. However hard you try, you cannot force a pig in any direction other than the one it chooses. This is because swine such as Pork and Bacon were not only fairly big by now, but they were also very low-slung. This meant they worked on the same principle as a rugby scrum, and, as any prop forward will explain, to push something which wants to go in the opposite direction, you have to be lower than its centre of gravity. I could no more force Pork and Bacon back into their run than I could have turned back the might of the Pontypridd front row. As I struggled to return them to their sty, I thought bitterly that the adage about leading horses to water but not making them drink was sheer bliss compared with moving a pig.

I turned to the Major for advice and was assured bribery was the answer. You may not be able to lead a pig to food, but who the hell needs to? Give the greedy little bastards the merest hint of a meal and they'll be burying their snouts in it before you have a chance to shout "Chow time!"

Soon there was a bucket of food waiting in constant readiness by the front door. When I heard Bel's familiar yell, I'd grab the pail and fly out of the house after the disappearing backsides, screaming as I ran "Grub's up, Pork! Come and get it, Bacon!"

The escapee would then scamper back and I would skid to a halt and charge towards the sty gate. Ideally I would hope to get it open before they arrived, but a pig can move surprisingly fast and more than once a hundredweight of ham-to-be came crashing into me, pitching me into the mud of the sty.

Once they were in, however, they'd lose all interest in me and devote their attentions to the bucket. This was my chance to plug the latest gap and I would beaver away with barbed wire and corrugated iron. They were more inventive than any Colditz escape committee, however, and the routine would be repeated five or six times a day. After a week or so, all three of us were pretty expert at our respective roles.

One day the Major saw the spectacle. "Never seen a pig move so fast," he said as he lent an expert hand to the fence repairs. "What on earth are they eating?"

"Oh, kitchen scraps mainly," I panted.

"Not giving coffee grounds?" he asked thoughtfully as he helped me plug the latest gap in their enclosure. I admitted there was a fair proportion of strong black Continental coffee mixed in with their slurry on most days. "Aha!" he barked with a laugh. "No wonder – got to watch the caffeine. Never drink the stuff myself. Saw what it could do to a man in Kenya. Won't touch it. Good dark tea, that's the stuff to clear the mind without sending the body haywire."

I made a mental note to omit the coffee and in no time the escapes had stopped – although I felt this was more likely to be thanks to the Major's fencing rather than the effects of diet – but soon I found myself missing our daily exercise sessions. Then Geoff and Mary came to dinner and while our partners inspected the vegetable patch behind the house, Geoff and I sneaked around to the sty, our hands full of carrots, apples and celery pinched from the larder.

"Do you take them for walks?" asked Geoff as he gazed longingly into Pork's beady black eyes. "Gloria and I used to go for lovely walks," he added wistfully as he shoved a carrot into her wet snout.

The thought was too tempting and the next day I began what soon became a daily ritual – a stroll down the lane. Whenever Bel wasn't watching and I thought the Major was unlikely to view the spectacle, I would arm myself with a bucket and go for a walk. Pork and Bacon would trot alongside and if they didn't quite walk to heel, at least I soon established a semblance of control. Needless to say, what the dogs thought of the whole procedure does not bear repeating.

This was light relief, however. Other, far more serious matters were beginning to cause us fresh problems. The first real cold snap was one good example. It came as a serious shock. As newcomers to horticulture, until now we had never bothered to listen to weather forecasts, they were merely the slot before the news, so it was a surprise to find the world muffled and white. Our tiny urban car had always struggled with the pot-holed farm track. Now with this submerged beneath eight inches of snow, escape was impossible. We were well and truly snowed in.

Naturally I was thrilled by the romance of it all, but Bel was less impressed. By now just the hint of a home delivery with me acting as midwife upset her greatly and I found it generally best to avoid the topic of labour as much as possible. Also, although we had bought two huge second-hand chest freezers to fill with the bounty from our garden and the contents of our sty, we had yet to harvest anything and the cupboard was almost bare. Fortunately the cold spell only lasted for four days, but Bel threatened to leave unless we learned the lessons of the experience. According to her, there were three of these: first, lay in serious supplies of wood; secondly, fill the freezer with choice supplies of tasty nibbles; and finally, acquire a four-wheel-drive vehicle – and fast.

It was too late now to do anything about the wood – for this winter at least – but the second was accommodated easily enough with a three-hour round-trip to the nearest big supermarket. It was the third category which most caught my attention. I asked around the area and was quickly steered towards a cheerful local farmer who had an ancient long-wheelbase Landrover gathering cobwebs in one of his barns. Until I saw her, I had pictured a short wheelbase, hard-topped car – and it certainly had to be diesel – but the sight of the grey bodied, tarpaulin-covered beauty in the barn swept all this aside. The grinning farmer accepted my offer of a little cash and the dog-ravaged Renault in part-exchange and I found myself the proud owner of a vehicle which burned petrol faster than a fire at an oil depot. Bel was horrified by its age, (it had been made in 1955), but I was as smitten by my 'classic' as I was with Pork and Bacon.

More importantly, however, I got my first confirmed sighting of a peregrine. I was driving up the Wye Valley when I noticed the characteristic long-pointed wings of a falcon high above. It was circling effortlessly in the gale, high above the valley, far too big and too aimless to be a kestrel. With a joyous whoop I knew I was staring at one of the world's top predators – and within a few minutes' drive of our front door. I stared in rapt attention at the sickle-winged shape silhouetted against the grey clouds whipping past and realised with a jolt that most of the 'kestrels' I'd been watching since our arrival were actually these, the pinnacle of a falconer's dreams. They were all over the place! My delight knew no bounds. Bel was far more concerned by the abrupt swerve with which I'd pulled the car into the lay-by. She pointed out that because of her condition, the movement was particularly uncomfortable and that perhaps I ought to be thinking more about the responsibilities of parenthood than distant black dots in the sky.

Such observations were becoming increasingly frequent as the date of the birth galloped towards us and Bel was becoming obsessed with the knowledge that epidurals and Caesareans were not on offer in the local cottage hospital. Nor did Dr McBain help when he explained that, if things *were* to go wrong, a helicopter would be the order of the day. As an anxious first-time mother with a phobia of flying, this did nothing to calm an already apprehensive Bel, but in the end the thought of the hour's drive while in labour across twisting mountain roads was too grim and she reluctantly agreed to the local option.

Having moved the birth 35 miles closer to the farm, I entertained vague hopes I might be able to close the last ten miles without too much difficulty and have a home birth, but fortunately I kept my thoughts to myself. It was clear that in her present state of apprehension, any mention of going it alone might produce a major breakdown in our relationship.

Meanwhile we had what were likely to be our last house guests for some time. Two friends – both doctors – came out and Mike and I spent a happy three days together, working our way through the wine range of the local shop, accompanied by his splendid rendition of 'Every Sperm is Sacred'.

In this we were alone. His wife, Clodagh, was also pregnant and she and Bel had to content themselves with watching us morosely from a very sober state.

For my own part, as the weather improved, I was finding it increasingly hard to get any work done, finding the temptations of outdoors too great to control. There were trees to cut down and plant, endless tasks to perform with my trusty cordless drill, the duck pond needed dredging, the vegetable patch needed urgent attention before the main planting season began. Also, of course Pork and Bacon needed feeding and walking twice a day. All of this took time and left precious little for earning pennies.

Dominating everything, however, was the looming date of 17 April. As it crept ever nearer, Bel was becoming increasingly nervous. I found my biggest problem was keeping her calm about the whole thing and particularly soothing her preoccupation about how such a comparatively large thing as a baby could emerge through the standard female equipment. She was not at all happy and things only worsened with the news that Fred's daughter-in-law had just had her first child two months prematurely. Apparently it had been an extremely tricky birth and the farmer had an expression of grim relish as he announced both mother and child were lucky to survive. I tactfully kept this last bit of information to myself, but

Bel still sensed all had not gone well and the incident threw her into an even deeper bout of depression.

Nor were matters helped by all the friendly 'information' friends and relatives felt obliged to pass on. Since well before Christmas, everyone (and I mean everyone), couldn't resist the 'she-was-in-labour-for-153-hours-the-drugs-didn't-work and-the-epesiotomy-was-botched-so-their-sex-life-is-over-and-then-the-child-turned-out-to-be-suffering-from-a-rare-blood-disorder-and-was-in-intensive-care-for-the-next-five-months' sort of story.

"These are the one in a million cases," I kept telling Bel, but with extremely limited success, partially because I too couldn't help worrying about the 'what if' scenario.

So, it was understandable that Bel was beginning to brood on the ordeal she was due to face in a few weeks' time. In an effort to distract herself, she devoted many hours to the creation of a birthing tape, comprised of her favourite tracks of soothing music. As the rain continued to pour down outside, she found herself recording and re-recording this almost daily. Meanwhile various assorted relatives cleared their calendars and were waiting to rush to the bedside (her mother, bless her, had actually taken to driving around London with her overnight bag packed in the boot and was carrying a mobile phone everywhere). Not to be left out of the general atmosphere of preparation, I found myself writing out addresses on stamped postcards, ready to fill in the relevant hastily scribbled details on the day.

Fortunately, however, the weather came to our aid for once. At the end of the month came a sustained bout of sunshine and for the first time since our arrival the farm and surrounding valleys were bathed for hours on end in warm spring light. The air felt positively balmy and I was keen to get our self-sufficiency properly under way. Bel needed little encouragement to take her mind off things by

working in the garden and we spent a very happy afternoon pottering around the vegetable patch. It fell to me to
wheel out the giant rotovator we had also inherited with
the farm and I began the laborious task of turning over the
soil.

This proved harder than I'd anticipated. To begin with,
in spite of the sunshine, the earth was completely water-
logged and although like everything else our predecessors
had acquired the rotovator was ludicrously overpowered,
it was soon struggling with the task. To complicate
matters further, the area seemed at some point to have
been a dumping ground for baler twine. At any rate, I was
soon finding myself having to stop every few minutes to
clear the machine's blades of a tangled mass of shredded
plastic and coarse sisal string. It was also extremely heavy
work and I was soon bathed in sweat.

Bel was anxious to get planting, however, and so no
sooner had I managed to bare a strip of earth and break it
down into something like a cultivatable state, than she was
stuffing broad beans into the soil. These were chosen
partially because these are supposed to be particularly
hardy, but more because they were the only seeds on sale
in the local ironmonger's. After a couple of hours of this,
we were both covered in mud and chilled to the bone, but
hot baths worked wonders and that night, as we felt our
muscles slowly knot and tighten from the unaccustomed
exercise, we congratulated ourselves on our industry. For
a few blissful hours Bel forgot about the agonies that
awaited her and as we lay in bed, we found ourselves calcu-
lating when we could reap our first harvest.

The next morning I began work on another cherished
project – soil fertility. Of all the lessons John Seymour had
taught, this was probably paramount. At the best of times
all plants take nutrients out of the ground, but the problem is exacerbated in an area of poor soil, such as our own.

It was therefore up to us to pump up the fertility of our shallow acid loam. Naturally livestock would play an important part in due course, but a compost heap was equally important. It would consume anything the pigs could not – paper, cardboard, grass cuttings and citrus skins – and turn them into top-quality soil, freeing us from our dependence on costly planet-destroying peat. So, as soon as time permitted, I scrounged half a dozen pallets from the local farm store and constructed a pair of professional-looking bins at the bottom of the garden.

No sooner had I finished, however, than winter returned with a vengeance and the returning frost not only nipped off those few shoots which had made it to the surface, but sent my composting plans into suspended animation. Instead I found myself having to redirect my interest in decay to a serious critique of modern packaging methods and the complete failure of our local authority to offer adequate recycling facilities.

In general, however, we were undaunted by the temporary set-back in the weather and continued with our ambitious plans for the vegetable patch. We were spurred on in this by the knowledge that it would be our principle food supply for the summer. It had long struck me that although self-sufficiency was a worthwhile goal generally, priority should be given to luxury crops – expensive treats like soft fruit and artichokes which take several years to develop their full potential. This resolve was given extra impetus after our first two months of dependence on the local stores with their winter range of fresh vegetables limited to onions, potatoes, parsnips and leeks.

As we sat down one night to one of my regular culinary creations – lamb stew, served with mashed parsnips and steamed leeks – Bel started a conversation on the subject of favourite meals. She asked what dishes I would take with me, were I invited on to the gastronomic equivalent of

Desert Island Discs. Visions of hot rich curries, steaming naan bread, basmati rice, pickles and chutneys flooded my thoughts. Next came fiery Thai dishes, laden with lemon grass, lime leaves and flaming red bird's eye chillies. The procession continued through Schezhuan, Mexican and Jamaican cuisine, before ending with the image of anchovies, pimentos and capers, cascading in a rich paste of sun-dried tomatoes down the sides of really fresh home-made pasta.

While my taste buds watered at the visions of all this hot, fiery food, Bel's imagination took a subtler turn. Top of her list came lobster (what form it took was unimportant), followed closely by really fresh steamed sea bass. Then came seafood generally, poussin in a light tarragon sauce, Peking duck and delicate lamb chops, served with redcurrant jelly. Artichokes, asparagus and peas straight from the pod were her favourite vegetables, although she conceded that few things could beat a good crisp mixed green salad, laced with herbs and drizzled with fresh vinaigrette.

As the conversation continued, we found the meal in front of us sadly disappointing. It was not that it was badly cooked – if I say so myself it was more than edible – but we had eaten a version of the same dish every week since our arrival and had the slightly uncomfortable knowledge that we would probably be seeing another incarnation next week. Moreover, there was little prospect of matters improving over the coming months if the unadventurous range of vegetables on sale locally was anything to go by. It was obvious that if our diets was to improve over the coming months, we would have to start our horticultural efforts in earnest.

So as soon as the dishes were cleared away, we turned to the bookshelves for advice. I pulled out the battered copy of *Self-Sufficiency*, while Bel rummaged around in a file for the mail-order seed catalogues. The next three hours passed in almost total silence as we immersed ourselves in thoughts of the horticultural bliss to come, but the tranquillity was undermined somewhat when we began to compare notes.

For once our normal roles were reversed. I found myself playing the conservative, talking about concentrating on beans, fir apple potatoes and courgettes. Meanwhile, Bel's imagination had run riot with more adventurous fare. Inspired by our dinner conversation, she was determined to fill every gap in the list of ingredients necessary to create our favourite meals. It would be tedious to go through the entire repertoire, but suffice to say it included four types of basil, lemon grass, chillies and coriander, on top of the slightly less alien, but still adventurous range of celeriac, squashes, sweet corn, mangetout, a whole fleet of lettuces and rocket.

I could cope with these, but was deeply alarmed by the inclusion of half a dozen plants which to me were complete anathema: it transpired she had designs on rhubarb, gooseberries and – horror of horrors – swedes! This was no mere irrationality on my part, but rather a Pavlovian reaction, based on traumatic childhood experiences of institutional catering. At my three otherwise benevolent schools, sadistic teachers, deprived of corporal punishment to break the rebellious teenage spirit, used diet as the weapon of last resort. For me, rhubarb and gooseberries will always have nauseous associations with congealed Bird's custard, but it was the thought of mashed watery swede which I found most distressing and I swore roundly that I would leave rather than live on a farm cultivating the abominable root.

More importantly, however, totting up the seed bill produced an astronomical figure which was clearly beyond our budget. So, in the manner of all good diplomats, we began by seeking out common ground, starting with those plants which appeared on both lists. Unfortunately this didn't get us far and we were left with red onions, rocket potatoes and blackcurrants. At £20 it might be affordable, but it left us with a distinctly limited range of culinary options for the year ahead.

It is no exaggeration to say negotiations continued around the clock for days with the silence of even the small hours regularly punctuated with exclamations of "Swiss chard – I mean it!" or "We haven't finished with the marrow implications!"

Gradually we wore each other down and eventually a deal was struck, although like all hard-fought agreements, there was much bad grace on both sides. I scored a notable victory on the rhubarb front (mainly because this is normally planted in the autumn) and managed to whittle down the gooseberry patch to just two bushes. To my disgust, however, it turned out that swede seed is so cheap my prejudices were bulldozed to one side. I also lost an important battle on the issue of asparagus. The 'crowns' – or root cuttings – of these were pricey and I was inclined to forget about the 'grass' bed for the sake of parsimony, but Bel was adamant that our new world was already suffi-ciently puritanical to be in desperate need of a shot of luxury. True, 30 crowns might come in at £25, but that was a small price to pay for ample supplies of tender green shoots each spring and, after all, it was far less than the price of a restaurant meal for two (not that we ate out anyway).

I gave way as graciously as I could manage, comforted in large part by my own fondness for a plate of asparagus, drenched in melted butter and freshly ground sea salt.

Unfortunately, when we turned to the books for advice it became clear that these took several years to crop prop-erly. The chronology went something like: year one, plant; year two, maybe cut a couple of spears; year three, harvest sparingly; year four, eat until you're sick.

Nevertheless, we reasoned that the sooner we began, the sooner we'd be dining regularly on plates of the luxury vegetable, so the next step was to find a suitable spot for the bed. In the end we settled on slicing a sizeable chunk from one side of our front lawn. I skimmed off the grass, out came the rotovator again and I spent an afternoon steering the bucking and spluttering contraption back and forth, slowly – ever so slowly – reducing the thick mud to something resembling the tilth described in the manuals.

The next stage was more tricky, however. Apparently asparagus loves rich soil and prefers it to be on the alkaline side, but ours was thin, poor and decidedly acid. It was obvious that we needed help again and so, one bright morning, I found myself walking down the lane to consult the Major. There was no answer when I knocked at the door, but I spotted a plume of thick grey smoke rising from the bottom of the field in front of the house and wandered down to see what he was doing.

When I reached the blaze there was no sign of our neighbour. The fire was burning strongly, however, and had clearly just been attended to – with the centre piled high with fresh twigs and branches. As I looked around I was surprised to see the Major's two immaculately behaved dogs lying to attention on either side of a chain-saw and billhook.

"Ah! It's you," said a voice suddenly from behind me. I wheeled around to see the Major standing immediately behind me, although God knows where he had materialised from. Apart from a couple of leafless hawthorns, there was no cover of any description behind me. He was dressed in a camouflaged jacket, with light green army fatigues on his legs and heavy black boots laced tightly up his calves. It was his face which really arrested my attention, however. Each cheek was daubed with a thick black stripe, another ran beneath each eye and more charcoal was rubbed into his neck. The whites of his eyes positively gleamed against the dark background and for an instant he reminded me strongly of Martin Sheen in the final horrific scenes of *Apocalypse Now!*

The Major's demeanour was anything but deranged however. He seemed totally oblivious to my surprise.

"Saw you coming, couldn't think who you were for a moment," he said simply. "Thought I'd better lie low until I'd sorted out your intentions. Standard security practice."

"But where on earth did you come from?" I asked, staring back up the hill in puzzlement. Apart from several million one-inch-high blades of grass, there was no cover that I could see.

"Drainage ditch," he retorted with a smile, delighted with the obvious success of his camouflage. He pointed to a narrow trench a few feet away which looked too thin to hide a rabbit, let alone a human. "Whacked on a bit of the old war paint when I heard the drive gate click and nipped in there. Trick I learned in Kenya from my Kikuyu trackers – many of 'em were ex-Mau Mau, you know."

I failed to see why one needed to resort to guerrilla tactics in modern Wales simply because of an unexpected visitor, but the Major looked both so extraordinary and so pleased with himself, that I decided to keep my observations to myself. Instead I asked his advice about improving the fertility of an asparagus bed.

He looked distinctly unimpressed.

"Not a grass man myself," he muttered. "Wouldn't have a clue. Prefer straightforward things, like beans, carrots and potatoes. Natural crops those, grow well up here. Forget the rest."

"Well, you're probably right, but just supposing you wanted to prepare a really good fertile bed, what would you do?" I asked diplomatically.

"Hmmph!" snorted the Major, obviously still deeply distrustful of exotic vegetables and my disregard for his advice. "Only one thing to do: shit!"

After the camouflage trick I had begun to suspect our neighbour was sufficiently eccentric to be issuing an imperative, but I decided to cock an inquisitive eyebrow while my imagination grappled with the schoolboy's interpretation of his words. The latter vision was so powerful, however, that I found it difficult to surpress a childish giggle.

"Your barn – full of it. Pump as much of that into the ground as you can manage," he barked, turning back to look at his fire and his statuesque dogs. He was referring to the fact that our predecessors had once housed a dozen cows in the more ramshackle of the two barns. This had never been mucked out and, according to our neighbour, remained full of three-year-old manure. Clearly few observational details escaped him and it seemed certain we were sitting on a fertility bombshell.

I hurried back to tell Bel about the Major's advice and, after fixing two huge ploughman's lunches, the pair of us headed for the barn, armed with wheelbarrows, shovels and pitchforks.

For the next three hours we immersed ourselves in a labour which proved far more back-breaking than either of us had anticipated. To begin with the manure was hard-packed into a solid block of almost concrete-like consistency and I had to hack away at it with a pick to make any impression on the foot-thick layer. Next, it had to be loaded into a wheelbarrow and ferried across the muddy yard and lawn to its intended destination and hurled across the substantial bed-to-be. Back and forth we marched, slowly heaving barrow load after barrow load on to what we intended to be the jewel of our collection and as dusk was falling, we finished, but it was clear that yet more labour was needed. The new bed was now covered in brick-sized lumps of ancient cow-shit and even to our inexperienced eyes, seemed far removed from the soil in the weekly gardening programmes which had recently become compulsory viewing. I summoned up one last burst of energy and hauled the rotovator out of the barn and tried to force the hard-packed lumps into the soil, but in the end I was saved by the failing light. I retreated inside to nurse my aching muscles and to contemplate the situation.

We knew from the books that in an ideal world we should wait until the worms and rain achieved what man-made machinery could not. Although all the guides stipulated strictly that the soil must be broken down into a fine tilth, we didn't have the luxury of time. The 30 asparagus crowns we had ordered (at great expense) by mail-order had been drying out in the garage for almost a fortnight and as every day passed they were losing their will to live. If we were to have any hope of success, I reasoned it was better to get them into ill-prepared ground rather than let another fortnight go by.

The next morning I was out there, working on hands and knees in the mud to ease our precious crowns into the soil. For anyone unfamiliar with asparagus cultivation, I should explain here that the delicate spears so beloved of gourmands spring not from seed but from a tangled knot of root off-cuts which resemble nothing so much as a lanky spider crab. These have to be lovingly teased apart and then soothed into a trench, mounded slightly in the middle to support them from the weight of the soil as they are covered over. As I slaved over the unfamiliar task it was also inevitable that the rain should start, coming down in a steady drizzle sufficiently light to encourage me to persevere, but chillingly penetrating all the same. I was soon soaked to the bone, but continued grimly, reasoning that there was little point in breaking off halfway because I would just end up with a second drenching when I returned to finish the task.

As if to reward me for my hard work, the next day dawned bright and clear, heralding our second proper bout of truly pleasant weather. This allowed me to return to hawk training in earnest (I had barely started a fortnight ago when the elements turned on me). Naturally, I leaped at the opportunity. This was, after all, what I had come here for.

Fortunately, thanks to my earlier efforts, Gwen was already approaching flying condition. Put simply, this involves training the bird to respond to commands by slimming it down until it reaches the avian equivalent of a boxer's fighting weight. Then it will be sufficiently motivated and fit to try hard to catch quarry, but prepared to return to the fist when it fails.

Or that is the theory.

Sure enough, when I weighed Gwen, I found she was spot on the 2 lbs 10 ozs that I had been flying her in Oxfordshire before Christmas and so, inspired by the weather and full of anticipation of a wonderful afternoon's hawking among the gorse and bracken, I headed up the hill behind the house.

At first everything seemed to be coming together perfectly. The air was full of birdsong as chaffinches, tits and blackbirds dusted down their vocal chords ready for the breeding season ahead. There were plenty of rabbits in evidence too, sunning themselves on the hill above us and hopping back at an almost leisurely pace as we approached.

This was where the trouble began. I didn't give a damn that we couldn't get sufficiently close for a kill – for me it was reward enough to be out in the sun, enjoying the sounds and smells of a perfect spring day – but for Gwen it was another matter. It soon became apparent that the rabbits, inured to the ways of hawks thanks to the hill's numerous wild buzzards, knew all about the strategic advantage of altitude. They understood perfectly that provided they remained above the frantically bating beast on my fist, they were safe. She was incapable of flying fast uphill and, too used to Oxfordshire's rolling hills, lacked the experience to gain height before even thinking about hunting. Worse, for the past three months she had been cooped up in a small pen as the wind and rain had lashed the hillside, steadily losing fitness.

In consequence, as I laboured up the hill – and it is a very steep hill indeed – Gwen repeatedly launched herself from the fist, only to land a few yards away, panting and exhausted as a white scut bobbed leisurely towards its bury. By the time I reached the top, her beak was open, tongue arched belligerently as she gasped for air, and in a thoroughly foul mood. I should have spotted the warning signs and instead of continuing with the hunt, turned the occasion into a training exercise, keeping her on the fist, while recapturing her good humour by feeding her up with a tough rabbit foreleg.

That is what I *should* have done. In fact after my long bout of forced inactivity, I was too excited. I was desperate to have one last crack at a decent flight and an opportunity soon presented itself as I spotted a rabbit grazing innocently on the short-cropped turf, about 50 yards ahead. For once our quarry had no height advantage and although it was too close to the nearby gorse for Gwen to have much hope of catching it, at least she'd be able to get close enough to restore her flagging confidence – or so I thought.

Heart in mouth, I swung my gloved hand smoothly forwards, casting her off towards the intended victim. The four-foot wingspan unfurled itself as she launched herself majestically into the cool Welsh mountain air and for a split second I bathed in the sheer perfection of the moment. The birds were singing, my nostrils were filled with the scent of warm damp earth and the panoramic view was dappled with the shadows of clouds drifting slowly across the pale blue sky. Best of all, far from seeing us and scuttling for cover, the rabbit had actually turned his back and was grazing oblivious to the pair of us. Gwen was about to christen her Welsh hunting career!

Then, with the same slow-motion quality with which one watches an accident, everything started to go wrong. Far from closing rapidly on her prey, making the most of surprise, Gwen peeled off to the left, wheeling out over the valley on stiff, sail-like wings. Twice she circled as she drifted further away from me, remaining at eye-level, but rapidly gaining altitude as the hillside fell away below her. As she turned for the second time, I began to whistle and frantically beat my glove with the largest lump of meat that came to hand as I groped desperately in the hawking bag dangling at my side.

Gwen ignored my calls. Indeed, she barely glanced in my direction as she turned for a third leisurely circuit to take stock of her new surroundings. I watched her continue to soar high above the farm and patchwork of small fields spread out across the valley floor. In less than a minute she was barely more than a speck in the sky and then, suddenly, she furled her wings and began to drop rapidly. As she passed below the skyline, she disappeared from view, the browns, creams and reds of her plumage blending in perfectly against the backdrop of dead bracken, leafless spinneys and distant sheep.

This was when the worries *really* began. The most proficient falconer with the best-trained bird may be totally confident his bird will return – but only as long as it remains in sight. Even the 'greats' of modern falconry (and they do exist in this, as in all sports), have to admit to at least a momentary quiver of trepidation when a hawk disappears from sight. They know that at best this is no more than a wild animal whose natural instincts have been suppressed through a training process based (precariously) on manipulating its calorific intake. If it kills for itself out of sight, unlike a dog it will never return in triumph bearing its catch. Instead it begins to feed and with every mouthful, its interest in its owner diminishes. Within a few minutes it will be literally gorged (the word is a falconry term in origin) and fed up (again a falconry phrase). It will then fly to a suitable (for this read inaccessible) vantage point and digest the meal, oblivious to all human entreaties. If it kills again within the next couple of days, it will have reverted to a virtually wild state and within a week or so, recapture will be virtually impossible.

So even great falconers worry when they don't know the precise position of their bird. I was very definitely not a great falconer – indeed, I was little more than a beginner – and worse, had lost a hawk the previous year (he was blown away in a gale to land somewhere in the middle of a well-stocked shooting estate). Thus, as I watched the 'blip' on my visual radar disappearing, my elation at the perfect hunting conditions was transformed into sheer, blind panic.

I ran, stumbling down the hillside as fast as I dared, desperately attempting the impossible task of watching my feet and the skyline simultaneously. The ground was pockmarked with rabbit holes, gorse roots lay like twisted snares across the steep incline and the grass was still wet enough to be truly treacherous. Nevertheless, I managed a speed which would be the envy of any fell-runner as I careered back down the hill towards where I estimated I had last seen my bird land.

Fortunately, as I clambered across a fence, I spotted her

silhouette in the most likely spot – near the top of a leaf-less ash. After my careering descent, I was completely out of breath: my throat felt as if I had swallowed a red-hot cannonball, my heart was pounding and my legs felt like jelly. I stopped running and walked more slowly to the tree, confident she would descend, as soon as she had forgotten about the infuriating bouncing scuts up the hill.

I was still waiting an hour later. By now all sense of heat had evaporated and my feet, in particular, were numbed with cold inside my sodden boots. Dusk was definitely falling by now, but Gwen showed little interest in the tasty morsel held out in any manner of tempting positions. Finally she looked down disdainfully, bobbed her head a couple of times and (this the tell-tale sign that action is imminent) shat forcefully. Sure enough, a second later she spread her wings – but only to fly across two more fields.

It was clear she was not going to return that night. Still, I was not wholly downhearted – at least I knew where she was. She would be in the same place the following morning, but more importantly, she couldn't hunt in the dark and would be twelve hours hungrier when I returned at dawn.

Again, that was the theory, but things did not go according to plan. Although I was there at six, well before light, it was another seven hours before I held her jesses firmly clamped between fingers and thumb. In the interim I found myself running backwards and forwards across the valley, inviting much amused comment from passing farmers as I whistled pathetically at tall, leafless, trees. In the end it was only by tying a particularly large lump of juicy meat on to the end of a long length of string that I managed to lure her to the ground. A careful approach and a desperate lunge for her legs finally put her in my grasp.

One might have thought this lengthy episode would have deflated my spirits, but in fact I was anything but depressed. My overriding emotion, as I trudged the two miles home, was of euphoria. I decided that her disobedience was due to her lack of fitness – the muscle that had bulked up her weight before Christmas had been converted to fat and she had far too much latent energy to be obedient.

Sure enough, as the fine weather continued, I reduced her weight and within a week she was flying perfectly, although it has to be confessed that our impact on the local population of canny rabbits was anything but impressive; we managed just two kills and neither of these was anything to boast about. The first was a baby, little bigger than a rat and the second so riddled with myxomatosis it was blind and incapable of escape.

Nevertheless it was a start and the whole exercise of watching the bird flying and hunting in its natural way so thoroughly enjoyable that I began to wonder if it might not be a good idea to get Bel a hawk of her own. That way she could share more fully in the pleasure of this most ancient of sports. Moreover, as the perfect incentive to climb the hill on a daily basis, it was good exercise and, last but not least, if I were to get her a male red tail, in due course we would have a breeding pair! As I dreamed of our family-to-be setting out on lengthy hawking expeditions, the vision seemed just too perfect: this, surely, was what paradise on earth was all about!

LAMB STEW

1 lb diced lamb
(preferably from a cheaper cut like
shoulder with fat removed)
2 ozs chopped streaky bacon
1lb onions
2 lbs assorted seasonal vegetables
(eg potato, parsnip, carrot, celery)
2 cloves garlic
1 large tin tomatoes
2 oz tin of anchovies
½ pt cheap (but drinkable) red wine
Handful of fresh herbs – preferably
including rosemary,
bay leaves and parsley

Brown the meat in a little oil. Remove from pan
and soften the onions in the remaining juices, then
add the chopped vegetables and garlic. Stir for a
minute on a high heat, then return the meat and
add the rest of the ingredients. Transfer to oven and
cook gently on low heat for 2 hours. Serve with
mashed or baked potato.

April: Bel

The buds were bursting and in much the same way my pregnant stomach was growing into gargantuan proportions. My walk had become a waddle and whenever I stood still, my hands would unconsciously cup around the small of my back. I couldn't see my feet (let alone reach them) and was in the humiliating position of having to rely on Dan to do up my shoelaces.

Life had changed so immeasurably it made my thoughts swim, but as the due date came closer I became increasingly preoccupied with the mechanics of labour. I could not yet picture the baby, not even the simplest of images. I'm not sure I was even convinced there was a baby: perhaps it was a large cyst or maybe a trapped cushion? Even when the foetus kicked I found it hard to rationalise that a small infant was in there waiting to emerge.

Gradually I began to home in on the negatives of giving birth. How bad was it really? Just how much pain *did* they mean? To avoid such unhealthy preoccupations, I tried to read novels, but foolishly chose rather too many lengthy 19th-century tomes, all of which eventually succumbed to gory episodes of death during childbirth. What did they die of? Was it shock from the pain?

I needed to know exactly what would happen, but

when I asked experienced relatives they invariably dismissed my fears with platitudes such as "I am sure you will be fine." It was far worse when I asked contemporaries, who produced a collection of the most horrific stories of eight-day labours, lengthy operations, unimaginable pain, buckets of blood, dead babies and women splitting in two.

For many it was competition to tell the most gruesome story. Like the Ancient Mariner, they were compelled to impart tales of doom and paint lurid images which would ricochet around my mind in the small hours of the morning as I lay dragged out of sleep by the usual indigestion. I did try to be brave, but I challenge any first-time mother not to be at least morbidly *curious*!

I thought perhaps I could gain some more reassuring answers from my local doctor. At my next checkup I casually introduced the topics of excruciating pain and death and their connections with childbirth. Dr McBain laughed.

"Oh you don't want to worry about that – giving birth is as easy as shelling peas," he said.

I had never shelled peas, but instinctively realised this was probably an exaggeration. The doctor told me he had two very important pieces of advice for me: "Don't go playing with any sheep's after-birth or rummaging around in piles of silage," he said. "This would not be good for the baby."

I tried to explain that I did not know what silage was and that I was unlikely to be anywhere near sheep's afterbirth, let alone play with it. Still, I thanked him for the advice and left the surgery with my confidence still at a low ebb.

The desire for satisfactory knowledge drove me next to the ante-natal clinic and I enrolled in a session that was running in the local cottage hospital. I walked in on the first day with a pathetic 'please help me' expression, only

to be met by a room full of other mothers-to-be all looking at me silently saying 'please help *us*'. At the front of
the room sat the midwife who smiled and seemed at total
ease: this was an encouraging sight. I felt reassured by her
confidence, like when you're on the plane and you glance
at the hostess to make sure she isn't wearing an oxygen
mask with her head between her legs. The midwife was
called 'Faith' – this seemed like a very promising start.

We settled down and she began to tell us that labour
was nothing to worry about. The room sighed with relief.
She told us she had been practising midwifery for years
and had seen every possible birth scenario and she reminisced for a while about her early days and some of the
more unusual places she had assisted in births. Then she
outlined how she planned to run these ante-natal sessions.

"I find that it is better to get the whole business of
complications during labour out the way at the start," she
said, "then we can relax and concentrate on methods of
pain control, breast-feeding and so on."

My nerves fluttered, but maybe there was some wisdom
in this. Faith left the room and we all shuffled our feet. She
returned holding a plastic skeletal model of a woman's
pelvis and a large cloth doll. Holding the doll up high in
one hand she began, "Now the idea is that this baby here"
– she waved the doll – "needs to pass through this gap,
here" and she pushed the doll through the opening in the
pelvis. This was a bit of a squeeze and she had to give it
quite a shove before it emerged on the other side. The
whole room flinched and went very silent. I could feel a
hyperventilating attack approaching. "Well, that's if everything's all well and good, but it does not always work like
this," continued Faith. "For example the baby can get
stuck here. "

Faith now had the baby stuck in the constricted hole,
and was pushing and shoving the bedraggled toy whose

stuffing was beginning to show through the loose stitching.

"Now in a situation like this we may decide to use a Van Tuse." She put her model down and went to a cupboard at the side of the room. After muttering about someone moving something, she returned with a large tray crammed with what looked like mediaeval instruments of torture. There were sharp intakes of breath and I noticed the woman next to me clutching the edge of her seat. The midwife reached for the Van Tuse which looked rather like a large hose from an industrial hoover, its apparent aim being to suck the baby out in times of emergency. It was pushed unceremoniously up the fake pelvis as Faith demonstrated how it stuck on to the baby's head.

Then she held up a pair of forceps and demonstrated how they could be inserted to wrench the baby out into the open. She went through some other possible reasons why labour can go wrong and as she did so, everything was all clearly communicated by the use of her grisly skeleton and worn-out doll. Faith asked if anyone had any questions, we all shook our heads in unison.

After tea and biscuits, accompanied by lots of nervous laughter, we were taken on a tour of the labour ward. There were a lot of large metal pans and I shuddered, imagining they must be to collect all the blood. Another midwife joined in the chamber of horrors, she introduced herself as Megan. I dimly remembered that the girl with the spinny head and the ability to project green vomit in *The Exorcist* was called by the same name. She was carrying a pair of unusually large knitting needles, which I found particularly unsettling.

Megan asked if anyone would care to try the gas and air. The class lunged forward, but I made sure I was last so I had the freedom to linger with the drug uninterrupted by a queue of twitchy women. The midwives moved on through the ward with most of the class, leaving me and another mother-to-be called Miranda. She had a large suck from the mask and passed it over, I took a long toke. She looked a little shaky and, passing back the Nitrox, I asked her how long. "A week or two," she answered, "I am shit scared." Then she inhaled deeply from the canister. "Not bad this stuff," she continued. "I was thinking of having the baby at home, but after this class I think I might just go to hospital."

We talked while passing the gas and air inhaler between us, I told her how and when I ended up in this part of Wales. She said she lived in an old school house nearby with her Polish boyfriend, Olek, who was a film director. She had been brought up in Wales and then had spent ten years in London attending art school among other things. They had only moved back to Wales in the last year. I felt that this was someone with whom I might have something in common and who would understand my urban habits.

She started to tell me about her fascination with roses and her lengthy efforts to create new roses from grafting species together.

"Roses are the most perfect flower. Oh, I don't know why, but I just love them. The smell, everything. I am trying to create a new rose, but it's really difficult to get it right."

As we talked and sucked our conversation became more intense and personal. I started to tell her about my feelings of estrangement from everything I knew and how hard I found it adjusting to a deeply rural lifestyle. By this time I was lying on the labour bed and Miranda was deeply ensconced in the beanbag.

The class came back in as she was telling me about the fears she had experienced as a child. The midwives took the gas and air away from us, but were reasonably understanding about our absence. When the class ended, Miranda gave me her number and invited us over for dinner.

Dan was interested by my new contact, which worried me given that his dinner party social skills still needed a little polish. He had developed a new habit which was oddly disconcerting. With the arrival of the new pigs he had become obsessed with arranging free food for them. This would entail a constant bucket in our kitchen where all scraps would be casually thrown. No problem at home, but on the rare occasions that we were at someone else's house he would produce a plastic bag from his trouser pocket and in mid-conversation would open their rubbish bin to pick out edible food waste for his little porkies. As he leafed through their kitchen rejects he had been known to interject the odd critical comment: "Oh you throw away jars – could you keep them for me? This looks like an interesting magazine . . . Where did you get this flour? I would love to make some bread with this." Naturally I was worried any potential new friend would find this eccentricity rather invasive.

Away from human company, though, Dan was in his element, whether this meant flying his hawk, working in the vegetable garden or caring for our menagerie. I was beginning to see the point in keeping animals. Although my interest in handling the ferrets was minimal, I did see that their purpose in life was not entirely without credit when Dan would return from a ferreting trip with a rabbit or two. His success with the hawk was less impressive. He never seemed to catch anything, in fact more often than not I could spot him a few fields away standing under a tree whistling like mad for what seemed like hours. I tried to take an interest in his hobby, but where was the fun in watching a tatty bird sit in a tree and Dan repeating over and over "She's coming down now," as he whistled and waved limp meat in the air?

The chickens had become rather productive in the egg

department, which made up for their intensely neurotic attitude towards us. Being bantams, they were more feral than most domestic chickens and had more or less abandoned their hut for trees around the house. I now realised that the image of chickens clucking around my feet was pure fantasy. With these birds, if you got within ten feet of them, they would squawk like crazy and fly off in a wheel spin of feathers. With the help of the hideous dogs we would find their nests and actually it became quite fun looking through the hedgerows for their little brown eggs.

I even felt rather sorry for the pigs who spent large amounts of their day looking down the valley at the open green fields. On moments like this I would catch a funny faraway look in their eyes and once I fancied I saw a tear roll down a snout, but Dan was still taking them for walks down to the cattle-grid which seem to cheer them up immensely.

Dan's enthusiasm for his new lifestyle continued almost unchecked. Every day he would try to persuade me to join in some ludicrous new scheme. For a few days he was obsessed by the notion of a house cow. He would drag me to the barns and show me where this monster would live and then fill a Marigold glove to demonstrate the milking technique. He even found a local Jersey for a snip at £350. I managed to combat this terrible idea with a little research, discovering that the time and effort in keeping and milking the beast, as described by many cow owners, constituted a greater commitment than marriage. Although this seemed a fairly strange comparison, the point was clear enough. I asked Dan when he thought he would have time to whistle at trees if he had to sit on a stool and milk a cow every day? He accepted my realism begrudgingly.

My own enthusiasm for our Welsh life increased in conjunction with the mercury of the outdoor thermometer, which was an enormous personal relief. For the first time in three months I could afford a little variety in my wardrobe and finally I was able to dispense with the Scandinavian army jacket in exchange for something which did not emphasise my late pregnancy to such a degree. Occasionally I would catch my reflection in the mirror and wonder what had happened to my image. Flicking through the smart office clothes I had brought from London, I wondered if I would ever be the same person again. Was this the start of a general physical decline which would end up with me in an extra large shell suit and a polyester ski jacket? If so, who would notice my degeneration anyway, apart from animals?

The rising mercury also played a large part in encouraging our combined efforts in the vegetable garden. Dan was still spending hours working the beds with a fork and rake and would periodically demand that I come over and examine the fine tilth he had created. He would challenge me to find a rogue weed in his beds and when I did spot an emerging foreign green leaf he would attack it with the unprovoked violence of a chainsaw murderer. I helped him as much as I could, but bending did present practical problems.

The first vegetable we planted was a row of shallots. We had the John Seymour open and I was relaying the information to Dan as he laboured. I couldn't quite grasp how this shallot thing worked – somehow, they just multiplied right there in the soil, but obviously over a long period of time. Dan was a little cavalier for my liking, he was too rough with the small onions and threw them into the trench rather than lovingly placing them. I was sure they needed gentle handling and a quick pep talk before being left to perform this little miracle. I was measuring the gaps between the shallots with a tape measure, Dan was placing them inches too close together.

He dismissed my perfectionism as mere whim and I explained this was information from John Seymour. Was he really going to ignore the Great John? Needless to say we re-spaced all the shallots.

We then tackled a row of early potatoes. We had chosen a Scottish seed potato called 'Rocket' which I had heard the presenters of *Gardeners' Question Time* praise for the succulent taste and firm flesh of its tubers. By now I was finding listening to the radio gardening team strangely comforting. There was something reassuring in knowing that the worst thing you were likely to hear was that the secretary of the Leamington Spa Allotment Society had a dicky geranium.

Anyway, following the advice of the late lamented Clay Jones, Dan dug a large trench and we flicked some dreadful-sounding stuff called 'blood, fish and bone' in the bottom and then carefully placed each spud in a neat row – though not before a long debate on what was meant by 'rose end up' which I thought lent itself to several interpretations.

Once this was done we both felt an enormous sense of achievement. We sat and watched the earth where the tubers were lying underground, absorbed in thoughts of the processes. What would happen? I dismissed the rogue image of a large bush sprouting forth cartons of scrubbed potatoes, wrapped in cellophane, hanging off branches decorated in bar codes: no, this was real, our hands were dirty and we were planting food.

The crowns we had planted in March were beginning to throw up tiny little spears of asparagus. They were not ready for eating – that would take at least another year – but there was something extraordinary about seeing those little spikes come out of the ground all on their own: just little green thin asparagus which looked exactly like the ones in the shops. Somehow I had expected them to look different. My seedlings of tomatoes, chillies and artichokes were also coming up, in spite of the vole attacks, and were doing well. I had to transplant them into larger pots where they did everything a plant was supposed to do – continue growing up and out.

My father, who is a keen horticulturist, had been immensely encouraged by my first attempts in the growing department and had offered to buy us a greenhouse. So Dan and I spent hours discussing which one to go for and – unfortunately for my father – we concluded that a wooden one would be best (these are considerably more expensive than aluminium). While we waited for this giant propagator to arrive, we made a sizeable construction out of glass in which to nurture our seeds and seedlings. The more the seeds germinated the more ambitious we became, planting aubergines, sweet corn, okra, melons, avocados and figs – that is the kinds of crops you would expect to grow in the Mediterranean, not a 1000 feet up a Welsh mountain and on the wrong side of Offa's Dyke.

To be a real part of the growing season was exciting and my spirits had lifted following the atrocities of the first three months. I loved watching the little lambs cavorting in the fields and discovering new shoots in the garden. The only spring growth that was proving a problem was the extremely vigorous lawn which was sprouting up with such strength that it reminded me of an elderly Russian woman's legs I had seen by accident in a Turkish bath in Istanbul. Clearly it needed regular cutting and all we had was a minuscule mower which a relative had tired of. I began an attempt to wade through the front lawn propelling the thing, but after an hour I was in serious danger of premature labour. I had not quite realised the extent of our rolling grassland and passed the job over to Dan.

He immediately began thinking of solutions which did

not actually involve him pushing this hunk of metal backwards and forwards. "A couple of goats would do a grand job. Half a dozen geese would be traditional," or so he tried to persuade me. "Why *don't* we buy some goats?" he repeated in desperation, as he gazed at the wilderness before him.

I suspected these convoluted plans were hiding some work shy ethics, and knowing the only way to argue with Dan on subjects of this nature was to quote John Seymour at him, I looked under goats.

'Restraining goats is the goat keeper's chief problem.' Success! Seymour described a scenario of goats breaking out year after year and ravaging the vegetable garden. Dan conceded the point and after a few negotiations, which involved roasted red tail hawk in a port and juniper berry marinade, we sorted out the domestic dispute by agreeing to purchase a new mower.

I favoured a ride-on model, but a quick shufty down at the agricultural suppliers proved that we needed at least £1000 to get 'a tidy motor'. My disappointment was audible and the sales assistant took pity and told me of an auction of agricultural equipment, not too far away, where you could pick up this sort of machinery for a song. It seemed a perfect solution and so the next Thursday morning we went down to the enormous disused airstrip in an attempt to solve our mowing problems.

After trawling through the endless rows of rusty junk we came to the ride-on mowers. I fancied an ex-demo Husqvarna, the *crème de la crème* of garden tractors and, like my army coat, a Swedish invention (my respect for Scandinavian exports was rising by the hour). Then there were some medium condition baby tractors and finally came the real dross. We tried them all, which consisted of me sitting on them and deciding whether the seat was comfortable or not.

The sale eventually came to our row. The Husqvarna went for six times our agreed budget and the medium selection went for three times. Finally the auctioneer came to the end of the row, the scruffy rusty ones, but they were still fetching over £300. The last tractor was a hulking great machine which looked as if it might easily have seen active service in World War Two – possibly even One. This was the only machine which we could conceivably afford and we brought it for £100.

We managed to haul the beast home thanks to the Landrover and a trailer we had borrowed specially for the purpose from a neighbour. Once back at the farm we were anxious to see it in action. We fuelled up the mower and I sat in the driver's seat and turned on the ignition. There was much noise and black smoke, but at least it moved (in retrospect I think it showed great optimism that we actually believed it would start). Dan followed me trying to discern, through the blanket of smoke, whether it was actually cutting the lawn. When I stopped and inspected the results, it seemed more that the grass was just wilting through excessive carbon monoxide poisoning. After many stops and starts we managed to mow the lawn and in doing so, probably doubled the size of the ozone hole, but as soon as the job was done we took the prehistoric beast to the local mechanic to see if there was any way to tune the machine into acceptable emission levels.

Apart from the lawn, the only other annoyance (not including the dogs) was the marked increase in local wildlife. I found that bees were constantly buzzing around waiting to sting me and enormous spiders lurked in corners waiting to pounce. One night as I lay in bed watching some terrifying science fiction film an abnormally large spider crawled up the bedclothes towards my face. I lay frozen unable to speak as the enormous invertebrate with its six-inch hairy legs brushed against my hand.

My hand involuntary flung the spider ceilingwards and I caught sight of it landing in Dan's sock drawer as I ran downstairs screaming.

I am not overly fond of insects and I had noticed that there always seemed to be the most phenomenally unpleasant hairy creature crawling around the inside of the windows. This must have been a country thing, because I had never seen one in West London. Outside, slugs started to appear slithering around damp areas, horrible nasty little things.

My other complaint remained that our social life was still confined to mingling with bloody animals. I longed for human company and this prompted me to follow up Miranda's dinner invitation. We fixed a date for the night before she was due to deliver.

That evening, as we drove to our dinner appointment, Dan and I went through a few ground rules. In particular we agreed that he was to leave their rubbish alone and not get so drunk that he fell off his chair.

We arrived to find our hosts lived in a small 19th-century schoolhouse which had been converted. Inside was one large room with enormous sash windows set in dark wooden panelling and it was full of candles, cats and incense.

Olek welcomed us in, "My house is your house – come in for traditional Polish welcome."

We were given a shot glass of vodka. Olek knocked his back. "Nazdrowie," he exclaimed. "Excellent, now sit down. Let's talk. Is odd, don't you think, that a Pole should end up in Wales? Still I like life here: chopping logs and everything. And during the week I go to London and make stupid commercials with food."

Olek poured Dan and himself another vodka. "So, tell me everything."

Dan proceeded to tell him everything and I went to see

whether Miranda was feeling any labour twinges. She admitted she had been hoovering all day – which according to some is the main pre-labour activity – and now she was making a sponge cake in the shape of a large heart. We talked a while about anaesthetics until Olek announced that his soup was ready. Miranda told us about her interest in octogenarians, which she partly satisfied by working as a voluntary home help. She had just been to the funeral of one of the old men she used to visit. "He was lovely – really lovely. I love old people, they're so sweet and gentle," she said with a smile. "Lewis, the man who died, had amazing stories of living in Wales as a boy. I could listen to old people all day – they have so many fascinating stories."

Olek brought out another vodka to go with the soup which was a traditional beetroot broth from his home town. In fact there were four courses and a different flavoured vodka with each dish. By the time the heart-shaped cake made it to the table, I could see Dan was about to sway off his perch. Olek on the other hand looked as sturdy as Gibraltar's famous rock. I decided it must be something in his Slavic genes that enabled him to soak up alcohol and not fall over. Dan, however, was totally English and inevitably, after the cake was finished, he got up too quickly and stumbled off his chair. He complained that the cat had pushed him off balance and as soon as he was upright swerved to the rubbish bin, pulling a plastic bag out of his pocket. He explained he just could not let all this excellent kitchen waste go to the local tip. Olek was actually praising his resourcefulness. "Yes, excellent," he said. "I love recycling. Take everything for your pigs."

It was nearly midnight by the time Dan had finished combing through their dustbin, making the inevitable comments about their discarded items. Olek seemed to be enjoying this critique of his rubbish and every now and then would pitch in with short histories of particular consumer goods. Then they talked for ages about compost and the best activators to break down waste.

"Yes, yes – I want to make good compost!" shouted Olek, becoming very excited and starting to bang the table. "I will make a bin tomorrow and start this process. So, you say it is best to pee regularly on the rubbish – I will do this every day – Miranda, we will have finest compost for our vegetables and herbs. I want our baby to be proud of our compost. Here, let's drink to recycling and composting."

Dan and Olek clinked glasses, downed their shots and went outside to pee together on the site of the new compost bin – obviously some male bonding ritual which I did not fully understand.

I was wilting fast, but Miranda was laughing and seemed as energetic as a bouncy ball. For some reason I could not instantly determine, she had now progressed to making masses of tiny cakes in the shape of small hearts. She put the tray in the oven and asked me if I wanted to see her roses. With a paraffin lantern we went out to the greenhouse to view her horticultural work and, just as she started to explain the process of grafting one species with another, Olek came bounding in followed by Dan, who was weaving around as if carefully avoiding large imaginary objects. It seemed the right moment to leave.

I tried to contact Olek and Miranda over the next few days, but was unable to get any reply. I was beginning to wonder if they had moved house so we could not find them, till three days later Miranda rang. An hour after we had left she had gone into labour and the next day gave birth to a little girl, Rosa Cello. I asked her how the labour was.

"Oh nothing to worry about. Really it was fine. It was not as bad as you'd think."

She answered just a little too quickly to be totally convincing, but I wasn't sure I wanted to hear the truth any more – my own labour was imminent.

My mother came to stay for the weekend when it was all supposed to happen and by now I was so uncomfortable that I actually wanted the birth process to begin just to get the baby out and regain some control over my physical being. As it drew near, I began to assess my surroundings for their suitability for child rearing. There were animals with sharp teeth, a pond that looked as if no self-respecting bilharzia worm would even think about residing in its waters and odd metal objects with tetanus oozing all over the place. The garage housed a multitude of rusty cans full of strange liquids and crystallised forms, in which only a qualified chemist could guess the lethal compounds at work. Inside the house there was an oak staircase which was as steep as it was slippery. This was the very staircase the local farmer had informed us that a previous owner had died climbing down in the middle of the night.

Somehow I imagined this baby was going to emerge as a fully mobile child, perfectly capable of climbing ladders and drinking poisons, or starting chainsaws and amputating limbs. My mother and I rushed to Mothercare to buy all manner of safety equipment. We plugged up all sockets with plastic protectors, installed a baby gate, fitted locks for the windows and removed the strange array of liquids from the garage. No sooner had we screwed in the last safety mechanism, than I started to feel light cramps in the baby area. I was relieved that after the long wait the end was finally near and I would soon be able to run, leap or jump with the once customary vigour of pre-pregnancy.

The first twinges happened on Monday morning and by midday they were still fairly gentle and certainly not seriously unpleasant. "This is going to be a doddle," I thought. "What is all the fuss about?" I felt greatly relieved and reassured and my mother and I walked down to the farmer's lambing shed to pick some primroses, which seemed like the proper pre-birth-giving thing to do. The cramps had increased a bit, but not so much as to interfere. By the afternoon I thought I had better ring the midwife to ask when I should go in to give birth. I was put through to Faith.

"If you can talk to me on the phone, then you are not in labour," she replied briskly. "Ring back when you can't talk."

This was ominous and my reassurance began to ebb. What did she mean when I can't talk? Why wouldn't I be able to talk? What *was* she talking about?

I spent the afternoon listening to the compilation music tapes I had been making over the last few months and put some other things together that I thought might be useful. These included magazines and books (in case it was a long wait), some snacks and bottles of soft drinks. As an after-thought I added a plant mister for Dan to spray me if my body temperature rose too high.

By six p.m. I was becoming bored with the wait, so I decided to do a little light shopping in the local supermar-ket. As I lingered in the dried pasta aisle the cramps started to hurt much more. I decided I had better go home and wire myself up to the TENS machine. This was a small box the midwives had given me which you attach to the small of your back and it feeds you small electric shocks. This seemed nothing more than electro-compulsive thera-py. The main purpose appeared to be to take your mind away from the pain of labour by providing an even more excruciating distraction. It seemed a rather perverse psychology, but it came highly recommended.

By ten p.m. the pain had become distracting, I waited an hour and a half and then we drove into the local cottage hospital. I was pretty sure that the baby was about to pop out at any minute and by the time I was on the labour bed I was convinced that the contractions must have reached their threshold – there was nowhere else for the pain to go. The evening midwife came in and taking a cursory look at me said, "You've got a while to go yet."

I asked if she could take a closer examination. This was not going as I had expected. She made an internal check and told me, as she snapped off her rubber gloves, that I was not quite two centimetres dilated and had to achieve another eight centimetres before anything serious happened. She advised me to go home.

My despondency was intense and very audible on the journey home. Two centimetres! My God what on earth kind of torture was I going to experience? This was my first real indication that giving birth was going to be a lot harder than I had anticipated. We got back to the house and went to bed. I lay in the dark while the contractions increased in intensity till seven-thirty a.m. I felt cruelly deceived by the entire female population. They might have banged on about children in oxygen tents and *pain*, but they never mentioned I would have to go through this excruciating, protracted *agony*. I made a mental note to take revenge on every woman I had ever spoken to about childbirth.

We drove back to the cottage hospital at eight-thirty a.m. By this time I was crippled by the pain and unable to walk properly. I slumped on the labour bed and in came Faith all cheery and full of smiles, I wanted to get up and push her out the window.

"Oh Bel, it looks like we have some good contractions going on here," she grinned. "Righty ho, what's going on here? Shall we have a look, then? Oh, before I start does anyone fancy a cup of tea?"

TEA! Was the woman insane? Dan perked up and said he would love a cup, but before she could go I grabbed her by her tunic: "Do you think you might have a check first to see how dilated I am?"

Faith looked rather taken aback. "Oh Bel, don't worry, you're not going anywhere."

I intensified my grip. "All the same please could you have a look," I said between contractions, in a slightly out-of-control voice. She wavered, had a look and told me I was about seven centimetres.

"Three to go," I told myself as the midwife bustled out of the room.

Faith came back with the tea. "I met your mother in the waiting room – she looks a little peaky. Is she nervous?"

Was *she* nervous? Who bloody cared about my mother's demeanour? Faith placed an ultrasound receiver on my stomach to hear the baby's heartbeat, all the time chatting away.

"Now, Daniel, they look like practical trousers, what do you call them?"

Dan told her they were moleskins – not real mole skin, of course, but a tough cotton-based material. I could not believe they were talking about trousers. The doctor came in and he too joined in the conversation about the merits of rural clothing. Dan was leaning against the bed where I was groaning in agony, and telling them the benefits of his trousers in all weather conditions. It was as if I was in their way. Had it been physically possible I would have got up and looked for a blunt instrument with which to bludgeon them into silence. Finally, the doctor looked over and asked the midwife how dilated I was. She answered it was probably about eight centimetres by now, and then the three of them returned to talking about outdoor clothing.

I remembered the gas and air from the ante-natal lesson and shouted to Faith to give it to me. She set up the canister and gave me the inhaler. I took a large suck – and nothing happened! It was akin to smoking an Extra Mild Silk

Cut. After hours of nothing progressing except my unbearable agony, they decided something was wrong. By now the nervous-looking doctor mumbled something about swollen heads and said that perhaps I'd better go to Hereford. At this point I started shouting for decent hard drugs. They brought me pethidine, which I had heard had a sort of hushed respect on the streets.

After injecting me with the stuff, they transferred me into the ambulance with Dan sitting beside me. The pethidine started to kick in as we pulled out of the town and the ambulance nurse's vibrant make-up began to look rather disturbing. I wondered whether the drug had been an error in judgement, as the hour-long bumpy journey turned out to be the worst of my life, with the unbelievable pain now coupled with a very nasty trippy sensation.

At the hospital the examining registrar gave me a choice. "You can either carry on pushing for maybe another two hours, or I can have the baby out in ten minutes." My exact words were: "Get the fucking thing out NOW!" – or so Dan later informed me. It was apparently the only time I swore during the whole process, which I think shows remarkable strength of character.

Of course what I had not quite understood was that in order to get the baby out he was going to shove some large pliers up inside me to wrench it out. In retrospect I wondered what else I thought he could possibly do: get a megaphone and talk the baby out?

My first memory of Jack was that he was blue and covered in paste. The relief that he was out and we were both alive was colossal. I asked where my mother was, but apparently she was being told off by the hospital administrator for using her mobile phone and interfering with all the dialysis and other life-saving machines. I had a shower and was taken to a ward bed. As I washed, I made another mental note to terrorise Dr McBain and his family for telling me that labour was like 'shelling peas'.

I felt deeply sorry and guilty about Jack who by now was rather pale, except for two large red marks down either side of his face. We were both exhausted and slept for two days in Hereford before we were transferred back to the local cottage hospital. In the smaller hospital we had our own room; a remote-control telly; midwives at my beck and call and meals brought for me. Apart from the constant sensation that I was sitting on a hedgehog, I felt reasonably comfortable and after a week the midwives were making unsubtle hints that I should go home. I begged them to let me stay, telling them I had to live with three vicious dogs and that the house smelt, but they maintained it was better to go. Extremely reluctantly, Jack and I did as we were told.

My mother was still around and had worked hard trying to wash the dogs' piss off the sofa, but as I walked in the front door that musty stale canine smell still prevailed over the perfume of the flowers she had scattered around the house. I wondered if Jack could be at risk from bad dog gasses floating in the air and I turned to my baby health encyclopaedias. These mentioned nothing about dog smells, but there was a large section on a very nasty disease which begins with 'T' and is impossible to spell. It had something to do with worms. Panic. Parasites that would burrow into Jack's head and make him blind. I went to bed and dispatched Dan to the vet to buy the strongest anti-worm dog drugs on the market.

Once I'd settled in, I spent most of the time lying in bed looking at Jack and waiting for him to turn blue and choke to death or turn red and spontaneously combust. How could something so small survive, when all around were concrete life-threatening dangers, not to mention the constant fear of cot death and meningitis? I tried so hard not to be a neurotic mother, but I frequently caught myself almost sub-consciously checking his breathing and temperature. The problem is that babies do not breathe properly, there is always a background noise of snuffling and gasping and I would watch Jack as he slept. Quite often he seemed not to breathe at all and, alarmed, I would give him a shove and he would draw in a gasping breath as if he had forgotten that the intake of air was a minimum requirement for life.

Dan's paranoia was cot death. I would often wake up and find Jack lying on his father's chest with Dan's eyes wide open looking very hunted. As a result we had an almost impossible difference of opinion: he was obsessed by the baby being too warm while I was equally irrational about the cold. The first week was a battle ground of blanket warfare. Just as I sneaked a cover around the baby Dan would pretend to go to the loo and whip it off.

The whole process of adjustment to motherhood was a terrifying helter-skelter of overwhelming panic. The immense responsibility which had suddenly and irrevocably landed literally on my lap was almost impossible to digest. Every time the baby cried it was like the red alert signal on the Starship Enterprise: what was wrong with him? We would agonise over every conceivable possibility and once we had checked the normal, food, temperature and nappy problems with no result, we would become desperate. Was it too light . . . or too dark. Perhaps his arms were too long and he was disconcerted. His hair bothered him . . . or was it his lack of hair? His skin was too dry . . . or was he merely, as Dan suggested, disturbed by the realisation that there is no God?

Chicken Curry

1 lb boneless chicken thighs, cubed
1 medium-sized onion
1 inch fresh ginger (grated)
1 clove garlic
1 tin tomatoes
1 tsp cumin seeds
1 tsp coriander seeds
1 tbsp garam masala paste
1 tbsp sunflower oil
1 oz butter

Melt the butter in the oil and when hot, fry the cumin and coriander seeds until they pop. Brown the chicken and onion and add the garlic, ginger and garam masala. Stir to coat the meat thoroughly, add the tomatoes and simmer for 30 minutes. Serve with boiled rice.

May: Dan

It was three weeks before our son got a name. Like many parents we agonised for an age over the acceptable alternatives. We wanted it to be unusual, but not one which would make him the butt of endless playground jokes. I was also particularly keen on finding a Welsh label, but my favoured options, Merlyn and Dylan, were rejected outright. Unfortunately Bel spotted the falconry connection of the first and decided the second had too many unhappy associations. "People will think he's either an alcoholic poet, an ageing hippy or a dopey rabbit," she announced firmly.

In the end we settled on Jack as slightly unusual (neither of us knew anyone by that name), but still recognisable. Of course no sooner had we decided, than it turned out every male child in a 20-mile radius was being called Jack and we were rather crestfallen. In desperation we began toying with middle names and it was at this point Faith turned up to check on Bel's stitches.

"Thank God you've picked a sensible name," cooed the midwife in her lovely sing-song Welsh accent. "I've just delivered a baby to some travellers and they've called it Badger! Can you imagine that!"

I caught Bel's eye across the bed. "Yes!!!" We both cried

in unison – and having sorted out that particular problem, the next day we found ourselves at the registry office, recording the arrival of Jack Badger Butler-Crewe.

Obviously, the following weeks were dominated by a period of numbed adjustment to our new status as proud parents. For the first fortnight things went relatively smoothly as the three of us gradually absorbed the full implications of his emergence from the womb. After this brief calm interlude, the shit hit the fan and he began to cry inconsolably, every evening for a minimum of two hours. This usually started around midnight, just as I was going to bed and two hours after Bel had nodded off.

Naturally, as anxious new parents, we spent hours trying to analyse what might be upsetting him, but there seemed to be no obvious cause for his distress. Regardless of whether Bel fed him, I changed his nappy or bounced him on my shoulder to burp him, as soon as he was put back down his knees would come up, his face would crumple up and gradually turn puce as the screams rolled out of his tiny body. At first we persevered with our pre-baby routines, desperate that he should fit in with our established sleep patterns, but he refused to conform and inevitably the lack of rest began to affect our mood. As we grew increasingly sleep-deprived, so our irritability increased and with no alternative outlets for release, we began to take it out on each other.

We soon realised there was no hope of shutting him up if he remained lying down, but that holding him upright had a mildly placatory effect. This was where I came in. Until now, apart from making sure his mother was properly fed and changing the odd nappy, there had been little I could do for our son. He had only two activities, sleeping and feeding, and I was not much help with either. Now, however, I had a chance to play the loving 'new' father, carrying the moaning and struggling baby around the house.

Although I couldn't claim this was always entirely welcome, it was not without its attractions, one of which was the chance to introduce him to the basic principles of falconry. Once he was quiet – if nowhere near asleep – the pair of us would sit on the armchair by the fire, studying the illustrations in the manuals as I explained to the tiny form on my knee, with his blinking, blue, unfocused eyes, how to differentiate a falcon from a hawk, where the buzzards fitted in and how to tie the falconer's knot.

The baby's arrival brought other, unforeseen problems, the most important of which was that the trickle of friends from London who had made it out to see us now dried up completely. Most had no children of their own and were trying to be sensitive to our needs and leave us undisturbed at such a precious time. Of course, what they failed to appreciate is that very small babies are actually incredibly boring and, at least at first, require little active maintenance, particularly from a father. They just sleep, burp and suck at their mother's breasts. I tried to play my part during the day too, but it was not always easy. I would spend hours wandering around the farm, cradling him in the crook of my arm, explaining the significance of major points of interest to him, "Look at those buzzards! Can you see the kites? Do you think that might be a peregrine?"

Of course there was no reaction from the tiny form cradled in my arms and I have to confess to a slight sense of frustration, even if in general terms we were two of the proudest and happiest parents in Britain. We were gradually acknowledging the truth of the cliché 'Your lives will be revolutionised', which is repeated time and again as a first pregnancy matures. Like all other first-time parents, we simply assumed this means you will have a huge rash of new responsibilities – nappy changing, preparing meals, planning activities, choosing schools and so on. What you don't realise is that those are the highlights. For at least the first six months one of you is constantly tied to the infant, barely able to put him down and thus so handicapped that the simplest of activities, like making a cup of tea, becomes a logistical nightmare.

Our lives were indeed transformed. One moment we were free agents with a happy – if uncluttered – social life, the next we found ourselves marooned on our farm and shunned by our well-meaning urban friends. Not surprisingly, we began to go a little stir-crazy.

Fortunately, the local wildlife soon provided its share of distractions. These came in the form of rabbits – or to be precise, baby rabbits. Suddenly there were dozens of them, hopping around our fields and even into our vegetable plot. So in spite of the growing fascination with parenthood, far from finding ourselves immersed in our new baby, we were instead preoccupied by a common obsession – rabbit control.

Now it hardly comes as a surprise that the idea consumed me – after all I had been driven out here by a passion for falconry – but Bel's determination to see a bunny massacre was less predictable. Until recently, she had thought my hunting activities a total waste of time, but this began to change with her discovery of the delights of gardening. Suddenly, she became excruciatingly aware of the potential damage just one rabbit can do in an evening, so the regular sight each morning of half a dozen tiny bunnies hopping in and out of her precious brassica seedlings became unbearable. Things came to a head one Saturday morning when I returned from a shopping trip to see Bel with an expression darker than the blackest storm cloud.

Rabbits had mounted a daring midnight raid on our vegetable patch the previous night and the two rows of cauliflower seedlings – planted only three days before – were no more. Instead there were just a handful of tiny green stumps, a few scratch marks and dozens of tell-tale currant droppings.

In her distress, Bel's initial reaction was to blame me for the devastation (why hadn't I been more successful with my hawk during the winter months, was the general line), but in the event the current adversity was to draw us closer together. We were facing a crisis. The wet winter had now given way to warmer weather and as the grass exploded into life, so did the local rabbit population's reproductive capacities. Suddenly the hillside behind the house was dotted with pairs of dark brown ears, poking up through the ankle-high grass.

Worse, unlike their canny parents, the new generation had no respect for the perils of the farmyard, let alone the vegetable patch. Forsaking the boring safety of our pastures, they had easily penetrated the 'rabbit-proof' fencing we had inherited from our predecessors and were feasting on the crops we had laboured so long over and on whose success we were relying for food during the summer and autumn. The invaders seemed to have a connoisseur's eye for the most valued plants and soon we were running to stand still as we replaced row upon row of delicate broccoli seedlings with fresh stocks from the rapidly emptying greenhouse.

The question of how to exclude them from the vegetable patch became an overriding imperative which began to invade what little social life we could still muster. Bel is one of those people who are perfectly capable of maintaining four thoughts simultaneously and leaping from one to the other without any prompting or explanation. For example, having been invited to a rare dinner party at a friend-of-a-friend's place, we were making small talk, chatting casually about the Conservatives' most recent appalling by-election result when Bel, who had been silent for a couple of minutes, suddenly interrupted with, "So, how are you going to kill them?"

It goes without saying that our new friends were completely bamboozled at Bel's apparent incitement to mass assassination of the Tory hierarchy. Even I was momentarily taken aback, before realising what she meant. "The ferret should do the trick," I cooed reassuringly. Our hosts looked even more bewildered.

So, for all Bel's fury at the plague of self-propelled mowing machines zigzagging backwards and forwards across our precious crops, the rabbits brought us closer together. For the first time, she began to look at the dogs with an almost affectionate expression and the transformation in her feelings for the ferrets was remarkable. Although she had seemed to like them initially in London, this affection had cooled markedly since our arrival in Wales. Indeed, for the past couple of months she had even professed a total loathing for their musty smell. My conviction that this aversion was mainly due to pregnancy hormones might well have been correct, but she maintained her reasons were more pragmatic.

One morning she happened to hear a radio story about Whipsnade Zoo selling lion manure as an effective deer deterrent. A little lateral thinking took place and I was presented with the previously unthinkable sight of Bel cleaning out the ferrets' cage and then going down on hands and knees around the vegetable patch, armed with a teaspoon and carrier bag full of sawdust and ferret-shit.

Unfortunately, such humane options soon proved hopeless. Not for nothing were the hills alive with the sound of munching: our rabbits were either too clever or too numerous to care about the evil-smelling piles and after three days they were actually scraping the stuff out of the way as they scampered into the garden.

Washing up one morning, I spotted six of these messengers of destruction bouncing through the asparagus. I could bear to lose a few sprouts to the creatures, but the sight of these four-legged vandals devastating the bed which had cost us so much sweat and effort to establish made my blood boil. Something snapped and, forgetting my normal overriding preoccupation of how to catch rabbit with hawk, I rushed for the stair cupboard. In an instant I was clasping my old air-gun and creeping to the back door. One well-aimed shot accounted for a miscreant and over the following few days I managed to add more by sneaking pot shots through the bedroom window. It would be an exaggeration to say Bel was delighted by the slaughter, but she greeted the news of each demise with a grim smile.

In addition, I went on a frenzied session of shoving Purdy and Mrs Peel down rabbit holes left, right and centre, in spite of the fact that this is generally only done during the winter months. The experts tell you that summer ferreting is wasteful and time-consuming as the little predators have no problems killing young rabbits underground. This was a crisis, however, and my objective was solely to control the numbers before they got completely out-of-hand. So twice a day for a week I went out with my nets, ferret box and dogs to wreak death and destruction in our hedges and fields.

Every day I would account for two or three vegetable-killers and, like some old-fashioned bounty hunter, would return home with the evidence for Bel. She had no compunctions about seeing dead bunnies. Indeed, she was as suspicious as any sheriff expected to produce the reward money: "How do I know you got four if there is only that pathetic little creature to show for it?" she would query as I waved the latest corpse at her through the living room window before I headed off to skin and portion it for the freezer.

This sense of triumph was far from total and I began to feel slightly uncomfortable. I had no problems justifying my actions intellectually – the rabbits were alien pests, which were threatening our domestic happiness, food and property – but like most urban observers I felt uncomfortable with the bloodbath. My disquiet was only intensified by the fact that most of the victims were barely old enough to have left their mother's breast, a particularly difficult concept given the suckling scenes indoors.

The truth was, I retained an urban disquiet at killing. I still felt uncomfortable every time I heard a thud and squeal from the vegetable patch. I got – and still get – no pleasure from a means of control which pits the full might of man's technological supremacy against the animal kingdom.

My response was to make sure that every victim played a purpose, even in death. Following the Great John's philosophy of 'waste not, want not', I made sure every rabbit was eaten. Now, although we were both fond of rabbit marinated in cider with red peppers, there soon came a limit to how many times a week we could face this form of recycled seedlings. The hawks and ferrets dined well that late spring.

Apart from her reluctance to eat rabbit more than twice a week, Bel showed no such compunction. She pointed triumphantly to the cabbage patch where the replacement rows positively thrived and prospered in the increasingly warm weather and lengthening hours of daylight. She was also becoming almost friendly towards the dogs – particularly Bracken – who by now had discovered what his hunting ancestry was all about. He started to score regular successes while out on walks and more often than not would suddenly appear to present us proudly with the proof of his speed and agility.

But the peace and sense of shared purpose was short lived when I decided to turn my DIY talents to the hawk. While in flying condition it was perfectly acceptable to 'weather' (tether) her by day on the lawn, moving her at night for her comfort and protection to the garage, but this state of affairs could no longer continue. Now that summer was on us, Gwen desperately needed to moult and for this to happen successfully, she needed space. With no horses, cows or sheep to house, the two barns were obvious candidates for conversion and I spent hours drawing up plans for a magnificent hawk palace.

In spite of his dubious business credentials, I ordered a ton of freshly cut ash planks from Mike. Naturally he turned up with larch instead, but I was keen to get started and decided not to labour the point and within a few minutes was tacking them on to the barn's timber frame. I had imagined that the cost of the wood would be about the end of it, but as with most building projects I was mistaken. I had forgotten the wire mesh necessary for the front wall and blocking up the eaves, ignored the numerous hinges, nails, lengths of rope, drill bits, wood preservative, brushes, paint and so on.

In the end it cost about four times more than I had anticipated, but as I stared up at its beautifully crafted walls and vast interior (which came fully furnished with two nest ledges, rocking perches, a mock tree and built-in bath), I knew this was a worthwhile investment. Bel frowned as I slaved away, but restricted her comments to pointing out that after five months I had yet to build a £5 duck house for the birds she was still determined to purchase.

This led smoothly to yet another minor domestic disaster, when she began to ask when the ducks, an integral part of her original dreams of our smallholding, would arrive. Whilst in itself no cause for marital strife (I was far from averse to the scheme), the real problem grew out of how we were to procure them, particularly as few local farms kept livestock other than sheep. So, after asking the Major for advice, early one morning Bel and I struggled out of bed, dressed and swilled down tea, before gently lifting the dormant Jack Badger into the car seat and heading for our nearest English city.

We had been to the small-animals livestock market once before, but then our purchases had been restrained. There were only a handful of ducks on display and these were mainly Aylesburys – the standard white table birds that Bel had declared were boring and not what ducks were all about. In addition, my tentative bids for the three attractive mottled fowl that Bel had wanted failed. I was bowled over by the rush of like-minded amateur bidders. While the local farmers first chuckled and then gawped, the bids had risen to an astronomical £15 – a figure I was certainly not happy to match.

On that occasion, I was the villain of the piece. The three ducks were worth every penny of £20 a head, Bel argued. Instead of returning in triumph with three ducks, we were devoid of any livestock apart from five dozen quails' eggs which I'd bought, like the Monty Python piston engine sketch 'because they were a bargain'. These went into the empty incubator we'd purchased from our predecessors and which it seemed only sensible to put to good use. So, for the next three weeks we found ourselves brooding both literally and figuratively.

It was while these pipped that we made our return trip to the market. As I waited for Bel and Badger to announce they were ready to set off, I transferred the last of the tiny creatures to a cardboard brood box. When I had finished, we had forty brown and yellow striped chicks. It was, I thought happily on the hour's drive east, an auspicious sign – although when I began to talk happily to Bel about our new acquisitions, it led to a minor argument over their use. Naturally I saw them as an important source of high-quality hawk food, but Bel, brought up in different circles from myself, regarded half a dozen hard-boiled quails' eggs a week as virtually *de rigueur*. It could have got nasty if it hadn't been for the glorious weather and the fact that it would be another eight weeks before they would be fully grown and ready to lay.

To our delight, when we arrived at the market, we found it stuffed full of ducks. The hall was crowded with grinning farmers, marked out from the amateurs by their ruddy cheeks and the purely utilitarian nature of their oil-stained blue overalls and grubby lumberjack shirts. Rollies hung out of the corners of their mouths and they stood to the side, muttering quietly and nudging each other as obvi-ous amateurs, flagged by their immaculate Barbours, muted tweeds and gleaming complexions, walked past. I wasn't dressed quite the part of the full-time farmer, but at least the torn jeans and coarse red ethnic cloth of my shirt seemed to ally me more closely to them than to the 'gentlemen' farmers we both despised.

The auction began as we arrived.

"Please remember that all lots are sold as price per animal unless otherwise stated," chirped the auctioneer happily. I ignored him and the rest of the early stages: the first lots being comparatively boring hardware, feeding troughs, incubators and the like. This gave us a few minutes to inspect the goods on offer. The ducks began in lot G74: seven Aylesbury/Harlequin crosses and, much to Bel's delight, a pleasing blacky-brown in colour. The next box contained a further twelve and there followed a plethora of Aylesburys, Khaki Campbells, Muscovies and farmyard mongrels. On the other side of the warehouse were yet more, most excitingly including a box which contained three Silver Appleyards – to me rather boring off-white birds, but perfection in Bel's eyes. Next to them were three Swedish Blues, pretty yellow, white and blue-black balls of fluff. These, she announced, were even more desirable.

While Bel was getting excited by thoughts of pretty waterfowl floating on our green puddle of a pond, I couldn't help noticing some rabbits further on. The germ of an idea was planted in my mind – if we could rear pigs, geese, hens, ducks and quail for our own consumption, why not breed food for the hawk?

True, for the time being there were more than enough wild rabbits to sate our needs, but this was unlikely to continue for ever. What we really needed was an assured animal feed supply to bolster the natural stocks.

My thoughts were interrupted by the auctioneer's announcement that lot G60 was up and the three of us returned to the thick of the fray, waiting for the first seven ducklings. It was then, with the unerring timing of a tiny baby, that Jack began to cry. It was time for breakfast and Bel had to beat a retreat to the car.

"Just make sure you get those ducklings," she whispered as she left. I nodded, lost in my thoughts of rabbit-breeding plans. I made some quick calculations based on half-remembered statistics on rabbit reproduction rates. According to the Great John, three does and a buck would give a six-pound rabbit every three days. Mind you, that was being careful to maintain a culling programme. Someone else calculated that if left untouched a pair could, under ideal conditions, become two million in a couple of years. I reckoned that a decent-sized pair would probably provide enough meat for the hawk and ferrets combined.

"Lot G74!" bawled the auctioneer. I clutched my little plastic bidder's number, '91', tightly.

"Shall we start at £2.50?" he asked hopefully. I played it cool and kept my number down. There was a satisfying silence all round.

"£2?" He inquired. "All right then, £1.50? . . . God you're a hard lot . . . £1 – and that's giving these beautiful little birds away."

"Right then, I have a bid – £1, I'm bid £1 – anyone got £1.50?"

That was the last coherent action I can remember in the heat of the auction shed. Whether it was the temperature, the time it took to get to the lots of interest, preoccupation with Bel's reaction to the quail or concern that I might fail to get what I wanted and have to return next week, I can't say. Whatever the cause, I went into a sort of slow-motion world where I waved my placard and nodded at the auctioneer, but I didn't register buying very much, although I did come to enough to realise that I'd bought the three New Zealand white rabbits – and all for under the £5 benchmark I'd set myself.

I went off to pay the bill, leaving Bel to stare at her beloved Swedish Blues. It came as a dreadful shock.

"That will be £111.00 plus VAT," said the lady behind the glass. "You can pay by cheque if you like," she added helpfully. Stunned, I duly scribbled and then was left staring at the pink release slip which detailed my purchases. How was I going to explain this to Bel?

19	Welsh/Harlequin ducklings	£	28.50
10	Quail	£	20.00
12	Guineafowl eggs	£	1.00
2	Muscovies	£	3.00
8	Rouen/mongrel crosses	£	9.00
3	Swedish blue ducklings	£	7.50
10	Goslings	£	20.00
1	Pigmy black doe rabbit	£	2.00
1	Pigmy Dutch buck rabbit	£	2.50
2	Pigmy Dutch doe rabbits	£	5.00
1	New Zealand white buck	£	4.50
2	New Zealand white does	£	8.00
	Total 71	£	111.00

"Ah, I'm glad I've found you," came a voice from behind me. I turned to find a weasel-faced man, grinning at me. "You bought my quail I think? I wonder if you'd like to buy another ten, you see I've a bit of a problem. The auctioneer was about to give the next lot away at £1 and I waved at him to say that I wasn't happy with the price and the stupid man knocked them down to me." He smiled in what I suppose he thought was a winning way. "They're worth every penny of the £1.50, but I don't want to have to drive all the way home with them and I wonder if you'd like them for £1 each?"

The fresh air and the bill had brought me to my senses. In a flash I realised that I had been bidding for the quail against their breeder. Spotting a sucker a mile off, he'd delicately teased me up to £2 for his bloody birds, but had been caught out by the very impulsiveness which had initially made the gambit successful. I shook my head, angry with myself not him – after all he had a living to make.

"I didn't really mean to buy them," I explained. "I just got carried away, but now I've got them, I suppose I'll just have to breed from them."

"Well, you'll need twenty unrelated females for that lot. But even if they are already good layers, give them a while to settle down before trying to incubate the eggs. I've got a few – how about £30?"

"Are these all males then?" I said weakly. I had never thought to ask before, having taken it for granted that the ten would be sexually at least 50/50.

"Oh yes, I wouldn't sell females – need them to lay eggs," he replied. "These are for eating – either that or falconry – falconers love them for their birds you know."

I smiled weakly and turned away, clutching the pink release slip which listed our new acquisitions. What on earth was Bel going to say?

"Quail? Quail? They've made a mistake, Dan. They've put us down for 10 quail . . . and what's this about guineafowl eggs? I can't stand guineafowl – ugly birds."

"Well they were only a pound," I muttered, but she wasn't listening.

"I can understand the Muscovies, I suppose, but what do we want with six Rouen crosses? Three Swedish Blues, good . . . Hang on a minute, how many rabbits did you buy? Three, four, five . . . seven!"

"They're for the hawk," I explained, wishing that I could inject a bit more conviction into my voice.

"But we've got a whole hillside swarming with rabbits! So far this week we've eaten rabbit casserole, rabbit in cider with red peppers and rabbit curry. If there's one thing you don't need to farm it's rabbits," she said.

"They're much bigger than the wild ones," was the best I could muster, contenting myself with the observation that she'd stopped looking at the quail.

"Is that why they're called pigmy?" She countered.

I grabbed the paper from her. Sure enough the word was neatly printed in front of four of the seven animals – the three Dutch and one black that I'd imagined were merely young creatures, turned out to be fully-grown miniatures – toy animals bred to be pets. I groaned, but at least they were the right sex, I muttered without thinking.

"What do you mean?" Bel was on me quick as a flash.

There was nothing for it. I had to confess about the quail and decided to make a joke of it all.

"Well, you know the ten quail I paid £20 for?"

"Plus VAT," added Bel.

"They're all male."

Needless to say, the return journey to Allt-y-Gwalch was not a comfortable one. Quite apart from the icy glow being given off by Bel, the car was, to put it mildly, overcrowded. Naturally we'd never intended to make so many acquisitions and so had come in our tiny Fiat. Now as we loaded the quacking, clucking, honking and scuffling cardboard boxes into the boot, so the available room for the human occupants became more and more cramped. I made the most of the sacrifices. As driver, Bel needed enough room to move, while the size and rigidity of Jack's car seat ensured his comfort. Thus logistics meant that I had to vacate the passenger seat, surrendering it to four boxes – one in the footwell and three piled up on the seat. More boxes filled the boot and covered the back seat, with others on my knee. Hunching my six-foot-three frame behind Bel, I spent the entire drive squinting over my left shoulder at the hillsides rushing past.

Bel soon took our new acquisitions in her stride and forgave my loss of control. For a start the majority were such sweet balls of fluff that it was impossible to remain immune to their charms. Here at last were the ducklings that she had been dreaming of and I spent a busy three days constructing an assortment of brooders, boxes and hutches for our new arrivals. The 32 ducks were soon ensconced in a variety of huts by the pond, while the rabbits were stacked in three hutches near the ferrets. All this industry on my part did much to mollify Bel and any residual bitterness she might have felt towards the impact of my rush of blood on our delicate finances was eliminated by the sight of dozens of happy ducklings floating on the pond, pulling at the weed and up-ending to dabble in the mud.

My efforts with the greenhouse were the icing on the cake of our ameliorated relations. Its arrival was heralded early one morning with a call from a local phone box from the lorry driver. He announced he was in a neighbouring village and wanted directions for the final mile or so. As Bel began to give them, it emerged that his vast articulated lorry would never make it up our lane. Instead, I was forced to arrange for him to drop his load off at the near-est lay-by and then spent the rest of the day ferrying parts of our new building home, tied precariously to the side of the Landrover. The only minor mishap came when one side slipped in front of the exhaust pipe and ended up badly scorched as a result. I slaved over the red-brown construction for the next two days and although I triumphed eventually, all I can say of the experience is that anyone who thought IKEA self-assembly furniture was difficult to make head or tail of, should try assembling a cedar-wood greenhouse in an exposed site up a mountain.

Eventually the job was done and Bel could move in, spreading out her seed trays and compost across my home-made staging and sowing a myriad of seeds to make up for the late start.

As she threw herself into her new-found passion, so I tried to support her through compost. Now that the improving weather had reactivated the teeming microbes and invertebrates upon which the processes of decay depend, my great composting schemes could begin again. I devoted myself to the task and became an avid mower, only too keen to volunteer for the hour-long chore of cutting the front lawn on our noisy, smokey mini-tractor. The goal, of course, was to become an artist in compost making.

And, I soon discovered, it definitely is an art. As any gardener knows, left to themselves, grass clippings soon become a slimy smelling ooze, far removed from the moist crumbly brown material sold by garden centres. My 'waste not, want not' philosophy dictated that there must be some purpose to which it could be put and so I found myself treating it as a valuable raw product which would eventually free us from the expense of shop-bought bags and fertiliser.

This was a major task. The grass had to be layered in the

huge bins I had made out of discarded pallets scrounged from the local agricultural merchants. For every three-inch layer of clippings, another layer was needed to provide air and nutrients. This could come in the form of manure, old animal bedding, weeds or newspaper, but given the huge volume of grass, it involved a major effort.

In addition, according to the books, all extra 'activation' I could supply was welcome. I needed no encouragement and was soon automatically scurrying to the bins every time I felt the need to pee. Indeed, the habit became so imbued that I would even stagger sleepily across the lawn in the small hours and on more than one occasion found myself interrupting lunch on the terrace to relieve myself on the pile, within sight of our guests, only to realise too late that in some circles this might be considered a trifle coarse.

All in all, I soon found compost a deeply satisfying repository of my efforts. When correctly constructed, the huge heap would rapidly heat up to surprising temperatures – sufficiently hot to heat a pitchfork's tines to the point where they would scorch the back of the hand. As this happened, so the mound would collapse in on itself, halving in volume over the course of a fortnight.

It was all so exciting that I was in danger of becoming rather too enthused – not to mention boring – on the subject, but fortunately I managed to find an outlet with our new friends, Olek and Miranda. Or, to be more precise, Olek was someone with whom I could share my passion. Whenever we visited each other, the host would take a proprietorial pride in ushering the other down to the heap to witness the rapidity with which the surface had shrunk since the last visit, and, of course, to invite his guest to pee ceremonially on the heap.

Meanwhile my composting industry was being paralleled just down the lane. As his own grass and weeds burst into life, so the Major became increasingly in evidence. On the same hot sunny afternoon that I finished the greenhouse and drove down into town to buy a well-earned celebratory bottle of wine, I spotted him walking ponderously across a field. Well, when I say I saw him, this was entirely a process of deduction. In fact all I could see was an amorphous figure, looking like an extra from *Dr Who*. He was clad head to foot in a one-piece rubber suit, with a large plastic knapsack between the shoulders, from which trailed a pipe ending in a pistol arrangement.

The sight would have been odd enough in its own right, but it was the head which really caught my attention. Largely enclosed in a tight-fitting hood which was tied by a drawstring around the face, any human features were completely obscured by a sinister black gas mask, complete with a bright orange circular filter which protruded like the stump of a horribly amputated elephant trunk.

As I watched, the figure stepped forwards with first one and then another ponderous step, rocking carefully from one side to another, and slowly waving the pistol apparatus at the grass ahead. The movements were so slow and deliberate that one might easily have imagined this to be an extra-terrestrial stopping off for a quick bout of t'ai chi before continuing its voyage on to another galaxy, but by now I knew enough of the Major's eccentricities to take it in my stride. I stopped the car and gave a gentle toot on the horn. The figure took no notice, but continued its rhythmic swaying across the field. I dabbed on the horn again and this time the figure stopped, swinging ponderously first left and then right, before giving a muffled cry of what I assumed was recognition.

It then began to flail its arms as it desperately struggled to divest itself of first the backpack and then the face mask. Eventually it succeeded and a moment later the more familiar figure of the Major was standing in front of me, his face bright red with the heat and dripping with sweat.

"What on earth are you doing?" I asked.

"Roundup," he said, jerking a thumb in the direction of his backpack. Fortunately I knew enough about farming to recognise the leading brand of weedkiller. "Now's perfect time to nail these thistles," he said. "That's the trick – hit insurgents hard at the first possible opportunity . . . then nail 'em before they can regroup. If only our bloody politicians had followed that line we'd still have an empire."

I was not entirely comfortable with this, thankfully rare, brush with the Major's political views, but fortunately he returned to the subject of spray warfare. "See those markers?" He barked. I looked up the field to see a line of sticks pushed into the grass at the far edge, each with a six-inch disc of white paper at its top, letters scrawled in thick black marker on each. Looking around, I now noticed more positioned along each side of the field: these were numbered.

"Grid references," he barked. "Cuts the field into squares. Using them, you can tell your position at any moment. You're in C28, I'm in D29."

I failed to see the necessity, but the Major was clearly convinced of its value: "Never spray the same thistle twice," he said. "Trick I learned on counter-insurgency operations in Kenya."

I was about to ask him if the army had found themselves doing a lot of thistle-spraying during the Mau-Mau revolt, but decided it might sound rather cheeky and I had no desire to offend our neighbour. Instead I found myself questioning his apparel.

"This? Oh just my old germ warfare kit, left over from my army days," he said simply, as if this explained everything.

But were the chemicals he was spraying quite so toxic? Surely Roundup was actually nice biodegradable plant hormone which was totally harmless to people and animals?

"Seen too many official cock-ups to fall for that one . . . Agent Orange, Gulf War syndrome . . . never swallow the party line," he said. "First priority is to look after number one: take all sensible precautions."

As I looked at the bright red face, streaked with sweat, I couldn't help thinking the elderly Major was at more immediate danger of a heat-induced heart-attack than he was from long-term effects of chemicals. By now, however, he was beginning to shuffle, clearly anxious to continue with his anti-thistle manoeuvres, so I bade farewell and made my way back to the car.

The encounter set me thinking and the following afternoon I wandered up the hill behind the house to check our fields for weeds. What I discovered came as a shock. Until now, whenever I clambered up the hill, it was with the eyes of a walker, naturalist or falconer. I'd completely forgotten my new role as farmer and stared blindly through problems which would have screamed out for attention to our neighbours.

The fields were covered with tiny nettles, thistles, docks and – worst of all – the tiny bright green curls of emergent bracken. Also, several of our fences were so flimsy as to be on the point of collapse. Indeed there were several sheep grazing illicitly in one field and the wool dangling on the barbed wire above the badger set pointed clearly to the entry point.

The sight of the trespassers stung me into action and, taking a leaf out of the Major's book, I found a roll of barbed wire, a pair of pliers and a hammer to repair the breach in our defences. As I struggled to cut the unyielding barbed wire with my short-handled pliers, I soon realised fencing required far more skill than one might imagine. Although I'd had limited experience with the pig pen, my efforts had succeeded only when helped by the Major. Now, as I struggled to string a length of wire across the gaping hole, I found myself desperately trying to remember how he'd managed to tension the pig perimeter. I had a vague memory of an arrangement with two sticks and a home-made pulley, but without any of the necessary materials to hand, I contented myself with leaning back with my full weight on the strand, while hammering in the staple. The result looked reasonably professional and so it was with a vague sense of achievement that I strode back to the house. My elation was premature.When I returned to the field an hour later to show Bel my handi-work, it was to see three sheep grazing contentedly.

Though disappointing, at least I hadn't wasted too much time on it, but the weed problem was another matter altogether. After doing a little research, I discovered there were two main approaches to the control of unde-sirable plants – the organic method of cutting them down, or following the Major down the herbicidal path. Keen to comply as far as possible with the Great John, I decided to attack our nettles, thistles and bracken with the huge brushcutter we'd inherited from our predecessors. This was the farmer's equivalent of the strimmer owned by my father, but unlike the latter, this huge machine was equipped with a six-foot-long drive shaft and a vicious-looking three-pronged cutting blade. Powering the whole thing was a two-stroke motor which wouldn't have looked out of place on a microlight.

After some initial trouble, I got the beast going and began to meander slowly up the hill, heading across the gently rippling grass towards the patches of weeds. I'd ear-marked the morning to do the job, but by lunchtime I was still struggling with the noisy machine on the lower parts of the slope. As I trawled back and forth, the Major's technique with marker sticks began to make sense. Every time I glanced back down the hill my eye would be caught by a stray thistle, a solitary dock or handful of bright green shoots of unfurling bracken, missed through lack of navigational precision.

Nevertheless, by the end of the day I'd dealt with the worst of the problem and was filled with the self-satisfied feeling of someone who's earned their rest. Bel and I sat on the terrace as we watched the shadows lengthen. For once Jack was obligingly silent and as the sun sank, we sipped at glasses of ice-cold kir and watched the golden sunlight pick out every fold and contour of the surrounding hills. Still glowing with my exertions, I savoured every second: this was heaven.

RABBIT CASSEROLED
IN CIDER

1 young rabbit
½ pt good cider
1 large red pepper
½ lb shallots
2 cloves garlic
Olive oil, flour, salt and pepper

Cut the rabbit in half at the rib cage. Discard the ribs and forelegs (use for hawk food or stock) and pare the flesh off the saddle and back legs. Cut into roughly equal pieces. Marinate for at least two hours (overnight if possible) in the cider, turning occasionally. Drain and reserve the liquid. Fry up the chopped shallots in oil. Roll the diced rabbit in seasoned flour and add to the shallots. While this browns, de-seed the pepper and slice into long thin strips. Add to the rabbit along with the crushed garlic and stir for a moment. Transfer to a small covered dish, tip in the marinade and put in a moderate oven (gas mark 2, 150°C, 325°F). Cook for 90 minutes, and serve.

June: Bel

Who would have thought that such a small thing as a baby could make so much noise at such inopportune moments? There were times when I would have donated an important limb to science to be allowed to sleep uninterrupted or eat a meal with both hands. I would watch his small body tense and his face turn deep purple and at the apex of his screams his whole body would shake with the convulsion of crying and there would be a muffled silence, like the eye of a storm, until the cycle would continue into a more frantic cry as he regained his breath.

In the middle of the night I wanted to offer Dan large sums of money to take the child away and leave it with a deserving family in the Midlands for the weekend, but managed to suppress the urge. On these nights Dan looked almost as desperate as I did, but we took it in turns to walk around the room with the screaming infant. On my hour off I could hear Dan's muffled voice through the pillow, repeating over and over, "Jack hath murdered sleep. Jack hath murdered sleep."

Early evenings were clouded with a growing sense of panic as we contemplated what the night might bring to test our parental mettle. One appalling evening we drove to see Olek and Miranda with our screaming accessory, to be met by their own wailing child. Miranda was in her greenhouse with her roses. Olek was outside in his underwear singing a loud aria to his distressed daughter. He greeted us with the customary welcome, "Yes, you need vodka. Miranda is with roses again, she plays with them for hours for what reason I don't know, but it relaxes her, I think. Christ Almighty bollocks I need a vodka. Come let's drink and settle these children."

Olek was holding Rosa flat in his arms and moving her up and down quite vigorously. She seemed to quieten down. He looked at Dan, who had a screaming Jack slumped over his shoulder. He told Dan to copy him and to rock Jack up and down. Dan tried this and it appeared to soothe him. Olek started to smile, "You see, it is as I say – these babies like this up and down thing – what we need is some sort of rubber strap. You tie to the beam and fasten to car seat – then we can drink vodka in peace. It will work, I think."

He threw Rosa at me and ran outside to his car. Through the window I could see him fiddling around with his roof rack. He came back in and tossed a piece of rope over the oak beam above our heads and then tied a large stretchy 'spider' (the kind you use to fix luggage to the roof) to the rope. With the hooks of the spider he connected Rosa's car seat. He strapped her in and with a few pushes the spider was bouncing her up and down in perfect rhythmic movements. It was inspired and worked instantly.

Olek and Dan quickly rigged another bungy on the other side of the room and soon Jack was also placated and quiet. Miranda came in and said he was a genius: we were so grateful we asked him to be Jack's godfather.

As if dealing with our son was not enough, Dan had added to our problems thanks to his enthusiasm at Hereford market. He was unrepentant about his adventures at the poultry market and remarked repeatedly that actually the purchases had been a bargain when you thought about it. Although he had managed to convince himself, as I surveyed the noisy belligerent geese, neurotic chickens and the army of ducks all in little huts dotted about the farm I felt curiously ambiguous.

I liked the ducks: they waddled around, dipped in the pond, walked up the lane, neither hostile nor in a constant state of panic. All the same, I would have liked them a lot more if there had only been half a dozen. The trouble with thirty-two ducks is that firstly they are the messiest creatures on the planet and secondly, to cram that many ducks into three different houses is as hard as advanced origami. The pair of us had to approach them obliquely from either side with the three dogs blocking the rear. Then we would edge forward incredibly carefully: you could spend a half-hour getting them to the brink of the hut door, but then ruin it all with a quick movement. If that happened there would be anarchy for a moment as the entire flock panicked and then they would waddle off quacking into the sunset. It was generally at this point that Dan would start making pointless dives like an England goalkeeper in a penalty shoot-out in an attempt to recover the situation.

The success of the operation was not helped by my complete refusal to touch any bird. I did not feel comfortable coming into contact with feathers or skin, so I used a large stick to prod them. As a result, some evenings we were out there for up to an hour attempting to herd them into their huts. In the end the whole episode got so lengthy that we gave up and left the ducks to take their chances bedding down in the open.

The quail were not so much of a problem. Dan had found a rather clever design for a quail farm, which consisted of a large cage, five foot off the ground and slightly on a slope. When the eggs appeared, they would roll down a sort of spiral cascade into a trough below. By coincidence we were there for the first egg. It rolled down just as Dan had predicted, zigzagging down the slopes and eventually smashed, literally, into the trough. Dan stared in disbelief and stuttered that in fact he had anticipated this, and in the end a little light bedding sorted out this teething problem. That evening we were dipping our first little eggs in celery salt.

The weather was now excellent, never really topping more than 70 degrees and usually with a cool breeze. The wet mud had dried up and the garden was growing. When we were outside working in the vegetable garden, with Jack asleep in the old English nanny pram, it was rather idyllic. The vegetable plot was at the end of the front lawn with the whole Wye Valley unfolding before it and you could trace its course all the way to the Brecon Beacons and the Black Mountains. In the whole panorama you could only count half a dozen farms, with not a road in sight. It was a peculiar feeling.

In the winter I had found this isolating, but now it was summer the remoteness made the place rather magical. All you could see were colourful woodlands of hardwoods and pine, craggy hills and mountains, deep blue lakes, hay meadows and fields of sheep. The roads were too far away to hear cars and any commercial plane was too high in the sky to be audible. The only noises were buzzards mewing and lambs bleating.

In order to enjoy the view properly, I convinced Dan to make me a large sofa out of enormous rocks, which I then filled with earth and planted with creeping thyme. I would lie there for hours, watching the view as the buzzards rode the thermals above a large lake, where, it is rumoured, King Arthur threw Excalibur to its last known resting place. Early evenings were best, when the mountainous sides of our valley were glowing a hazy pink and the

Beacons went a strange misty blue colour.

The satisfaction of staring at our maturing vegetable plants hadn't dwindled. The potatoes had become tall green bushes with pretty blue flowers, the courgettes were branching out ready to flower and the red oak leaf lettuce was spreading large auburn leaves across the earth. There were seedlings climbing bamboo poles and bushes growing in perfect little lines. On evenings when Jack was sleeping and I could sit on my thyme sofa and watch the view with an extremely cold glass of Mâcon-Lugny, just for a second it did seem close to paradise.

The weather was so warm that we could now eat outside on the terrace. On one such night in early June we decided that the moment to try our first home-grown new potato had come. Deciding which plant to pull up was a lengthy process, Dan was all for choosing the first one in the row, but I was not sure that the plant was ready. In the end I choose one which looked emotionally prepared from about halfway down the patch.

I dug the fork deep into the ground under the plant and levered up gently. Dan pulled the plant out and we peered in to see what our labour had amounted to. The sight was not short of awesome: the most perfect little potatoes you had ever seen. Dan and I were almost drunk with our success and we agreed several times that they were the most beautiful potatoes in the whole world. We carried these specimens of excellence to the kitchen and I watched them boil while Dan barbecued some succulent Welsh chops to compliment our harvest.

We ate them on the terrace by the light of a few storm lanterns. Dressed in a little local Welsh butter and a few sprigs of mint, they were unbelievably exquisite: a sweet nutty flavour. And the texture was fantastic too. I had never realised that a potato's consistency could be so important. Dan and I talked about every aspect of these tubers for most of the evening. We were so excited that we took photographs with Dan's flash and I used the video camera my mother had lent us to record her first grandson's formative moments, to film Dan eating one while giving a lengthy commentary.

When Jack began to gear up for his evening crying session, Dan brought him out to show him what his parents had achieved. The potato tasting was a big moment and it seemed that with every mouthful, much like Persephone and the pomegranate seeds, we were committing ourselves more deeply to our new life.

Seriously buoyed up by this success, we worked harder than ever in the garden. The artichokes I had planted from seedlings were being somewhat choked by weeds and I spent most of an afternoon clearing them and spreading wood chips around the base. It was while I was pulling up stubborn dandelions that I noticed the large black cloud moving fast towards the house. It was low, about half the height of a tree and was an irregular shape which seemed to mutate as it travelled across the hillside. My first thought was that it was extra-terrestrial and I must save the baby. I grabbed Jack from his pram and walked briskly – but without breaking into a run (so as not to draw the alien's attention) – back into the house. As I arrived, so did the black cloud and it hovered above the top corner of the end wall. I screamed for Dan and ran inside to thwart any attempt to abduct my baby into outer space. The only place large enough to hide Jack was the stove, which was a fine French cooker procured by my mother from a little-known Continental distributor. Its main feature was its particularly large oven. Jack fitted neatly on a mattress on the bottom shelf. I left the door ajar to avoid suffocation problems.

Once Jack was safe I tiptoed outside to investigate the enemy. Dan was there staring up at the eaves of the house.

He looked at me with excitement.

"Look! Isn't it great? We've got a swarm of bees – I have always wanted bees."

There were thousands and thousands of the little creatures, all buzzing around just six feet away from the main door. My knowledge of bees was on a par with my grasp of Romanian country dancing, but I did know that they could sting and each was a potential baby-killer. Only recently I read the story of a lorry driver who was stung by a bee on the M40 just past Oxford and was dead before he reached Birmingham. I was feeling distinctly unsettled about the situation, as Dan rushed inside to consult John Seymour capturing swarms. As he did so, I was frantically leafing through the yellow pages for some sort of professional bee disposal person. Dan explained that if we could persuade them to leave the house and take up residence in a beehive we could have delicious honey all season. I put forward my 'considered' case. "I don't want bees," I said. "They're killers. People, ordinary people, die just within seconds of looking at a bee. What chance has a new baby got? Do you want your son to die from a thousand bee stings?"

This seemed like a very coherent and well-thought-out argument to me, but Dan was not really even listening. Within the hour a neighbouring beekeeper was at our house wearing a white bodysuit with a hood. He placed a ladder up to the colony and climbed up with a small box strapped to his back. Once he was on a level with the bees – who by now were becoming rather agitated and looked poised to commit murder – the bee man tied the box to the ladder and retreated to ground level. We went inside the house.

"If the bees are going to leave your house for the swarm box," he told us, "it will have to happen in the next hour, but maybe they're already settled in your house. If they do swap to the box you will have to go up the ladder and seal it up. Then you've got to wrap it in a blanket or such like and move the bees at least three to five miles away from here. Bees have a remarkable memory and homing instinct, so they need to be a good distance or else they will swarm straight back to the eaves."

I thought the man must be ever so slightly mad to think that we could do all that. Then again, he must have thought the same when he spotted Jack in the oven on his way to the bathroom. I told him that Jack seemed to feel a greater security in enclosed spaces, but it was still mildly embarrassing.

Within half an hour, the bees had decamped from the actual fabric of the house and were firmly ensconced in the swarm box. Their defection was markedly encouraged by the honey the bee man had spread inside. I still felt very nervous about their presence and watched them from a distance. There were so many coming and going, making an unbelievable noise. The flowers on the terrace were being constantly pestered. Dan kept leaving the door open and some were buzzing around inside, I went upstairs to escape the anxiety and no sooner had I kicked my shoes off to lie on my bed than I trod on one of the little bastards.

The pain was instant. I looked at my foot and seeing the sting, hopped to the stairs shouting at Dan to come and suck the poison out, only to land on another one. I sat at the top of the stairs with throbbing feet, Dan picked the stings out and asked me if I was allergic.

"How the bloody hell do I know?" I almost screamed. "I've never even seen a honeybee before, let alone been stung by one. I could be dead in twenty minutes." I lay on the bed moaning as I wondered when the convulsions would start. My theory that the countryside was danger-ous was at last confirmed. It may look safe but it isn't: it is full of things that can kill you in horrible ways. In the city you don't get all those nasty insects and poisonous plants and such like. Yes, there are cars, but you know where you are with a car. You cross the road and you can see it.

I freely admit I am not very brave when it comes to any living creature that can harm you, or for that matter any animal which is bigger than me. I am slightly irrational about horses and cows, while insects are wild and capable of unpredictable attacks. This is why I do not want to go to Australia. There, they have more deadly snakes than harmless ones, lethal spiders, scorpions and Christ knows what would kill you if you put one toe in their ghastly waters. When I went to East Africa, I had hardly stepped off the plane before a large Black Mamba snake threatened me. The people I was with made me go on some dreadful safari, where I absolutely insisted I sleep in the car rather than risk attack in a tent.

Needless to say the bee stings did not kill me, but they did leave me with bright red feet which itched uncontrollably. That evening I hobbled outside to look at the box just before dark. The whole surface was covered in them: they had all come outside and were clinging to the wood.

This looked ominous. I looked in the book, but there was no mention of this phenomenon. What were they up to? Anyone who has seen that cinematic 1978 classic *The Swarm* will know that they were getting ready for a big Hitchcockian attack and that while we were sleeping soundly in our beds they would come through the vents and under the cracks in the door to sting us in the eyes and crawl down our throats.

I rang the bee man, but was told that apparently they come out of the box when it gets a bit hot inside. Whatever the banal reason, it still looked spooky, so I pleaded with Dan to do the job tonight. Fortunately, the bee man had lent him a bee jacket and veil and later when it was nearly dark, he began to get ready to mount the ladder. He tucked his trousers into his socks and looked for some gloves. All he could find were Marigold kitchen ones, but bees couldn't sting through rubber, he told me.

While he was doing this, I went to find a blanket and some rope, which Dan bundled over his shoulder. I shut all the windows and doors and went to stand well away from the house to watch the event. Dan slowly went up the ladder to the box but almost immediately I heard the bees swarming and could make out a dark shadow around his whole body. The blanket dropped to the floor as Dan came down the ladder rather fast and I watched in amused horror, as he ran around the lawn with a trail of black insects after him.

For a split second I wondered what I could do to help and then I ran inside the house, shut the door and peered out the window. Dan was still running around waving his arms a lot. A few minutes later he came inside bringing a dozen or so bees with him. I reached for the vacuum, sucked them off him and asked what had gone wrong.

"Bees *can* sting through rubber," he muttered, showing me his gloves which bristled with little stings. In fact his whole body was covered with what looked like small black splinters. He took his suit off and a bee flew out which I managed to suck into the vacuum without too much effort. After he had had a few large whiskies, he told me that they had all come out and had mounted a full-scale offensive on him before he had even reached the box. "Perhaps they are African killer bees," I proposed.

Dan did not try again and I spent an uneasy night with very itchy feet and dreamed of giant bees chasing me through a South American jungle. The next night Dan had asked Olek to come over and help.

After dinner Dan and Olek togged themselves up with all the most protective clothes they could find. Dan was wearing the same bee suit and veil he had the previous

night, while Olek fixed up his own. This consisted of a
large Russian army coat with a mosquito net over his head
and a massive rabbit fur hat. They went out with the blanket and rope. Miranda and I went to watch from the end
of the garden. Olek put another ladder up next to the
swarm box and they stood at the bottom holding the blanket between them. Then – ever so quietly – they each
began to climb. But by the time they had scaled halfway
to the box the bees were out and this time it looked
personal.

Olek jumped off his ladder and ran around swearing,
"Christ Almighty bollocks!" very loudly, while Dan
dashed up and down the garden, flapping his arms. In his
white bee suit he looked not unlike the old footage of
attempts by the early aviators to conquer the mysteries of
flight. Miranda was laughing so much I had to carry her
inside. Seconds later Dan and Olek came running in slam-
ming the door behind them. They were distinctly shaky.

Following this second failure Dan agreed that he definitely did not want to try again and the next day I called
the bee man who had lent us the swarm box. He sounded
surprised when I told him we were having problems
getting the bees down the ladder. That evening he came
dressed in an all-in-one bee suit and a smoke puffer which
looked rather like an old-fashioned perfume dispenser.
Dan felt the use of smoke was cheating. The bee man
swanned up the ladder puffing little grey clouds at the bees
who looked almost pleased to see a professional at last.
Within five minutes he had sealed the hole and covered the
box with an appropriate cloth. He took the bees down
from the top of the ladder and put them in the back of his
truck.

"I'll take them to some hives I have five miles from
here," he told us as he accepted a glass of wine. "Would
you like me to transfer them to a hive and bring them

back in a week?"

Dan said "Yes" at the same time that I said "NO". My voice was the louder and not wanting to incite a domestic incident, the man said he would ring in a few days. Fortunately when he did open the box back at his bee ranch the troublesome pests immediately swarmed off to terrorise some other poor family. He brought us the contents of the swarm box which was a pound of clover honey the bees had made in the days they had spent with us, it was so delicious I almost contemplated changing my mind.

Fortunately, the vegetable garden was growing with such vigour that Dan soon forgot about bee farming. Weeding and mowing was a twice weekly event. The potatoes were still as good as they had been the first night we tasted them, but by now we had spinach, broad beans and lettuces to add to our meals. The latter were sweet and crunchy and every day we had phenomenal salads with golden oregano leaves, baby spinach leaves and chopped fresh chives. The weather was hot and dry and I tended to potter about the garden in the late afternoon rather than in the full force of the sun.

One evening I was pleasantly disturbed from hoeing by the distant sound of Otis Redding's 'Dock of the Bay'. I couldn't pin-point the source, but the vague direction was from somewhere down the valley. The music was loud and it was clear there must be some sort of party going on. It seemed very obvious to me that whoever was playing that song must be an intelligent, interesting and generally nice person: no one could listen to Otis Redding and be horrible.

At this point Dan came out looking exasperated clasping our son who had started up one of his screaming sessions. I suggested we put Jack in the car and go off in search of the nice people who were playing good music to try and make friends with them. Dan was reluctant, but the bellowing baby persuaded him to give it a go. We took a few cold beers and drove down the lane and by the time we crossed the main road Jack had fallen into a snuffly sleep. We had the windows open and stopped every couple of hundred yards to check our bearings. The music changed to Percy Sledge, the O'Jays and Aretha Franklin: who were these people with such incredibly good taste?

We found ourselves driving down a bumpy track for about a mile, through a clearing in the trees into an open field full of primary-coloured wooden caravans, carts, tepees, little bonfires, black-and -white cart horses and a lot of travellers. By the time we had parked, Dan was much more keen to get out of the car than I was. We parked and with Jack strapped in a sling to Dan's chest ventured forward.

A man came up. He wore stripy trousers, a purple shirt and his hair was in thin little dreadlocks. He was holding out his hand. "Hi, you're Derry's mate, aren't you?" he said. "I remember you from last year. How is Derry? I guess he couldn't make it this year? What a pity, I love Derry – he's wild." This was followed by a long knowing laugh.

I said I didn't know Derry, but we lived across the valley and we had heard the music. He looked unperturbed. "Well, you look just like Derry's mate. You've got a double, you know, honestly the spitting image. Well, I'm Victory – great to see you."

And he was off. It has been a constant irritation to me that I am quite regularly mistaken for other people: I must have very common facial features.

We walked further into the field and Dan spotted a large bearded man carving something out of wood and went over to befriend him. I was about to follow when a woman in a long dress and equally long hair approached me.

"Hey, how are you doing?" she said. "Is Derry with you? I haven't seen Derry for about six months. Where has he been?"

Before I could tell her the truth she dragged me over to a bonfire with a collection of people circling the flames. This group had large tents and tepees covered in pieces of brightly coloured material. She announced me as Derry's mate. They all looked very animated when they heard this.

"Oh excellent!" said one. "If Derry's here we really are in for a good party."

"Hey, where *is* Derry?" said another. "Where the hell has that madman been? I've missed him."

They looked so eager to hear news of Derry I felt I couldn't disappoint them. "Derry really wanted to be here," I said. "He's going try to make it out in a few days."

This caused a big ripple of excitement. A bloke who, I gathered later, was called Stash gave a loud whoop and slapped his neighbour on the back.

"Excellent!" He said. "We're going to have a great summer if Derry makes it. So how the hell is he? What's he been up to?"

"Well you know Derry," I lied. "Just being mad. What a mad . . . man." Then, desperate to change the subject, I tried a different tack. "So how long have you been up here?"

Brook, the girl with long hair, told me they had all come more or less together about two weeks ago. Most of them came every summer for a couple of months. The rest of the year was split between pitches in Somerset, Devon and a few sites scattered around Scotland.

Somebody called Mole passed me a beer and offered me a cigarette, which I accepted and puffed even though I don't smoke. I thought it would be more in tune with my adopted traveller personality. The conversation flitted from people they knew to drugs and music. They reminisced about the events of the previous summer.

"Yeah that night was brilliant. I was howling like a wolf on top of that hill. I was with Birdman who sang 'Bohemian Rhapsody' in German all bloody night."

Stash was laughing as he attended to some minor repairs on his surf board (it surprised me that the Welsh coast had any surfable waves). He added his own pennyworth of memories. "Remember that strange bloke, Twat, at last mid-summer's party, who was off his head and spent the whole night diving into shrubberies?" he asked. "You would be having a beer with him and talking about the possibility of transporting molecules over the airwaves and then he would just leap into a shrubbery – completely weird."

There was more laughter. Rather bored with the conversation, I asked how they'd found the site.

"I met Victory down south ages ago and he told me his parents part-owned this excellent piece of land up in Wales and there was this massive field where we could come and stay," said Stash. "I've been coming here for five years now."

"How long have you been travelling" I asked.

"Oh you know, on and off since I left school."

I didn't quite understand how it could be on and off, but Stash seemed evasive on the subject. Hog asked me where I was going to stay.

"Have you got a tent or something?"

"Oh it's fine," I answered, "I've sorted myself out down the valley."

Fortunately I think they were too stoned to realise my impostor status. I stayed for a bit longer to hear more tales of colossal drug taking and their struggles with authorities. Then I got up to leave. "If you hear from Derry, tell him he's got to come up here," Mole shouted after me. "Do you think he will make it?"

I told them he was going to try his best, "but you know how caught up Derry gets," I added with a smile. They all laughed: I had no idea what at.

As I went on to find Dan who was far away across the field, I wandered past other colonies of travellers. Mostly they were families with masses of children of all ages draped around the caravans and carts. I walked by the caravan from which the music emanated. Two enormous speakers were positioned towards the hills playing yet more Motown and Soul. It was extraordinary that so many of the people that I passed on the way were fantastically good looking.

I found Dan still talking to the woodcarver. He was in his late fifties and had a large grey beard. He was wearing a very baggy blue overall suit and was surrounded by chunks of wood, some already carved into animals, others half-carved. His caravan was a beautifully painted old gypsy one, the inside was immaculate with a single raised bunk, masses of compartments and benches down the side and a cast-iron wood burning stove. The whole interior was painted with Celtic designs in dark pastel colours. Outside he had a woodshed stacked with neatly sized pieces of timber. There was a large canvas awning where most of his work was taking place and an array of tools and machines.

Dan introduced me to Bill and I said it was a relief to find he wasn't named after a small woodland animal. He laughed loudly and nearly crushed my hand when he shook it. "Great to meet you, Belladonna," he said. "I have been talking here to your partner about wood and thank God I have – what he knows about the stuff I could write on my little finger. Imagine living here and not understanding about wood. Incroyable." Why we needed to know about wood, except how to it chuck it on a fire, was a mystery to me, but judging by the number of lumps of the stuff in different stages of carving, I guessed that here was a man who lived his life with a chisel permanently in his hand.

I asked him how many people passed through the site.

"In the summer we get anything from thirty to a couple of hundred chaps and chapesses, but tonight is mid-summer so it's a big night. I should imagine they will go on for days – they've got energy these young whipper-snappers, by God. Rather a driftless bunch this year, you know a bit soft in the head, they need a bit of toughening up if you ask me. I have half a mind to take the job on, take them up into the hills for a little survival training. You know, I was in the SAS once, bloody ages ago – I thought I was officer material myself, but I couldn't stand being told what to do which is rather an essential aspect of army life as you can appreciate.

"That's how I discovered this bit of the country – we used to come round these parts and train up in them hills. One training session I was so bloody hungry I broke into someone's house and couldn't find any food so I borrowed their pet hamster and ate it."

He then gave a great laugh.

"I moved around the whole country after that – left not a stone unturned. Saw a bit here, a bit there and a bit of how's your father under there, all life's rich tapestry et cetera, et cetera. In fact I still like to move around a bit, just to keep the old oar in. I travel down south to a few places I know, but good sites are hard to find these days – a bit like doughnuts, can't find a well-baked doughnut for love nor money – so I stay here most of the time. It was thirty years ago I first came to Wales and I have seen all the changes. There is a core of us who have been here since the beginning, we got together and bought the land. Those log cabins you passed on the way up belong to some of the other founders. Me and June over there are the only ones still in the field. I like it here: it makes me feel younger. I don't think I would be happy in a log cabin. Too many walls."

Jack started up again and we left the field. Dan was deeply impressed by Bill and started to recount the traveller's theories on woodland management to me. I said that I thought it all sounded madly fascinating, but perhaps he could skim on some of the fine detail? As we passed Victory I quickened my step lest Hog, Mole, Brook and the rest asked me more questions about their hero.

When we got home I felt quite buoyed up by our experience with the local travellers. Even if there was a case of mistaken identity perhaps there were friends there to be made. As I went to the greenhouse to re-pot the aubergines and sow some more basil and coriander, it seemed that we had it rather easy. If we could get the baby to stop crying, keep bluebottles and dogs out of the house, there would not be much to complain about.

Strawberry Ice Cream

1 pint of cream
8 egg yolks
6 ozs sugar
½ lemon
2 lbs fresh strawberries
handful of fresh mint

Pour the cream into a double saucepan and add the zest from the lemon. Add the egg yolks and cook on a slow flame stirring all the time. When the mixture suddenly stiffens, remove from the heat, add the sugar, stir and strain. While it cools, pulp the strawberries and mint in a food processor (reserving a little of each for decoration) and add to the cream mixture. Pour into a suitable tray and place in the freezer, stirring every half hour until frozen (about 3 hours).

July: Dan

As the weather began to warm up, it became increasingly difficult to remain behind my computer screen. Obviously, as a loyal partner, I tried to combine work with my new-found parenting role. So I began to build up a routine of relieving Bel of Jack in the early evening and attempting to soothe him to sleep by taking him for a walk, strapped to my waist in a sling. The dogs accompanied us, romping through the bracken and gorse after rabbits, yapping in paroxysms of sheer canine delight. Of course these hunts failed more often than they succeeded, but that didn't seem to bother Dill, Havoc and Bracken a jot.

It was towards the end of one of these walks that I had one of my most magical experiences. It had been a longer excursion than most and as a result the dogs were already exhausted and unusually biddable, trotting obediently to heel as we descended the steep gradient back to the house. We were not more than 100 yards from the back door – when I was stopped short by an unexpected movement not 50 yards ahead. For a second I thought it was a rabbit, but then the creature began to clamber all over a tree root. Another joined it and they began to wrestle for control of the knotted wood, before another joined them: three very healthy fox cubs. In an urgent whisper I told the dogs to sit, and to my surprise found them only too willing to throw themselves full-stretch on the grass, tongues lolling out and sides heaving as they cooled down after their exertions.

I watched the three cubs, totally entranced, for a full five minutes before Jack began to realise the soothing rocking action of my walk had stopped and began to murmur in the first signs of protest. The sound brought me to my senses and I quietly turned around, calling the dogs to heel in a whisper, leaving the cubs undisturbed.

In spite of the views of our neighbours, I harboured a lingering affection for foxes and decided to keep quiet about the earth, knowing full well that were the locals to learn of the presence of an occupied earth, they would be around with terriers, spades and poison gas. I was pleased with the presence of our vulpine family, but I felt oddly guilty about my decision to stay silent. After all, we were newcomers and although foxes were far more of a threat to our poultry than they were to the countless sheep and their fully grown lambs, it was not a matter of financial survival to us. If a fox were to take a couple of ducks or a bantam, it was not a matter to be discussed with the bank manager, but rather one fewer tasty winter meal. So I contented myself with telling Bel all about the charming sight and vowed to return every evening to watch their progress. Like so many good intentions, however, this fell foul of Jack's erratic sleep patterns and when I did finally make it back, there was no sign of the family.

Meanwhile, for all the charm of our wild visitors, the sporadic human company continued to weigh heavily with us. A social element was clearly missing from our lives and as a result those few 'hits' with others of like minds rated particularly highly. The first came when we went for dinner with Olek and Miranda. As the drawbacks of parenthood became increasingly apparent, so our affection towards our two friends became stronger by the day, in large part due to Jack's increasing intolerance of long-distance car travel. On short runs it might put him out like a light, but any journey of more than thirty minutes would produce projectile vomiting all over the interior. Like all new parents we had rapidly become acclimatised to the warm, milky smell of baby puke, but we could be forgiven for avoiding the experience whenever possible.

Of course this had a serious impact on our domestic lives, given the remoteness of our new home. All the nearest fair-sized towns were about an hour's drive away. So 'comfort shopping' trips for luxuries like food and clothes were out. Perhaps fortunately, however, these were already largely precluded by our precarious finances and, on top of this, came a sudden heat wave which made any drive – even with the windows wide open – deeply unpleasant.

So instead, we contented ourselves with increasingly frequent trips to see our new-found best friends in their converted schoolhouse. It was on one of these weekend trips – coincidentally on one of the hottest days of the year – that we arrived mid-afternoon to be greeted with the surreal sight of Olek, stripped to the waist with sweat pouring down muscular chest and back, next to a huge pile of logs, strewn higgledy-piggledy all over the lawn. He held a huge axe casually in his left hand, its blade resting in the grass. The temperature was well into the upper twenties, but the neighbouring wheelbarrow was full of gleaming white, splintered logs. To me this was a picture more associated with snow-clad mountains, bare branches and whipping sleet, but Olek seemed completely at ease.

He grinned when he saw me. "Ah! Dan, you must have vodka!" He enthused, heading quickly for the kitchen as Bel delicately lifted the already queasy-looking baby from the rear of the car. Never a fan of excessively hot weather, she rapidly followed him in, leaving me staring at the huge pile of birch logs in a state of some confusion.

A moment later he had returned. "We split and talk?" he asked, pushing a shot glass into my hand. It was already misted with condensation and as I took it, I could feel the lower beads solidifying into ice: both the glass and its contents were straight from the freezer. Overcoming my British sense that neat spirits are for late night or winter – and preferably both – I followed his lead and knocked it back in one.

To add to my consternation, his next comment seemed perilously close to my thoughts. "Fuel for Christmas!" he laughed.

"Yes, that's when I normally drink it," I shivered as the liquid oozed down my throat, before warming into a red-hot cannonball as the alcohol triggered my digestive nerves.

"No, no," he roared with a huge grin, pointing to the wood lying around. "This – this is fuel! You British, you British are all alike, you know everything about central heating and nothing about warmth!

"All over Europe, they understand wood – except here," he continued, setting his glass down and picking up the axe. "You go to Poland, Russia, Hungary – even France – when you buy firewood, you buy firewood – not some dripping wet, half-rotten branch which will not burn!

"I was in France last year," he continued earnestly. "There you buy firewood from a specialist who delivers to wood store. He weighs it as it comes off the lorry and tests moisture content. He even gives you computerised read-out – you never buy when it's more than 50%. Wood has 90% water when cut down, so 50% means drying for two years."

Olek snorted, as he turned to kick a nearby log dismissively. "This wood? Is good for Wales, but has moisture of maybe 80%.

"The French, they understand wood is like red wine – it needs time to mature," he continued scornfully. "It cannot be good until it has grown up." He swung the axe down on to a birch log with an impressively effortless 'thwunk', sending the two halves cartwheeling across the garden. As he chopped, he expounded on his theories of good burning wood. Apparently in an ideal world, one cut, split and stacked logs in a dry but draughty place each spring. These were to remain here not until the following winter, not even the winter after that, but ideally for almost three years before they could be tossed on the fire.

"Like wine too you should have good cellar. You drink claret with beef, yes? But you do not drink it with fish," he said with a theatrical shake of his head. "So why burn just one tree? You match wood to weather. It is very, very cold? Burn dry birch or pine – good heat, but gone soon. It is night time? Burn oak or ash – last long time, but less hot. It is normal pissy-rainy day in Wales? Burn mix for warmth and stamina."

As the level in the vodka bottle dropped, his shoulders heaved and the pile of wood dwindled, he explained that to him oak was cabernet sauvignon, with bulk and staying power. In contrast, ash was a chardonnay, capable of being consumed young, but best with a couple of years behind it. Birch, pine, willow, on the other hand were just the plonk varieties, the sangiovese. They were all right, he admitted grudgingly, but, like cheap Italian reds, they lacked body. Were he to have his way, he said, his woodshed would be mainly ash, but it would contain a sizeable proportion of birch for quick-fix heat and a smattering of oak to impress visitors with its slow-release, gratifying power. "Now that is vodka wood!" he said with a laugh, draining the latest tot of the neat Polish spirit with an expert flick of his head.

"So you're chopping wood on the hottest day of the year for the winter after the winter after next?" I giggled, as I tipped back my own glass (what with the heat and the neat spirits, I was beginning to feel distinctly light-headed).

"What do you take me for? Conjuror?" Olek bellowed a little belligerently – it seemed he too was feeling the effects. "Look around you – was this house built by Pole? Where do you put wood? All we have is small coal bunker – look no bigger than car!" In a moment the high spirits were transformed into a deep Slavonic depression. "No, we are roped in by British builders. They know nothing of wood – this, this will all be gone by January."

He remained gripped by the inability of his adopted home's inhabitants to grip the elementary chemistry of burning wood: that the smaller and purer the ingredients, the quicker and more exothermic the reaction. "I think," said Olek (finishing yet another vodka), "the problem is you British cannot think or act the right way for your climate! It is like conversation – you like things cool. We Poles like passion and heat – it keeps out cold very good – like vodka." He poured out two more shot glasses of the fiery liquid and passed one to me. "No wonder you talk about weather even though is never really cold or hot – and why? Because inside is always like fridge! And why is this? Because you burn wet wood!" He punctuated his sentence with a contemptuous snort and an emphatic blow of his axe. Another guillotined birch log went cartwheeling across the grass.

Olek's depression soon disappeared, however. As I helped chop, ferry and stack the wood, the pile soon dwindled to nothing and with it his gloom.

The heat wave that bathed us that afternoon continued throughout the month and as we basked in the heat of the glorious mountain sun, so it presented us with unexpected problems. Obviously, neither Bel nor I were hardened horticulturists to put it mildly, but when we arrived we fondly imagined that what we lacked in knowledge, we could more than make up for in enthusiasm. In our inexperience we had paid more attention to culinary variety than vegetable reality. We had planted dozens of sensitive plants: indoor tomatoes, delicate cucumbers, heat-loving aubergines and chillies from the tropics and soon the cedarwood greenhouse was so full of exploding lush foliage that to my eye it more resembled something from *The Day of the Triffids* than a horticultural triumph.

Obviously some of them would have to take their chances outside – and their chances looked pretty bleak given that we were asking semi-tropical plants to thrive up a Welsh mountain. Fortunately, the heat wave seemed to suit them fine – it was one of the hottest, driest spells on record. If our first tentative forays into food production had been daunted by the cold climate, this was certainly no longer the case. Now we were basking in fiercely hot weather with our thermometer regularly recording temperatures well in excess of the BBC forecast.

The result of this and our over-enthusiastic vegetable planting was that the garden was soon awash with wilting vegetables and we were facing a fresh set of difficulties as the spring supplying the house was reduced to a trickle. Thanks to our altitude the nearest mains water was a couple of miles away and we were clearly completely reliant on the residue of last winter's rains seeping slowly down through the hill. Suddenly the steep slope above the house seemed all too small and I found myself visualising the giant sponge of soil and bedrock gradually drying out beneath the gorse, bracken and grass.

When we had bought the property, I had thought it a bonus to be free of water rates, chlorinated water and hose-pipe bans. Suddenly I began to see the other side of the coin. True, no one could prosecute us for watering the vegetables with a sprinkler, but with no possibility of an alternative supply, I hardly needed the threat of a hefty fine to impose a ban on what I increasingly saw as Bel's profligate use of this most essential component of human life.

As a confirmed shower man who had always had a more cavalier attitude to hygiene than my partner, I found nothing unreasonable in my imperious declaration that baths were now banned, but in retrospect this was a mistake. Bel rebelled at the outlawing of two of the activities she most valued in her day. In the end, I backed down – at least in part – and a compromise was struck: she could have three baths a week provided she kept the plug in after she had finished and siphoned the water on to the vegetable patch instead of using the hose.

If the weather was causing problems, so too was our lack of experience. As our first crops began to fruit, it became evident that a very small patch of ground could produce a surprisingly large yield. At first we were delighted by the rapid progress of the second batch of broad beans and the profusion of what until now we had regarded as a delicacy: rocket.

"Delicious!" we announced as we tucked into our first plateful. As early summer progressed, however, our spirits began to flag at the monotony. In fact, Bel's will folded completely and as I served up yet another bean casserole, she suddenly announced she had never liked broad beans at school, didn't like them now and that regardless of their remarkable cropping, she would never plant them again.

The rocket was more successful – or at least Bel continued to eat her daily salad of fresh leaves dutifully, albeit with wilting enthusiasm. In an effort to add variety, I looked for alternative means of using the bounty in the vegetable patch, but my experiments were less than totally successful (rocket soup was a particularly disgusting failure).

Nevertheless, there was hope on the horizon and we were amazed at how fast our later efforts had begun to prosper. Although, according to the gardening encyclopaedias, we had missed the planting dates for many vegetables by almost a month, the beans took off like satellites from Cape Canaveral. Given our limited diet, we found ourselves wandering around the garden with watering mouths, gloating on the wonderful meals to come.

While waiting for these to arrive, my life was given new impetus by meeting Evan, a local ne'er-do-well. This was the culmination of a three-month search for a poacher, triggered by a rare newspaper commission to supplement our ailing finances. There was a small catch, however: the reminiscences of an old boy were no good – I needed to find someone who was still *active*.

This was a bit of a worry, because I knew no poachers at all, still less one who was still at the game, but I'd glibly assured my commissioner there was no problem, desperate not to let a rare fat cheque slip through my hands.

So started a long search, although it began hopefully enough. A chance remark to Dr McBain – now restored to favour after his shelled-pea *faux pas* – held out some promise. We had taken Jack along for his routine jabs and, trying to take my mind off the distressing sight of our son screaming as the needle went into his arm, I mentioned my search.

He told me poachers were definitely still at work – only last winter he'd opened his door one day to find a large salmon, wrapped in newspaper, on the doorstep. Unfortunately, however, he said he couldn't tell me who had left it. He said this was in part to do with ethical reasons and muttered something about 'patient confidentiality' –

although what that had to do with illicit fish on his doorstep was anybody's guess – but then went on to say it was mainly because he wasn't absolutely certain himself. "But I strongly suspect it has something to do with a thrombosis," he whispered cryptically. "Try The Mayfly."

My tentative enquiries at the pub frequented by most local fishermen drew an icy response. "There's no one like that around here," said the landlord firmly. "Give up." And he proceeded to stare at me so frostily that I found myself finishing my pint very rapidly indeed.

In the end I found Evan by sheer fluke. It happened when I went to renew my acquaintance with Bill, the woodcarver who we had met down at the local travellers' camp. I was taking my turn to entertain Jack and the little tot was in a gripey mood where nothing seemed to mollify him. In desperation I drove down to the camp and sure enough, by the time I arrived the baby was fast asleep. This allowed me to have a good chat with Bill, who was working on a block of wood with a chainsaw as I arrived. Seeing my car, he cut off the motor and pushed his safety goggles up into his hair, dislodging a snowstorm of sawdust.

He grinned and pulled out a small leather pouch that hung from a thong around his neck and began to roll a cigarette. "I thought you'd be back – want another look at that hawk, do you?" He asked, gesturing to the finished sculpture which stood beside his caravan.

Although, with my falconer's hat on, I had to say it was not entirely realistic – the feet were too big for that – it really was very impressive all the same. Somehow he seemed to have captured the wildness and spirit of the bird and the sculpture had a really lifelike quality. I complimented him on his work and he looked pleased, seeming to take it as particularly high praise coming from a falconer (little did he realise what a poor practitioner of the sport I actually was). He gestured to me to sit down on another of his creations, a giant mushroom carved out of a single block of oak. As I lowered myself on to its domed top, I was surprised to see smoke wafting out of the ground in front of me.

"What on earth are you doing there?" I asked.

"That? Oh that's my smoker," he replied proudly. "Like a look?"

He led the way to an oil drum lying on its side a few yards away from the caravan. A thick metal drainpipe led out of one end and then snaked down into a shallow trench behind. "That's my stove," explained Bill, opening a little door in the other end of the drum. A cloud of grey smoke emerged, obscuring everything, but as it wafted away on the breeze, I caught sight of a mound of sawdust which was clearly smouldering away slowly. With its centre eaten away by fire and having collapsed in on itself in a pile of charcoal-grey ash, ringed with a faintly glowing circle of embers, it resembled a miniature volcano. Bill pointed to the other end of the drum. "The smoke goes through the pipe to the smoke box over there," he continued, gesturing to a second oil drum – this time standing upright – about five yards away. The whole apparatus was far more complicated than my only experience of smoking to date: one of those tins sold by fishing shops which you fill with expensive sawdust.

"The pipe means the smoke is nice and cool when it gets to the meat," he explained. "Of course you can hot-smoke, but that just cooks and flavours the meat. Cold-smoking is much better – it acts as a preservative and when you don't have electricity, that's useful."

I asked him what he was smoking and he gave another one of his huge grins. Without a word he opened the smoke box to reveal three huge trout and what I took at first to be a small chicken hanging by its neck. From the occasional feather clinging to the skin, I quickly noted it was actually a pheasant. With three-and a half months to go before the shooting season began, I wondered where it had come from – and the fish too, come to think of it. Bill hardly looked the type to spend his spare time and money flicking flies across the Wye.

"Them? They come from a friend of mine, Evan. He's a real character, a poacher from the old school – you should talk to Evan, he'd like your birds – in fact I'm drinking with him this evening, why don't I ask him for you?"

That was how I found myself the next day, winding my way up a long dead-end valley which snaked into the Cambrian Mountains, ending about three miles short of the watershed which marks the backbone of Wales. Evan lived two-thirds of the way up, in a redbrick cottage. As I knocked on the door, I was alarmed to see that it was suffering from terminal subsidence. A huge crack ran up the nearest corner, and although I couldn't see the other side, I had a strong suspicion the front wall was held to the rest more by willpower than anything else.

The door was opened by a short man, with grey curly thinning hair. He looked much older than his 37 years: there were huge bags under his eyes and he scuffed his feet as he walked. Wearily he motioned me in and flung himself on to the sofa. He buried his face in his hands for a moment, before rubbing his eyes and shaking his head. It didn't take a genius to work out that he was heavily hung-over after his night out with Bill.

He gestured me in, nodding weakly as I explained that I wanted to interview him about his illegal activities. "Christ, what day is it?" he said weakly, trying to roll himself a cigarette, but spilling most of the tobacco over his knees in the process. "Sunday? Sunday? We'd better get a move on, the kids will be arriving soon."

"Kids?" I queried.

"Yes," he replied softly, screwing his eyes up, even though we were sitting in the semi-dark with the curtains half-drawn.

"Daughters or sons?" I asked, noting with wonder a hidden change in myself. For the first time in my journalistic career, I found myself following up a comment about a subject's family life with a genuine interest in his response. As he struggled to answer, I was instinctively forming the follow-ups. How many were there? Was there sleep after babies? How did he split parenting with his wife? My thoughts were interrupted by his response.

"About four, possibly six, but I'm contesting a couple."

Any thoughts of 'new-age male bonding' with my interviewee came crashing to the ground. "How many mothers are there?" I asked.

"Well, it's somewhere between three and five depending on who you ask." He managed a brief chuckle, before giving a long hacking cough. "Jesus, that whisky's done my head in!" In spite of the hangover, he spoke in a strong Welsh accent, ending his sentences on a high note.

I decided that for the time being it was best to return to the interview and asked him about poaching. "How do you start poaching?" I asked – the simplest of questions are usually the best.

"Jesus, well, it starts when you begin to chase things, as soon as you can walk, almost. You don't catch anything for three or four years, of course, then all of a sudden you're getting rakes of 'em. I suppose I was eight or nine when I caught my first rabbit, probably more by accident than anything else." As he went on, his story appeared relatively simple. Put briefly – Evan himself seemed incapable of brevity – he was the third child of a family of eight and his father had left home just before the last daughter had appeared. His mother was a formidable woman, however, and had thought nothing of bringing up the family alone. Naturally, as soon as they were capable, her elder children had rallied to the cause. The eldest got jobs and the next lot became unpaid child minders for their siblings. At this point, Evan and two younger brothers decided to take on the role of hunter gatherers. From the age of twelve, he was 'at the game', as he put it.

"We used to get a bow out of the hedge and buy sporting arrows in Hereford," he explained. "We'd run pheasants into bushes and hedges and shoot them. Then you'd quietly escalate to a few tricks, like. There's always someone who'll show you a trick, see. There was one bloke who I used to do a lot of miles with. He was a bit older than me, but he was pretty hot."

He went on to outline his favourite techniques and as he did so, it became clear that virtually anything could become a poaching tool in his hands. Bows and catapults cut from hedges were silent while an air rifle needed less skill but was noisier and more difficult to conceal. A whiff of gas from a lighter on a stick could knock a roosting bird off its perch, while a snare tied to a bamboo pole was just as effective. Netting was used to make 'igloos' – baited funnels to trap pheasants – but although these could produce high yields for minimal effort, there was always the danger they would be found and watched. For salmon he would use either a large hook (gaff) fashioned from stiff wire, or explosives.

"A friend spotted a big salmon in the middle of summer and decided to go for dynamite – but he used too much," he said casually as he rolled a cigarette. "When he finally found the fish it was fifty yards away in a puddle in the middle of a field," he laughed, a smoker's wheeze blurring the edges of his voice. "Explosives are surprisingly easy to get hold of – you'd be surprised how many farms around here have a bit of black powder in an old cocoa tin in a barn somewhere. The only problem is getting it to the bottom of the pool. You whack it into a good weighted bottle with a steady hole in the top. You want it to hold 'till it gets to the bottom. If the water comes in too quick you get stones hitting you on the back of the head and they hurt!

"And if you're using explosives, it's not just stones you've got to look out for. A mate put a bit too much in a pool and set the alarms off on a local dam. Unfortunately there was an IRA bombing campaign going on and there was a hell of a row! They called in the anti-terrorist squad, the lot! The security guards had dogs too – they caught him hiding up a tree in the end."

It was at this point that the interview was brought to an abrupt end by a ring on the door. Evan hauled himself off the sofa and walked to the front door. As he stood in the doorway, I could make out an attractive woman in her thirties standing in the sunlight. She was accompanied by two young boys of about seven or eight, and as she discussed the arrangements for picking them up, she was stroking the hair of the younger. A moment later she was gone and Evan came back in, followed by the two children.

"This is Maldwyn and this is Owen – my two oldest kids," he said. "This is Dan – he's a writer come to talk about poaching." The boys eyes lit up: it was clear their father's pastime excited them. "They come out with me sometimes – don't you, lads?"

"Yes, but it's a secret," said Maldwyn earnestly. "We mustn't tell anyone, must we, dad?"

"It's all right, you can tell him," Evan reassured the boy. "But who must we never ever tell?"

"Mum," chorused his two sons.

"That's right. She just wouldn't understand, would she?" The boys shook their heads and Evan winked at me.

"Christine doesn't approve of poaching – thinks of it as stealing, like," he explained. "She'd hit the roof if she knew I took these two out with me, but they're useful chaps, especially with salmon. When they was younger I used to sling 'em in one of them big old Victorian prams and wheel 'em around town, like. They'd be sleeping peacefully on top of half a dozen fish!" He chuckled again. "Now they help in other ways. What do you do, boys?"

"Go ahead and look for bailiffs," said Maldwyn proudly.

"Yeah and run back and tell Dad if there's any about," volunteered his brother. They clearly doted on their father and adored their nocturnal expeditions with him along the local brooks and streams. Meanwhile, Evan's face was covered by the indulgent smile of a loving father and my initial good impressions returned. I began to picture myself and Jack creeping along a moonlit brook, gaffs in hand, ears straining for the sound of a waiting bailiff. The mental picture led naturally to my next question. "I don't suppose you'd take me out next time you're after a salmon?"

Evan burst out laughing. "I knew it! Everyone's a poacher at heart and you're no different from the rest of us, like. Yes, of course I'll take you out – but it'll be a while yet. Wait till the fish start to run, then I'll show you how it's done, like. Now I can see there's only one way to get rid of this hangover. Fancy a quick pint?"

I wanted to continue the interview, but couldn't see any reason why this couldn't be accomplished in the pub. I glanced quickly at my watch, feeling a little guilty at leaving Bel with Jack for a whole morning after a particularly sleepless night. Also, without thinking I had taken the Fiat, leaving her the Landrover. As an ancient model with no seat belts, this was incapable of taking a baby seat and thus she was effectively marooned on the farm.

Still, it was only just noon and I reckoned I could easily stop at the pub for a swift half on my way home. Evan motioned to the two boys and we went outside. "Which pub?" I asked.

"Oh, no pub as such," laughed Evan. "See that house across the valley, half buried behind the wood?" I squinted at the hillside opposite and thought I could just make out a building behind the trees.

"We'll be going there – do you mind giving us and the dog a lift? I thought we might walk back, slow like, after the pub. There's rakes of rabbits about this time of year and I know a pub in town who'll take as many as I can supply – provided there's no shot in 'em, like." He winked and pulled the ends of a couple of small purse nets out of his jacket pocket. Normally these are used to cover bury holes as ferrets bolt the occupants. How they could be used, in conjunction with a dog, escaped me. I asked Evan how he intended to use them, but he refused to be drawn, remarking simply with a wink that: "Once you know where he is, a rabbit is a very predictable thing."

When we got to the other side of the valley, we found ourselves outside a rather run-down farmhouse. A couple of Landrovers and an old blue mini were parked near the door, but there were no benches, umbrellas, advertisements or pub signs. The obligatory rusting machinery that accompanies all working Welsh farms was strewn across the yard and a couple of rangy sheepdogs eyed us distrustfully. I wondered whether Evan had actually meant we were to have a drink with a friend of his and that if the word 'pub' had been the muddled words of a hung-over man. I looked quizzically at him and he winked again, as he strode confidently for the door.

He opened it without ringing and marched into the living room which was spartan to say the least. It was flagged with slate and undecorated apart from three old chapel pews and a couple of crude tables. Four men (from their dress, clearly farmers) looked up to stare quizzically at me, before nodding in recognition to Evan. Then they continued their conversation in a low murmur.

Evan nodded back. "Ernie, Ron, John," was all he said, as he sat down and the boys threw themselves on to the bench beside him. Puzzled I lowered myself opposite. An old man, wearing a battered tweed jacket and flat cap shuffled into the room.

"Hi-yah, John. A jug, and two softies and crisps for the kids," muttered Evan to the newcomer as he rolled a cigarette. There was nothing in his demeanour to suggest any form of apology for the intrusion, but rather it was exactly what I would have expected had we walked into any of the numerous pubs in town.

The old man nodded and went out again, as I opened my mouth to ask what on earth was going on, only to be met with a "Shhh!" from my new acquaintance. A moment later the old man reappeared with the crisps, two tins of Coke, a couple of glasses and a large cracked jug.

He put these down on the table in front of us and disappeared again, to return a moment later with a battered unmarked collecting tin, which he plonked on the table in front of us. Then he was gone.

"I'll get the first," said Evan, stretching into his pocket and pulling out a handful of coins which he fed into the tin. "One . . . two . . . three pounds," he counted out laboriously. "That's about it." Then he turned to me. "Before you ask, this isn't paying for the beer, just making a charitable contribution, like – although it's closely linked to John's hospitality."

At first he declined to go on, but as the level in his pint sank and the sideways glances from the four farmers on the other side of the room became less frequent, his vocal chords loosened. Apparently there were so few people living in the valley the last real pub had closed at the same time Dr Beeching had axed the area's branch line. For a while it hadn't mattered all that much – times were good and everyone had just driven five miles into town. But things had started to change a few years ago, what with the new drink-driving laws and the arrival of a couple of officious new constables, drafted in from outside. Attempts by the locals to treat drunken driving in the same way they regarded valid tax discs had floundered and, after several had been harshly treated (as they saw it) by the magistrates, John had decided to supplement his meagre farm income by going back to the ways of his fathers. For centuries they had supplemented their incomes by selling home-made ale to passing drovers and he claimed to be old enough to remember the last of these, quaffing his grandfather's brew by the farm gate, on their way down to Hereford. As a result, he saw himself as something of a traditionalist when he began to open his doors to his neighbours and to serve his own home-made beer.

"Of course the police raid him every now and again," explained Evan, as he helped himself to another glass of the slightly cloudy bitter. "But there's only one way in and out of the valley and someone down the hill is usually on the blower first. Just in case, though, he doesn't charge for the drink – just invites contributions to his favourite charity." By this stage I had grasped the general principle and he didn't need to spell out the beneficiary.

The beer was good too, far better than most homebrew. It was thick and nutty with only the merest hint of gas. We polished it off quickly. "You'll have another?" asked Evan.

I began again to think guiltily of Bel and Jack stranded at home, but paused for only a moment. Looking back, I'm not sure why I succumbed so readily. It could have been the fact that it was my round and that I didn't want been the fact that it was my round and that I didn't want to seem rude to the man who I hoped would take me poaching later on, but in honesty it wasn't that. It was the sense of adventure; I felt the acceptance of my presence in an illegal watering hole by these taciturn Welsh farmers was a mark of approval.

I caught sight of John in the doorway and motioned to him. "Another jug?" I asked. He nodded silently and disappeared.

I don't know exactly how many of these we consumed, but it was three hours before I finally managed to extricate myself from the converted living room, emerging blinking and thick-headed into the afternoon sun. I was now faced with a dilemma of how to return home. I knew that logically I must be over the limit, but with five miles to travel, my options were limited. There was no way that Bel could come to pick me up and besides I had now been gone so long that I didn't like to think about her reaction were I to make the request. Fortunately, Evan knew of a short cut via a particularly quiet back road and thus I managed to assuage any residual puritanical feelings about drink-driving with the knowledge that I was extremely unlikely to see any other traffic, let alone hit it. Nevertheless, I drove home extremely slowly (sure enough, without seeing another soul en route).

I had imagined I would be confronted with an irate girlfriend and screaming baby, but was relieved to find that for once Jack had been sleeping non-stop, leaving Bel to garden in peace. She sniffed slightly when I lurched towards her, wafting clouds of beer in her direction and observed quietly that were I to have encountered a police car and lost my licence it would have been the end of our Welsh sojourn, but she was otherwise remarkably calm about my condition.

When I woke the next morning with an appalling

headache and overwhelming sense of nausea, it was to be confronted with a problem which had been looming for several weeks. Our flocks of chicks, geese, turkeys and ducklings had put on weight at a staggering pace and their appetites had expanded accordingly. Although we had begun by giving them just a couple of scoops a day, by now they were swallowing three sacks of grain a week. What had been meant to be a source of cheap, wholesome food, was suddenly not looking quite so much of a bargain.

They were not the only mouths gnawing away at our dwindling bank balance. As the summer got into full stride, so the bantams' productivity fell right off. This had always been unpredictable, thanks to their habit of laying in cunningly concealed nests at the bottom of hedges. At first it had taken us hours of searching to find these, but once we realised that chickens can't count and that if one left at least one egg in the nest the stupid birds would continue to lay, day after day, in the same site, our daily supply stabilised at about a dozen.

Now, suddenly, it had plummeted to three eggs daily, and even though this was still way beyond our own consumption, I wanted to get to the bottom of the mystery. At first I suspected that the 'gals' had learned our 'one-egg-in-the-nest' trick and had started another nest (as yet unfound). We both kept a close eye on their movements, but as time went by we failed to locate it and I became convinced a thief was at work.

While we tried to figure out who the culprit was, a more serious crime occurred elsewhere on the homestead. When I went to feed the ducks one morning, I arrived to find a corpse lying stiff and cold by the pond. At first I thought it had been suffocated in one of the mindless panics to which flocks of poultry are sadly all too prone. Closer inspection revealed that the back half of its head was missing and the brain had been eaten.

That afternoon revealed a possible answer when I was summoned outside by a breathless Bel. As we ran down to the pond, she panted that she had been cutting rushes by the water's edge when her eye was caught by something rustling in the grass by an old drystone wall. She said it was a marvellous sight, but refused to elaborate further, saying it would be all the better for being a surprise.

She was right. When we tiptoed along the water's edge to peer through the foliage at the wall beyond, we were rewarded with the sight of four young stoats playing together on a rock, tumbling over each other and cascading through the grass in a game which seemed to be a cross between tag and all-in wrestling. It was a wonderful spectacle and we watched entranced for quarter of an hour before the group disappeared into the old wall.

"Wasn't that incredible?" Bel asked as we walked back to the house. "How amazing to be able to watch stoats play with each other in your own back garden." She looked down the valley to the distant hills. "This is an extraordinary place to live, sometimes."

Parsley & Walnut Pesto

1 large bunch parsley
(preferably flat leaf)
2 cloves garlic
2 ozs walnut pieces
2 ozs extra mature cheddar
Generous pinch of coarse sea salt
2 – 4 fl ozs olive oil

Put all the solid ingredients in a food processor and chop coarsely. With the motor still running, gradually dribble in olive oil until thick and creamy. Serve on pasta or instead of butter on a baked potato.

August: Bel

I feel very sheepish bringing this up, but the weather in August was just too hot. I know I whined for months about the cold – and I still feel justified in that complaint – but the heat can be an awful burden on the body temperature as well. One day the mercury topped one hundred degrees: it was excessive. I have very pale skin and have a strange condition which precludes any ability to sweat properly. This disability has the effect that on reaching a certain heat, I boil internally. I recollect a frightful trip to India when I fainted on a train to Calcutta and was brought round with cold water and a kind word from the conductor. Fortunately Allt-y-Gwalch was a farmhouse made of stone and, much like a Spanish hacienda, it stayed cool in the summer and retained its heat in the winter due to the massive lumps of stone that made up the walls. On intensely hot days I could slump in the armchair, breast-feeding the baby and dreaming of punkawallahs, without too much discomfort.

Incredibly, by some horrible twist in the earth's climatic cycle, we had not actually seen a drop of rain for over three months. My main concern was for the courgettes and assorted squashes, which were wilting under the burning sun. It was mental torture to witness, so I would make up some pretext for Dan to drive to town for supplies and, left in peace, I watered them at my leisure with no fear of the hose-pipe police jumping out of a bush at me. The benefits of playing Russian roulette with our water supply were totally justified in my view.

As a result we had a wonderful supply of tender sweet squashes of all different colours and sizes; butternut pumpkins and vegetable spaghetti baked with melted butter, sprinkled with grated nutmeg; young firm yellow courgettes blended with duck stock and cream, simmered with fresh basil leaves and parmesan. We stuffed green striped, round Italian courgettes (Tondo Nizza) with fresh sage and breadcrumbs. I picked a few of the young pumpkins and made a soup with smokey bacon and toasted sunflower seeds. We even dipped the young flowers in a batter and deep-fried them.

But this was about more than vegetables: it was turning into a religion. I was not about to let these plants die, I wanted to worship them – to build shrines, to carve their image into pieces of hardwood and to compose exalting songs glorifying their existence. These vegetable Gods were turning our evening meals into scenes from a rapturous tasting fest.

The squash family was not the only winner in our vegetable award ceremony. The artichokes were pushing up their large thistle fruits which we picked young and which were so tender we could eat almost all the leaves and heart. They had a definite earthy nutty flavour which was different to any artichoke I had ever eaten before. The heart itself had to be tasted to be believed when served with a thick warm vinaigrette.

Our dinners became more elaborate by the day. For a light supper when we couldn't be bothered we had fresh spinach and walnut soufflé, made with our own chicken eggs. Meanwhile the greenhouse was a jungle of edible deli-cacies like crispy cucumbers which made a sweet relish or a light yoghurty soup. We had so much basil – a special kind which had leaves the size of a lettuce – that we were cramming shoulders of lamb with pounds of the stuff. Dan brought some pine kernels and made countless jars of home-made pesto. This led the way to an important realisation in our eating extravaganza: we had to have fresh pasta to match the finesse of the creamy basil sauce.

The only conceivable way was to make our own. Dan went to find the pasta-making machine he had been given along with his 'Italian the Easy Way' course, but had never used. We mastered the machine while learning useful phrases like 'Can you recommend an interesting church to visit?'.

I think it is true to say that to make really fine pasta you have to be passionate about it. We mixed durum flour with semolina and folded in some duck eggs and extra virgin olive oil. When I was feeling seriously decadent, I occasionally mixed in a basil plant or two. We then wound it through the machine again and again until the dough was stretchy, but not sticky. Once we had cut it into strips of tagliatelle we laid it on our clothes rack and hung it to dry until the salted water was boiling. My God it was amazing! I had not realised what pasta was supposed to taste like till that moment.

Suddenly meals became almost Roman in their indulgence, involving lengthy discussions on content and technique between us. To have a supply of such fresh and tasty vegetables and herbs would only have been possible in London from the most expensive of delicatessens. Our increasing love and interest in cooking and eating was partly greed, but we were also driven by the desire to create perfect meals from our own resources.

The pinnacle of creation came when we decided to eat our first home-grown duck. There were definite mixed feelings about the decision, Dan and I both felt very reticent about the prospect. We discussed in some detail how the deed was to be performed and I noticed that this was always done in subconsciously low voices lest any animal should become acquainted with our dastardly plans. By unanimous vote Dan was picked to murder the bird, while my role was to be as observer and assist only if it was totally necessary. I observed that late afternoon would be the right time to carry out the execution.

The night before the deed, I dreamed we called the duck out, placed a blindfold around its eyes and offered to meet any last requests. In my dream the duck stood against the wall drawing heavily on a filterless Gitane. The slim duck was wearing the clothes that you might expect of a member of the Maquis and, before we gunned him down, he looked us in the eye and said, 'It is a far, far better thing that I do than I have ever done; it is a far, far better rest that I go to than I have ever known.' I woke in a heavy sweat.

The day of the appointed chop, I kept popping down to the hut to see the duck and check that he was comfortable. I had crazy images of taking a Bible or the Koran down there in case the duck needed to prepare spiritually. Four o'clock came and we marched with heavy wellies to the hut. Dan eased out the plump-breasted duck. We had purchased a plier-type tool which was designed to kill fowl efficiently. Dan asked me to hold the bird, but I said I had better stand guard in case any other birds saw what was going on and became agitated. Dan held the victim firmly and placed the pliers around its neck. There was a fair bit of flapping – and then nothing: it was dead. Dan looked a little traumatised and told me that he had not enjoyed that at all, I think I would have been worried if he had.

He then threw the warm bird into my hands and said, 'It's your turn now, go and pluck.' This scenario had not occurred to me. To be honest, I had never thought about how the feathers are removed from a bird. I had imagined that maybe they just fell off once their owner was dead. We took the duck inside and I arranged a corner in the kitchen with a large cardboard box for the feathers. The skin tore within seconds, but I persevered for what seemed like days. Once each feather was removed from the bird, it seemed to have a life of its own and they flew off around the living room. Jack enjoyed the snowstorm flying past his Moses basket and played games hitting them with his feet.

Finally it was ready. Smeared with apricot confit, the breast went under a hot grill while we prepared our own new potatoes, slim Kenyan beans and vegetable spaghetti. Then we opened a bottle of heavy wine and sat down to eat our first home-grown meat. I cut the bird's flesh and sampled a mouthful. It was fantastically good, the taste was so much stronger than any shop-bought duck. This was true of our vegetables as well, everything just tasted so much better than the uniform food that is available in supermarkets. This meal was the best dinner I had ever eaten and a lot had to do with the fact that almost all the ingredients came from the garden. It was a gastronomic paradise.

That night as I drifted off to sleep, I wondered whether Dan would come across me, sleepwalking in the pantry, in a long white nightie moaning, 'Out, out damned spot.' This did not happen and I concluded that my conscience could cope with taking a more active role in meat murder. We both enjoyed being in control of our food supply, we knew what was being sprayed on our vegetables – or in our case, not being sprayed – we knew what our animals were eating, how they were being housed and what kind of space they were allowed to live in. This was a great feeling, we felt truly independent. We didn't need shops, we were not at the mercy of commercial farmers. There was something oddly liberating about it.

Dan and I were so excited by the concept of being self-sufficient that we decided to set ourselves a task of lasting a whole week without one single purchase from the shops. We allowed ourselves the contents of the larder which held a supply of salt, pepper, olive oil, vinegar, butter and milk, and Dan started the exercise by making bread using the flour. This actually turned out to be an unexpectedly good idea. He used poppy seeds from the garden in the mixture and the result was extremely edible. He also uncorked his vintage elderflower wine which he had made back in London and had now reached the required maturity. I decided that we would need something more than just the vegetable garden to carry us through the week and I browsed through Richard Mabey's *Food for Free*. This catalogues edible British plants, giving guides to their culinary use and – more importantly – identification. We dug up dandelion roots to make a coffee substitute, which according to Mabey is indistinguishable from the real McCoy. On taking the first sip, we discovered he either spoke with forked tongue or had had his taste buds surgically removed. In desperation, I sautéed the roots with a little soy sauce, but again this fell into the disgusting category.

The book also identifies many plants whose leaves can be cooked and eaten much like spinach. We tried a number of these – fat hen and ground elder, for example – but came to the conclusion that there was a good reason why these plants had not been used much since the Middle Ages.

We had one last go with stinging nettle soup. With much foreboding the nettles were washed and stuffed into a pressure cooker, to emerge five minutes later as a healthy dark green mush. Still unsure about the concept, Dan insisted on adding cream, stock and pepper to produce a soup which was not too bad – a nutty version of spinach, we decided. Compared with previous experiments, it was so much of a success that we consumed vast amounts. It was not until the next day we discovered a slight hitch. In my enthusiasm, I had failed to note paragraph three – apparently after the beginning of June nettles become 'decidedly laxative'.

Within three days of our self-sufficiency target, I started to feel a bit ticked-off with the lack of sugar and something decent to drink, other than the elderflower wine, which in fact resembled an acrid form of paint stripper. The last straw came when Dan spotted an old cock pheasant on the front lawn and shot it with his ancient air gun. We should have realised it was perhaps not in prime condition when Dan managed to get within a foot before delivering the fatal blow. The bird came out of the oven looking shrivelled and emaciated and eating it was comparable to chewing on an old leather shoe. Fed up with our enforced regime I drove to town and scored half a dozen chocolate mousses and a few cartons of Ribena, which I happily scoffed on my own in the greenhouse. Unfortunately Dan discovered the empty cartons and retaliated by driving to town to buy himself a six pack and a couple of pork pies.

I concluded that self-sufficiency worked best when complemented with a quick trip to Safeway. This still did not dampen our efforts in the horticultural department and I continued to spend many happy hours weeding and hoeing the vegetables. Normally this would be a peaceful time when, without the demanding baby, I could dream while eliminating some unwanted squatters from the sprouting purple broccoli seedlings. But something had happened to the usual serenity of our surroundings. With the resumption of long days of clear blue skies the RAF had taken the opportunity of bombarding the countryside with the noise of their hideous machines of war.

Most afternoons, the silence would be shattered by the thundering sound of 60 feet of raw metal jet about 50 feet above my head. First you would be aware of a vast machine hurtling towards you accompanied by a vibrating in the air, then a split second after it had passed you, there followed the most deafening of noises which churned throughout your whole body. One particularly low aircraft was such a shock that I instinctively fell to the ground covering my head. Once the noise was gone I became grudgingly aware that I had fallen into one of the muddier patches of garden.

We had seen low-level flying before, but this was lower than low. The telephone directory had a special number for complaints to the armed service. That seemed a bad sign: they were obviously used to people like me. I was put through to an operator, she took my details and told me someone would get back to me. A few days later I received a large poster of all the aircraft that are in service in the RAF and an accompanying leaflet explaining why we needed to protect our coastline from invaders. This I found insulting, so I rang back the operator and this time she sent me a claim form for any damage. I filled out a demand for payment for one shirt to be dry cleaned as a result of being forced on to the muddy ground by the power of the Tornado jet. I might have left the matter there had it not been that the next day, while out with Jack in the pram, we came under attack from a Chinook, a Puma and three Tornados. The Puma was hovering behind our small wood while the Tornados seemed to be searching for it. The noise was incredible, ripping through the countryside with such aggression that Jack became inconsolable. How dare they upset my son with their poxy war games? As we were weaving our way home through the bushes, I could feel the vibrations of the bombing practice at Sennybridge over 40 miles away.

I rang the operator again, asked to speak to someone else and was put through to Group Captain Hawkins. I explained that had I wanted to live in a war zone, I would have moved to the former Yugoslavia. He laughed and clearly thought I was joking. I told him my pitiful story and he listened in the way any official might when he knew that nothing will be done.

"They fly well below the 500 foot limit," I told him.

He sighed. "Ah well, Mrs Crewe, you see you fall in to a special area where our boys can fly at a 100 feet on certain days."

"What days? And they're not *my* boys."

"Oh, specially appointed days, weather permitting and so forth. I think you will find they give you plenty of notice, they advertise in most of the local papers."

I told him they sometimes flew below 100 feet.

"Well you might *think* they fly lower than they are, but it's just an illusion," he answered. "Trick of the light."

Now I had him. "Well, how do you explain that the other day, when I saw a Hercules, I was actually looking down on it, I was higher than the plane. It must have been flying only a few hundred feet downhill from me, but it was considerably lower. I could see the pilot's bald patch."

"How high is the hill? You see it's all relative. Actually these boys are very good, they hardly ever break the rules – but if you are unsure write down the time and grid reference and I promise you I will look into any alleged incident."

I said it seemed as if they were using our white house as a marker for their war games. We ended the conversation with him promising to come out 'to see the property and assess the situation' – as he put it. When I told Dan that I had been complaining about the low flying and that some-one was coming out to see us, he was surprisingly unhappy at my actions, arguing that if we complained too much, the jets would take themselves off to fly over Canada and disturb the caribou. Apparently a pro-caribou protest group had come over from Canada to ask the British not to fly over their country. Dan said they were very angry and argued that the caribou were suffering great misfortunes at the hands of the RAF. This line of argument carried very little weight with me. I found it hard to imagine that the caribou were particularly discerning about noise pollution, though Dan said that apparently the planes flew down to six feet and disturbed their migratory patterns. I was not even entirely sure what a caribou was, but I dismissed this argument as Dan being strange.

Group Captain Hawkins arrived on the dot of the appointed second. He was in the appropriate dark blue uniform with badges sewn on to each lapel. He was greasily nice and reminded me of Michael Howard. I told him that I had written to my MP about low-level flying and he nodded and said this was the correct procedure. Several times I tried to provoke him into a debate, asking him what genuine need could there be for low-level flying when in real warfare a plane had to reach levels of 10 feet off the ground?

He was patronisingly dismissive of my arguments and started to show a keen interest in our pigs. I asked him who did the RAF think was going to invade Britain anyway? At this point Dan came out and starting talking about the bloody caribou again. The Group Captain looked understandably bemused by his passionate interest in the plight of the caribou and clearly had no brief about how to deal with this line of questioning. At this point a Tornado roared just above our heads. The officer took off his hat and waved it in the air shouting, "Look at that baby go! Wow, what a thrust!"

So the planes kept coming. But there was one silver

lining in this noisy cloud: the dogs absolutely hated them, particularly Havoc who sat shivering under the table in unadulterated fear. My attitude towards the dogs had not really changed since I set eyes on them, though, over the months they might have calmed down a very small amount. They were still messy, smelly things which were always in my way and it occurred to me that it would be a far better arrangement if dogs could go out to work – if there was someplace where they could do a full day's paid employment and come back in the evening exhausted. The idea was, of course, that this would give the dogs a life of their own rather than impinging on mine and they would benefit by gaining greater self-esteem and a bit of beer money for the weekend. Instead they lay around the house all day: unemployed.

The greatest change since the beginning of the year had obviously been Jack's birth and the dogs took on a new irritating mantle: that of a walking health risk. They carried diseases to inflict on my unsuspecting son, but more than that they had teeth – great big incisors which could rip through a baby in milliseconds. So when my innocent son, by pure accident, grabbed Havoc's tail as she foolishly flicked it passed his grasping hands and the dog growled, my maternal alarm bells were sent into overload. Within the hour I had a notice in the post-office window advertising 'a friendly family dog with sociable habits, free to a good home'. Dan and I then argued over the word 'good': I did not want to limit the range of prospective interested parties.

It took three weeks for someone to come forward with an offer for Havoc. This turned out to be a large man who, I will concede, looked a little rough round the edges, but as I argued to Dan, he obviously had a heart of gold. He said thank you when given a cup of tea, which seemed ample proof to me that this was indeed a man who would be kind to dogs. I think Dan might have put up a bit of a fight if the man had not shown a more than fleeting interest in his hawk, but that sealed it and Havoc went off in a clapped-out old Fiesta with the stranger. Fantastic! "One down two to go," I sang to myself as I waved goodbye to the disappearing car.

Even Dan had to admit that life was considerably easier with only two dogs. I was surprised how smooth persuading him to part with Havoc had been: almost too easy. Flushed with my victory, I took advantage to have a crack at the ferrets. Similar arguments resounded in our living room: the smell, the danger of death to small children and what do they actually do that contributes to the sum of human happiness? I had suspected that perhaps I was pushing my luck and this premonition was confirmed when Dan calmly explained that a life without ferret is only half a life. "They catch rabbits and look sweet," he explained. It was true that their ability to entrap rabbits was welcome and they didn't actually live in the house, but 'sweet' was a mystery to me.

The one thing we did usually agree on was food production. We spent some time deciding on what to include in our list of winter vegetables. Here we were both equally ambitious: we ordered five hundred bulbs of *Crocus sativus*, the stamen of which provides the spice saffron. This might normally be a flower grown on the lower spurs of the Apennines, but I decided optimistically it was because no one had really tried to grow it in mid-Wales. We also chose a selection of oriental vegetables from a seed catalogue, many of which were types that neither of us had ever heard of. We planted a tray of sea kale which, come next spring, could be blanched and eaten much like an asparagus. This was followed by tay- and loganberry canes in long rows next to the raspberries.

The increase in the physical exertion inflicted on our

cheap gardening tools caused metal fatigue and the vital spade snapped in two. This meant a drive to town to buy a decent implement that could withstand the rigours of intense gardening.

When we arrived in town the whole road was awash with sheep and cows in a confused state. The former were running up and down the street bleating in anxiety while the cows were galloping past the car with the look of madness. We parked and Dan spotted Evan the poacher.

"It's market day, like, and them sheep and cows didn't fancy being sold and have taken themselves off for a bit of a run," he explained with a grin.

It struck me as odd that no one seemed to be attending to the chaos. Evan looked at the hills. "Well we might have a mind to intervene, like, but I think that with all that stock rushing around it might be just as well to stay put till they run the fear out, like."

The whole town was at a standstill: all cars had stopped and nobody was moving. As Evan had anticipated, the cows and sheep did eventually calm down, forgetting their anxiety they started to graze on the vergeside grass. We walked slowly into the shop with Jack waving his arms at all the cows outside. As I picked up a pint of milk a large sheep trotted passed the dairy counter.

When we walked back to the car the more relaxed animals were being carefully herded back to the market hall. Evan came and chatted for a while.

"I have a mind to come and visit your place and see these birds of prey you have up there," he said. "Maybe I could bring you a little something."

I asked what sort of something. He looked serious. "Whatever you would like?" I was trying to think of an answer when Bill, the woodcarver from the travellers' camp, came up. He nodded at his friend. "Evan, damn fine to see you. You'll have to come and see me one of these days to help me finish off some brew I have been saving for you."

"Ah well, I think I might have to do just that," replied Evan.

Bill turned back to us. "I was going to come up and see you," he said. "I have a proposition. I've a friend who is a bit of a horse man – well, actually he has all sorts of animals, but his main love is horses. What he really loves is riding them on treks across Wales. He has planned one of these expeditions with some kids and a llama to raise money for the local school. Maybe you saw something about it in the local paper? He was going to camp down at our site, but for one reason or another that is not such a good idea at the moment. You know – a bit of grief with the neighbours. So I wondered whether you could give over a field and have a few people camping on your lawn?"

Dan immediately said this was no problem. Bill shook us warmly by the hand and said we could expect them by tea time on Saturday. He also said that he would come up with some mates and organise a barbecue.

He put his arm around Evan. "Can we count on you for something for the pot?"

"Oh I suppose I might manage to think of something," laughed Evan.

We made some scones and bread in anticipation of this trekking party, and at about five p.m. on Saturday we saw a large man wearing a safari hat, walking a llama, with about fifteen people on horses behind him. The man shook Dan by the hand and introduced himself in a sing-song Welsh accent. "I'm Trevor, these are my team and this is my llama, Orlando. We can't thank you enough for helping us out. We'll be no trouble to you – you'll hardly know we are here. Now, perhaps I'd better have a look at the fields and see what's best for the horses. The llama I could tie up to that tree over there. I would suggest that you did not venture too near to Orlando, he has a bit of a temper with strangers."

The entourage trotted past towards the field, the riders mainly children, with the odd adult dotted about. I set to making tea for everybody. As luck would have it, I had a large boiler, a previous impulse buy, which I used to make industrial quantities of tea. The children were excited and ran around looking at our hawks, pigs, chickens and army of ducks. Dan was busy giving hawk demonstrations and keeping an eye on them to make sure they were being sufficiently gentle with the ferrets. Trevor and the other three adults erected a large tent, or more accurately a small marquee. This was where they were all to sleep together.

At seven p.m. Bill arrived in an old minibus with five other cars in tow. They set up a barbecue and a line of trestle tables which they loaded with drinks and food. Olek and Miranda came, Olek had just returned from filming some giant frozen peas in London and Miranda had spent all day at another funeral for one of her elderly friends. They arrived with a box of bison grass vodka. At eight p.m. Evan arrived with more people and an enormous bag. He emptied it into a large empty dustbin. Dozens of fresh trout! He winked at Bill. "I found these fish looking for somewhere to rest their weary bones, like. I reckon they'll sit on your barbecue all right."

After supper a band materialised from nowhere and started playing. Within minutes they were in full swing and people dancing all around the house. The idea that this unassuming little band of trekkers had been going to slip in to our life unnoticed and leave in a similar vein now seemed a little unlikely.

Dan had helped Olek unpack the vodka and had become rather attached to a particular bottle. As a result he was giving guided tours of his compost heap to anyone with legs. I met many local people who seemed to know all about us. Until now I had mistakenly believed we had not made much impression on the immediate community, but it turned out they all knew that we had come from London and moved in on New Year's Eve. Many of them had connections with the house. I met one lady whose grandmother had been born in Allt-y-Gwalch and had lived in the house with her sixteen brothers and sisters for twenty years. Another man had helped build the barn opposite, another had come up when the same building had caught fire. There were many people who had worked up here when it was a chicken farm and a few who had helped plant potatoes in one of the fields.

They all told stories about the farm and its history: one elderly man explained that the pond was the source of a local river and was likely to be hundreds of years old. The same informant had known some previous owners when they used to do all the cooking on the open fire in the inglenook fireplace. I was filled with a great sense that the house had been around so long that everyone in the area had been involved with its history somewhere along the line.

Evan the poacher had also had dealings with the house on several occasions. He told me that as a boy he had helped out here when it was a pony trekking business and as he spoke, the impression grew that Evan might have had dealings with almost every house in the district.

"Aye it is a grand place, like," he said. " The view here on a clear night is one of the best around. I reckon you have one of the best houses in these parts. Were I a house-buying man, I might have been interested, but I can't afford to buy houses, not with my outgoings, like."

I told him I was interested in fishing and showed him my rods and tackle. Evan was genuinely impressed. "This is good stuff you know – you could catch many a fish with this lot, like. This sea rod is a cracker, I might have to borrow this off you one these days." Then he took a fly rod and cast it in the night air, back and forward. "Yeh, not bad – it has a nice rhythm to it. I reckon we could catch a few trout with this, like. Maybe next weekend I will take you up the valley and show you a few spots, I know."

I asked him whether I could catch any salmon. He laughed. "Not with a rod, I don't think – they are devilish hard to catch this far up the river with a rod, like. No, no, no. You would have to use more persuasive ways to tease a salmon out of the water."

"How?" I enquired, and Evan became almost coy.

"Now what would an honest man like myself know anything at all about that, like." He was smiling – hard.

By midnight this impromptu party was still going strong. Olek and Miranda were doing the tango on the lawn and Dan was swaying around in the vague vicinity of his beloved compost heap. A few yards away, there must have been fifty people dancing, drinking and singing around the barbecue and band. Bill had brought some flares which he positioned around the front yard where most of the people were gathered. Jack was now past all the disturbances of the first three restless months and was relatively easy to convince that sleep was more productive than crying. So this was one of the first evenings of freedom that I had had since he was born and what with Evan's 'hot' fish there was a relaxing sensation of lawlessness about the evening. Dan passed out by the compost bin at about one a.m. and I managed to last till two a.m. and then fell asleep to the sounds of the fiddler who by now was in a fervour of musical excitement.

In the morning Trevor and his gang of riders were up early, organising their belongings. The marquee was packed and they had removed every scrap of evidence that they were ever there. When they were all packed and mounted, ready to go – Trevor at the front with Orlando the llama – we went to say goodbye.

He shook us by the hand. "Ah it was grand of you to put us up. I don't know where we would have stayed, really I don't. I am sure we were no trouble, I don't suppose you even knew we were here, really. Goodbye." And with that they trotted off down the lane.

The house felt decidedly empty after their departure. Dan went into his study to do some work and Jack and I pottered around the garden watering limp plants. I was feeding the tomatoes with some strange pink stuff I had bought when I heard a yelp inside the house. I dashed inside to see what had happened and found Dan gasping with shock and Evan sitting on the sofa behind him. Evan nodded at me. "Mornin', I don't suppose you would have a cup of tea, like.'

Dan, still fazed by Evan's unexpected appearance, went to organise the beverages. Evan was unconcernedly rubbing his eyes. "Oh I dare say perhaps I shouldn't have had that last pint, I feel a little groggy, like. Still perhaps a brisk walk back up the valley will clear the vision – I seem to have missed my lift."

We sat round the table. I asked him if he was working today. "Every day is a working day, like. I have a lot of pay-outs to meet, but perhaps today may be classed as a holiday, like – on account of my failing health and aching limbs. The old leg is not what it used to be."

"What's wrong with it?" I asked.

"Oh you know a bit of shrapnel lodged in there, like. Makes it hard to put on too much pressure on it."

I wondered where he might have picked up a bit of shrapnel, but he was the kind of person who might just as easily be lying through his smiling teeth as telling the truth. Dan brought the tea and we walked on to the terrace. Evan took a huge gulp and immediately spat the tea on the floor shouting, "Good God man, are trying to kill me! Christ, that's horrible. You've put bloody salt in my tea, like."

Dan tried to apologise but Evan stopped him. "Do you know that has actually cleared my head a little, like. I think you may have discovered a good hangover cure."

Then he talked a while about his old fishing days. He told long stories mainly about how big some of his conquests were: monster trout of 20 lbs and salmon over 40 lbs in weight. All this talk made me hungry to catch a fish and I suggested a trip up the valley with a picnic basket and my fly rods. I told Evan he had promised to take me fishing to some of his 'good spots'. He agreed and we packed up some of the previous night's left over sausages, drumsticks and salads. Dan brought a coolbox with some beer and juice and we drove up the valley into the hills to the lakes and rivers. Evan showed us a beautiful spot by a small stream which was owned by a friend of his. We ate and fished for most of the day while Evan showed me how to watch the water and identify the feeding insects, then try and emulate the size and colour from the box of tied artificial flies. He demonstrated how to look at the water and spot trout lying behind rocks in still water, avoiding the rush of the current.

I learned the rudiments of casting, which involved Evan shouting from the picnic site while he downed a beer. "Shoot to the moon with the rod, like, then slowly bang the nail in the wall letting out a little line as you go. No, don't whip the water, do you want all the trout in Wales to know you're here? Good God, we'll be lucky if the fish don't just bugger off down the river with all that noise you're making." He would inevitably have to get up and give me another demonstration, but we had two bites – both of which I lost due to general overexcitement and dropping the rod in the river.

It was a fantastic day nevertheless. The valley was stunning. The mountains were high and craggy, covered in acres of hanging oak forests. There were waterfalls of brown peaty water around every bend. The rivers were deep and everywhere you looked the most beautiful age-old rock formations meant you could leap across them from stone to stone. From one of these natural platforms I watched the water flow around the rocks and through a perfectly shaped hole in a smooth stone which must have taken hundreds of years to perfect. The heather was in flower away from the incessant eating habits of the herds of sheep which roamed the hills. For the first time since I had come to live here it didn't feel so strange being in this wilderness and knowing that this was my home.

Duck and Apricots with Stuffed Courgettes

Apricots and Duck
2 duck breasts
2 tbsps apricot jam (preferably confit)

Stuffed Courgettes
1 lb courgettes
1 finely chopped onion
1 lb fresh tomatoes
(skinned and roughly chopped)
1 clove garlic
1tbsp chopped fresh basil

For the duck: Smear the flesh side of the breasts with apricot preserve and cook under a hot grill for 5 minutes. Turn skin side up and smear this with the remaining preserve and return to the grill for another 5 minutes. Serve immediately (note, unlike chicken, duck is at its best when pink – or even bloody).

For the courgettes: Cut the courgettes in half lengthways and simmer gently in a little water until the flesh is soft enough to remove with a teaspoon. Remove from heat. Meanwhile, gently fry the onion in a little oil until golden. Add the crushed garlic, tomatoes and courgette flesh. Simmer for about 5 minutes, adding the basil about a minute from the end. Add salt and pepper to taste and spoon into the courgette skins. Sprinkle with a little grated parmesan or mature chedder and grill briefly until cheese is melted.

September: Dan

I must confess that over the course of that long hot summer, my initial *joie de vivre* abated somewhat. I don't mean that I'd had any second thoughts about moving to our paradise in the middle of nowhere, but somehow the minute-by-minute realities were beginning to tell. As the baby grew, so he began to get frustrated with his total dependence on others and although the nights were generally easier, it was no longer enough just to feed him, change a dirty nappy and put him down to sleep during the day. Instead he needed entertainment, even if this consisted of little more than gurgling at him on the sofa for half an hour or taking him for a walk in the ancient Edwardian nanny's pram that Bel had bought in an auction just before she left London. In short, it was becoming clear that parenthood was a touch more awkward than I had imagined before the event.

More importantly, however, the financial responsibilities of our situation were weighing heavily on me. Above all else, I felt increasingly frustrated at my inability to fly Gwen during the summer months. The moult is the equiva lent of a car's service when the vital elements of locomotion (the main wing and tail feathers) are replaced. To ensure healthy growth, the hawk needs copious amounts of food. As the relationship between man and hawk is based almost entirely on limiting the bird's calorific intake, this means it becomes extremely unresponsive and highly liable to fly off for good. Thus for five months I had not been able to do anything more than drool over her from afar as she sat, impassively, in the top of her aviary.

In an effort to dispel the pervading gloom, I suggested we have a barbecue the following weekend. Bel muttered, slightly cynically, about a lack of friends, but I pointed out that by now we actually had enough for a decent lunch party. To begin with, there was the Major, Miranda, Olek, Evan and Dr McBain and his family. With a bit of thought I felt sure we could bump this up to a dozen guests or so – and we might as well make the best of the gruellingly hot and dry weather. Although there was no end in sight to the drought, we both knew that in the end the rains would surely come – after all, this was Wales.

So we invited them and our invitations were duly accepted for a Saturday lunchtime feast. I wanted to make a mark and after some thought, the answer seemed simple: an Aussie-style 'barbie'. Tapping the memories out of my visit to Australia seven years before, I dug a large pit in the ground and filled it with kindling and woodshavings. Then I hauled up the ancient decaying bedstead from the pile of inherited detritus near the duck pond and positioned it alongside. Well before midday, I put the pyre to the torch and the bone-dry wood took the match as if soaked in paraffin. Within minutes the flames were licking to shoulder height.

It was at this point that two important events took place. The first was entirely planned – the arrival of our guests – but the second less so. The heavens opened for the first time in four months: and I do mean opened. As if we had suddenly become players in some melodramatic film, the sky darkened over and the clouds gave their best.

The rain came down not in a delicate welcome shower to break the drought, but quite literally in buckets. Within five minutes, the six-foot high flames had been thoroughly doused and my bonfire was little more than a smouldering heap of blackened embers. To venture outside was to be soaked to the skin in a matter of seconds and clearly the meal was not going to be cooked – let alone held – *al fresco*.

Fortunately, there was just enough time to rescue the culinary element, so I bunged all the assorted pieces of marinated pork, the lamb chops and aubergine-wrapped cheese parcels into the oven. Then I returned to our guests to watch the elemental tableau unfolding in front of us. Evan and I stood by the window, watching as the valley was swept with sheets of heavy rain.

"That's what they call a drench, like," said Evan sagely, pulling on his beer bottle. "I've been here five years and never seen a downpour like that," agreed Dr McBain.

Moments later the thunder began – huge peals which echoed down the valley, moving closer and closer, louder and louder. It sounded as if some enemy gun emplacement, mounted on the opposite side of the valley, was gradually swinging its sights towards us, picking off the scattered farmsteads as it swept inexorably closer.

At first Evan counted the gaps between the thunder claps and ensuing lightning. "One-up, two-up, three-up," he reeled off, but soon gave up as the delays became ever closer. In no time the two were almost simultaneous and the sky was almost as dark as if it had been night.

Suddenly, there was an exceptionally loud bang and a shower of sparks cascaded out of every electrical socket in the room. Simultaneously, the lights went out. This was more than just a power surge and sure enough, all attempts to persuade the main fuse box to kick into gear were without success: our electricity supply was well and truly severed. As if to ram home the point, a couple of minutes later there came a second loud bang. I was standing by the washing machine, bending over it to inspect for damage and, at least according to Dr McBain who was holding the torch, a spark leaped from the machine to my arm, making my hair stand on end and crackle with tiny blue sparks.

At first I thought this was just his idea of a joke, but as we carried out a cursory damage inspection, it was obvious something fairly serious had happened. Not only was every electrical gadget in the house defunct, but the phones were also dead.

At this point Bel came rushing into the corridor wearing wellingtons and a large mac. "We've been hit by bloody lightning!" she cried as she dived under the Belfast sink with Jack clasped tightly to her chest. "All the sockets have just exploded in a shower of blue bloody sparks!"

Bending down, Dr McBain asked her what she was doing. Bel began to explain that the wellingtons and rubberised coat were insulation against a third lightning strike and that under the sink seemed to her to be the safest place in the house. "We're under attack," she was yabbering. "Take cover – for God's sake save yourselves!"

Dr McBain was not terribly sympathetic – in fact he laughed and asked her if she really thought a pair of wellingtons would be up to the job of stopping a million volts? It was hardly calculated to inspire confidence, but he didn't wait to see the results of his comment, being too fascinated by the sheer power and ferocity of the storm to want to miss the display and he returned next door to stare in awe out of the window. I followed, leaving Bel on her own with the baby in the near dark. Not so surprisingly, she decided after a couple of minutes that it would be preferable to die in company and so emerged reluctantly from her sanctuary to rejoin the rest of the party next door.

Fortunately, although the fire was now totally extinguished, I had had enough experience of outdoor catering to know it is safest to pre-cook where possible, leaving the barbecue itself largely as a flavouring device. As a result we managed to have a tolerably good meal, though dominated conversationally by Evan, his tongue now well lubricated by cheap red wine. "Never rains but it pours," he chortled, as a volley of huge raindrops hit the window like the roll on a snare drum. Outside, the gloom was interrupted by a flash which lit up the valley, momentarily freezing everything in an eerie blue white light, like some giant natural camera flash. "Every cloud has a silver lining," he cackled instantly, and then, delighted by the speed of his wit, laughed loudly for rather longer than was necessary before managing to splutter, "Never mind, it's an ill wind . . ." before his voice was thankfully drowned out by another huge peal of thunder.

After this, conversation became difficult as the storm raged overhead. Deafening cracks tore through the air and, without artificial light, the room was illuminated solely by the increasingly frequent flashes of lightning. At its hiatus, the very floor seemed to shake with the impact, so much so that Bel changed her mind about the pleasures of dying in company and returned to her sanctuary under the scullery sink.

Once we had got over the worst ferocity of the storm, the rest of us watched the giant *son et lumière* in awed silence. These were the most violent weather conditions any of us had ever witnessed and we felt humbled by the immense power being chucked around by Mother Nature outside. Of course a storm that fierce could not last long and after half an hour it had burned itself out. Incredibly, not sixty minutes after the first lightning strike, we saw the first hint of blue overhead and soon the entire valley was bathed once more in glorious sunlight. After the dousing it had just received, everything looked as if it had been thoroughly scrubbed, an impression heightened by the light reflecting from the droplets which hung off every blade of grass in sight. To cap it all, the most perfect double rainbow arched over the opposite hill.

Needless to say, it was a particularly successful – and totally memorable – party. As we washed up by candlelight that evening (it was not until the following morning that we were reconnected), we agreed our guests would dine out on the tale for months to come. More importantly, however, the drought was now well and truly broken and all our rain butts were overflowing. Over the next couple of weeks, there was an evening shower here, a two-hour drizzle there and in no time the garden soil had been transformed from the colour and texture of concrete to something resembling the crumbly loams on *Gardener's World*.

The biggest transformation of all, however, was among the vegetables. In spite of the frequent downpours, temperatures remained high and our wilting crops perked up remarkably. It was almost as if they sensed that this was their last chance at life and they gave it their all. The courgettes and pumpkins put on a last spurt and grew faster than we could eat them. The spinach was worse: every time we marched along the length of the rows, scything down the delicate young leaves, it seemed only to provoke more vigorous growth and likewise, the beans put in one last burst of activity and we found ourselves picking daily basket loads from plants we thought we'd stripped bare the previous day. Meanwhile the greenhouse, cold frames and flower beds were overflowing with herbs: basil, mint and coriander which we knew would disappear all too soon.

The rain and ensuing burst of fertility swept away any lingering doubts that I had begun to harbour at the end of the summer. The lazy days of lounging on the terrace in t-shirts and shorts were now over and instead our hours were taken up with industry as we rushed desperately to preserve the bounty before the first frosts ripped through our vegetable patch like the four horsemen of the apocalypse. Although mornings were largely taken up with watering and feeding the livestock, afternoons were totally consumed with the process of food preservation and storage.

Whilst Jack napped upstairs, Bel and I would feverishly slave away in the kitchen, cleaning, chopping, cooking, packaging and bottling. Some of this was simple enough – beans and peas for example needed little more than blanching and freezing – but in many cases things were rather more complex. All too many vegetables don't freeze well and needed to be turned into finished dishes before they could be stored. Soon the huge white chest freezer in the garage was half-filled with industrial quantities of carrot and orange, courgette and basil and curried parsnip soups. Alongside nestled little tubs of ratatouille, vegetable chilli and home-made blackberry ice cream (a way of using up our surplus eggs).

A more awkward problem came with the tomatoes. Until we became gardeners, neither Bel nor I had ever seen a green tomato: now we were faced with a hundredweight of hard glossy green spheres which clearly had little hope of ripening before the first frost cut their semi-tropical parents down to earth – literally.

As always in such cases, the Great John came to the rescue. He recommended tomato chutney as the perfect way to store vitamin C – and unripe fruit is ideal for this purpose, even excelling the red version in its taste and vitamin content. With so many hard green balls to process, we needed no further encouragement and in no time the stove was topped with a steaming cauldron, filled with tomatoes, sugar, vinegar and spices, slowly reducing to a thick treacly liquid. As each bubble burst on the dark brown surface, it gave off a loud 'glop!' that sent a shower of sticky droplets into the air. It looked and sounded like the hot volcanic mud of the primordial soup, and by the end of the afternoon the cooker's surface was pebble-dashed with hardened lumps of baked chutney.

The biggest food surplus, however, came on the livestock front. Although we had already sampled a couple of ducks and pronounced them delicious, a huge flock remained. These were consuming huge quantities of food and were not, as they say, getting any younger. To be precise, they were fully grown and toughening up as they gradually transformed the soft juicy tissue of rapid growth into the firm muscle of an older bird.

I felt no enthusiasm for the task ahead – only a sadist could – so I decided to break myself in gently with the quail that I had so painstakingly hatched back in the spring. The mental preparation was comparatively simple – they are brainless, timid birds which panic at the slightest excuse, bursting upwards into flight only to crash into the ceiling of their run, even though this is deliberately placed just inches above their heads (you'd think they'd learn, but apparently not). In spite of my contempt for their intellectual capacity and cowardice, I still didn't look forward to the event, but in the end found it to be a much less unpleasant experience than I'd anticipated – they were easy to dispatch humanely and very quick to pluck. Indeed, in only a matter of a couple of hours, Bel and I had rendered all fifteen to an oven-ready state. Another couple of hours later and they were playing the lead role in a rather nice, oregano-flavoured pâté at the Larder Palladium.

In spite of this auspicious start, we knew this was just a tiny sample of what was to come. There were thirty-odd ducks still careering around our front garden and I'd grown fond of the waddling, quacking herd which had spent the summer rampaging backwards and forwards across the front lawn. They'd become quite a feature of the place, chatting to each other as they went and with a canny instinct for a free meal. No sooner had one of us sat down to shell peas or top and tail beans than they were there for the scraps. One moment you'd be lowering yourself on to a deck chair on the terrace to prepare the vegetables accompanied by a glass of wine, the next, your thoughts would be interrupted by the rapid arrival, stage left, of a host of quacking extras keen to get a slice of whatever action was going.

The problems were even more pronounced when weeding. They soon learned that every turn of the fork meant the imminent prospect of worms, while uprooted weeds often gave shelter to insects and slugs. As you worked they would squabble at your feet, greedily pouncing on any edible morsel (and in their greed, many which were not) and wolfing them down in a series of jerky bobs of their heads. Although this didn't make work outdoors any easier, it certainly lent it a fair degree of charm.

On a more practical level, I was dreading the plucking. Although dealing with the quail hadn't been too onerous a task, dealing with two or three dozen thickly feathered and down-laden waterfowl was a different matter altogether. All the same, their prodigious appetites and our slender bank balance meant that squeamishness was a luxury we could not afford. So, one evening, we fortified ourselves for the grisly task with a large tot of Scotch, donned our wellies (and in Bel's case rubber gloves) and headed for the barn.

It was to be a long night. Almost as soon as we had begun work, there were feathers everywhere: a sea of them covering the floor, while a fine dust of down hung in the air, clinging to our nostrils and lips and tickling our throats and lungs. To make matters worse, each corpse clung to its covering with a dogged, finger-numbing tenacity. The outer feathers seem superglued in their sockets, while the underlying layer of down and fluff went on for ever. In the end it took over an hour to get each bird to oven-ready standard and thus by midnight only five birds were ready for the freezer. As we flopped into chairs, for another well-earned 'anaesthetic and soda', we agreed that we never wanted to see another feather and admitted defeat for the night.

Fortunately, the next afternoon as I was steeling myself for another long plucking session, the Major called round. He wanted to borrow my chainsaw for some project (as usual he was evasive on exactly what this might be) and was also keen for a bit of a 'chin-wag', as he put it. I offered him a cup of tea and he asked me what I intended to enter for the coming show. The question surprised me on two levels. Firstly I had no idea what show he was talking about and secondly, I couldn't conceive of anything I might own which was worthy of displaying to the world at large – apart, that is, from my hawk, who was both moulting and extremely stroppy. I couldn't see that either she or the audience would enjoy the experience.

The Major then went on to explain that in these parts the summer shows were the highlight of the year. "'Course the Royal Welsh is the main one – everyone goes to that twice – but some of the locals are good too." He went on to list the names of six or seven villages, most of which consisted of no more than a dozen houses. "Take your lurcher – he'd help," he added as an afterthought.

The idea that any of this motley collection of hamlets could put on a fete worthy of note by anyone other than the decidedly simple stretched my credulity somewhat. I had visions of the numerous plays, sponsored events and children's parties I'd forced my parents to endure in the past and couldn't help feeling that the nearest local show, half a mile down the road and located in a cow-pat-strewn meadow was likely to be of the same calibre. As with so many conversations with the Major, I thought it prudent to keep my counsel – after all, Empire apart, he had so far invariably proved a reliable source of information.

So I changed the subject and mentioned the tedious task in hand. I suppose I half-hoped he would offer to help or show me some cunning trick to speed up the plucking process, but instead to my surprise he agreed the task was too boring for words. "Never pluck myself," he said. "Ghastly job. Get a man. In Kenya I always got one of my trackers to do the job. Course, bit more tricky here – but I know a chap with a machine."

The idea of a plucking machine had an electric effect on me. Until now it hadn't occurred to me that these might exist – or at least not on a local level (although now he mentioned it, I suppose I knew about poultry processing factories). The sudden realisation that someone locally might pluck, gut and truss our fowl was glorious. On the most superficial level it absolved me from killing my semi-pets, but much more importantly it would free me from about twenty hours (half a working week!) spent sitting on a stool in a draughty ill-lit barn, tugging at stubborn feathers and inhaling fluff. Barely were the words out of his lips than I was scribbling down the phone number and by the evening the birds were loaded in the back of the car, quacking loudly, on their way to their final destination. Two days later they returned and were stowed in the perma-frost at the bottom of our freezer – and all at the princely price of one pound a bird. Even considering our temporary financial difficulties, it was a bargain.

The next weekend it was the day of the local show and, with nothing else to do, we toddled down to view what we quietly expected to be little more than a WI bring-and-buy sale. Sure enough, the showground was badly advertised and, had we not had clear instructions as to its location, we would have ignored the tiny scrap of card marked with an arrow indicating the turning. Without a word we gave each other a knowing look and turned in along the narrow cart track.

Our patronising preconceptions were shaken slightly as we got to the car park. It was packed with Landrovers, trailers, pick-ups and ancient vehicles. Evidently there were several thousand people already here, drawn from miles around by the event. We dismounted with Bracken secured on an old piece of bailer twine, and paid the minimal entry fee.

We found ourselves confronted with a huge paddock filled with sheep stalls, carefully arranged bales and marquees. Ringing out over the crowds came the tinny voice of the fete announcer asking our neighbour, Fred Hir-Rhiw, to help set up the hurdles for the sheepdog trials. As I gawped at the thronging scene in front of us, Bel studied the programme. Apparently there were go-cart, bareback and trotting races; beer tents; sheep and cattle competitions with – more directly relevant – nine dog classes. Admittedly, six were for collies (with prizes for dogs and bitches in the 'best', 'youngster' and 'veteran' categories), but the organisers had generously decided to add three for non-farmers. The pedigree and toy categories were obviously out, but with her uncanny eye for an opportunity, Bel noted that Bracken was just about eligible for the last, 'sporting' category.

She bustled off to enter the pet that, until now, she had professed to despise, while I took Jack for a male bonding session in the beer tent which was filled with folding tables and chairs, mostly occupied by tired-looking farmers in jeans and half-unlaced steel-capped boots, tired wives with

tiresome children at their feet. I was not surprised to see
Evan ensconced in the depths of the tent, sitting at a table
with Fred Hir-Rhiw. I waved and they both grinned back
– from the flushed cheeks and crowded table in front of
them, it was clear they had been here for some time. I
waggled my hand in front of my mouth to indicate the
offer of a drink and both grinned back even more enthusiastically, accompanying the expression with a bellow (a
couple of decibels higher than was necessary – evidently
they were suffering from alcohol-induced deafness) that
bitter was what they were after. To my next quizzical
look, Evan pointed back to the doorway behind me.

Sure enough, the real action was mounted in a sheep
trailer alongside the tent, where the bar was to be found.
It was shut off from its clientele by nothing more than a
crude table made from a couple of bales topped by four
planks. Clamped to the back of the latter were the beer
taps, while the interior was crammed with three grinning
barmaids and box upon cardboard box, stamped with
'Woodpecker'. Customers jostled on the tail gate to grab
their plastic pints of warm refreshment.

Drinks, it turned out, came in four basic flavours: lager,
bitter, cider and lemonade. You could have any cocktail
you chose, provided it was a combination of the above:
Perrier, fruit juice, wine and spirits were all out. I noticed
with interest that our prospective Liberal parliamentary
candidate was standing nearby, surrounded by half a dozen
swaying farmers, all assuring him that provided he was in
favour of fox-hunting, their vote was his (a vague acquaintance told me in a slurred whisper – and barely disguised
disgust – that the sitting Tory was never in evidence at
such events).

I bought a couple of pints and as I manoeuvred back
through the crowd, heard another plea for Fred boom out
over the tannoy. In spite of the distortions of the public

address system, there was a clear note of exasperation. When I got to the table I mentioned the appeal, but he dismissed the comment with a wave of the hand, which was then smoothly transformed into an invitation to hand over the pint. He had no intention of moving for another few minutes, but instead was held by the lure of the beer and his conversation with Evan. I tried to join in, but the pair were both the worse for wear and distinctly incoherent. Fortunately, at that point I spotted Bel gesticulating wildly at the entrance. At first I thought she was merely being an anxious mother, keen to remove her baby from the cigarette smoke and alcohol fumes, but it turned out the dog class was about to begin.

I downed my pint and we strode over to the bale circle where a small crowd had gathered to watch the spectacle. Bel nudged me into the ring and, after handing over my entrance fee, I trudged around the circle. Following the example of a man with two battle-scarred Jack Russells ahead of me, I found myself pulling tight on the twine to make the lurcher show off his snake-like neck. Every now and again I would break into a jog so that the graceful arching lope of a running dog was shown to at least a modicum of advantage.

Eventually the five owners and six charges were lined up and the judges began their slow march down the line, pausing in front of each entrant, ostensibly to check its conformation, but as far as I could see the real purpose was to exchange pleasantries. Certainly that was the case when he paused at the two terriers.

"Ernie," came the greeting, accompanied by a quick nod. "Good drop of rain last week – terrible dry summer we've had."

"Oh aye."

"See Gyp's still looking good. How many foxes was it he had last year? Twenty-three? Ooh, he's a terrible good dog, is Gyp."

When the judge turned to me, however, there was no such familiar greeting. Instead he gave the dog a quick glance. "Ever caught anything?" he asked in a matter-of-fact voice.

I replied that Bracken had taken his toll of the local rabbits, but he interrupted me before I'd a chance to go any further, "No, no, I mean foxes?"

I decided to use a little poetic licence and said he'd coursed a couple on the hill behind us, although both had got away. "He'll manage it one day," I ended, a trifle lamely as I realised the man wasn't listening and was already turning to the next in the line – a small border terrier type – whose owner was soon recounting tales of derring-do with the local vulpine population.

As a result of these exchanges, I was not surprised when the gold rosette went to Gyp, followed by the silver being awarded to the border. In fact, when Bracken was summoned up to receive a blue ribbon (third), I was pleasantly surprised, but when I left the ring, I found Bel was fuming. "Third? Third? He's much the best-looking dog here and he only gets third? It's a stitch-up!" When I told her about the conversations with the other owners, she grew even more incensed. Her reactions reminded me of the James Herriot story where he was asked to act as vet in the local show, only to find the experience akin to being asked to take the hemlock cup.

Evan was more sanguine, however. "Gyp won, did he? Well, he does every year – that's a terrible good dog, that is." This did little to placate Bel, and her muttering was only intensified a couple of minutes later when we saw Gyp's owner buying the judge a pint at the bar, as the announcer – this time in a voice distinctly tinged with panic – was proclaiming that Fred's presence at the sheep trials was now a matter of considerable urgency.

We carried on around the fair, taking in a mixture of attractions, some of which were standard enough, like the bouncy castle and lucky dip, some of which were familiar – if with distinctly rural twist – like the quad-bike racing and others which were definitely unusual to the eyes of former urbanites.

The vegetable tent seemed particularly odd to two former Londoners. The trestle tables inside were covered with small groups of assorted produce in every conceivable shape, size and condition. In front of each was a neat hand-written notice, a rosette and a card bearing the name of the winner. At first the categories seemed straightforward enough: 'Best Parsnip', 'Best Apple Chutney' and so on, but as we progressed down the hall, a surreal quality began to infect the classes. 'Oddest-Shaped Beetroot' was one which stood out. 'Best Photograph of a Raindrop' was another, but my personal favourite was 'Vegetable The Judges Would Most Like to Take Home'. I was chuckling at this last when I noticed Bel had a particularly hard glint in her eye.

"Rosette," she hissed. "I want a rosette." I pointed out that as we hadn't entered anything this was going to be a bit difficult, but she wasn't listening. She had spotted a pile of winner's cards on the unattended judges' table and was sidling towards it, attempting to look unsuspicious and consequently – in my eyes at least – looking as guilty as hell. Nevertheless, she managed to swipe a couple of cards without detection and then we were out in the sunlight walking briskly away from the tent. As soon as we'd assured ourselves that we'd made a clean getaway, Bel sat down on a hay bale to fill in the two cards. She ignored my suggestions of 'Rudest-Looking Root Vegetable' and 'Densest Loaf of Bread', opting instead for what I consid-ered to be the rather boring 'Best Kenyan Bean' and 'Best Raspberry Conserve'. Bel was happy enough with this, however, and we continued our circuit of the field, pausing briefly at the sheep trials. (By now the announcer had reverted to a pleading version of moral blackmail: "Fred, we know you're in the beer tent and you promised . . .")

It was the horse racing which really caught our attention, however. This turned out to be little more than half a dozen men on motley ponies who were to gallop around the end of the field. Thinking it might be interesting, we wandered over to see the start and we were surprised to see Fred in front of us, walking unsteadily and leaning heavily on Evan. As we got there, the latter was pushing Fred on to a bridled, but unsaddled pony. The farmer's eyes were completely glazed and his speech was slurred and incomprehensible.

A moment later the race began with a whistle from a steward and the horses tore off, making two tight circuits of the end of the field, before crossing the finishing line in front of us. To my amazement, the semi-comotose Fred not only stayed on his barebacked mount, but emerged the clear winner. Grinning in triumph, he gave a winner's wave of recognition to the crowd – and promptly fell off the far side of the horse. Evan and another man I didn't know rushed to his aid and half-dragged and half-carried the giggling farmer back to the beer tent. As they passed the poacher whispered conspiratorially to me that Fred's victory in the horse race was as much a part of the annual tradition of the show as Gyp's victory in the dog ring.

By now we had had enough and turned to leave. As we reached the car, however, I heard the announcer appealing for volunteers to help Fred at the sheep trials. "We'll need two strong men to give Fred a hand," he was saying resignedly. "Occupants of the beer tent need not apply."

The visit to the show set me thinking in other directions. After seeing Fred's victory in the race, I began to think how wonderful it would be to have a sturdy pony to ferry me up the hill on my falconry trips. Better still, we could also get a small trap and transform our daily trips into town. True, it would be an unwelcome extra expense, but I reasoned some could be recouped by slashing our high fuel bills. I mentioned my ambitions to a horse-loving friend and she instantly reinforced the dream by telling me that 'Class A' foals (i.e. small in every way) can go for as little as £20. At this, I instantly began to think in terms of galloping across the hills, hawk on fist with the two dogs trotting at heel, but even as I pictured the scene, I recognised one huge stumbling block – Bel.

My preliminary soundings rapidly established that she believed all horses to be little more than fast-moving baby-kickers. Thus, in my new campaign for the fulfilment of childhood dreams, I would clearly need reinforcements.

The first ambush of the low-level guerrilla war came at our next meal with Olek and Miranda. Although the former shared some of Bel's reservations, his girlfriend was a natural ally. As a rural teenager she'd gone through the 'pony phase' that most girls – Bel apart – seem to go through. Moreover, she was now captivated by the idea of travelling around the locality in a rose-garlanded cart. So, while our non-equestrian partners were attempting to put the two screaming babies to sleep before the meal, Miranda and I quietly diced vegetables and plotted tactics.

By the time our two shell-shocked partners sat down at the table, they were in no condition to resist our suggestion that we try a donkey-riding experiment at the next weekend's show. Any suspicions they might have had were wafted away by the perfectly timed arrival of a steaming plate of home-grown ratatouille, potatoes and duck.

It was by chance, a couple of days before the sale Miranda and I had decided to attend, that I met a neighbour who was 'into' horses. I told her of our ambition to buy a couple of colts and she blanched. "Have you had a lot to do with horses?" she asked. "And how often have you broken one in?"

From these two tricky questions, we moved on to the monthly costs of shoeing, vet bills and feed. In no time at all, she had outlined that any horse would cost about £1,000 a year without ever being mounted – sit on it and we were talking about double that figure.

I left feeling distinctly deflated, but convinced she had painted far too bleak a picture. As time went on, however, the seed she'd planted in my mind began to grow. It was one thing to launch into a small-cost venture, another to commit ourselves to an on-going large-scale financial commitment. I had already fulfilled most of my childhood dreams of smallholding, dogs, pigs and falconry – was it fair to add one more burden to our crowded lives?

I was still mulling over the implications when we arrived at the auction, but felt unable to voice my doubts when I saw Miranda's enthusiastic smile. She seemed to have invested so much emotional energy on the project that I simply couldn't burst her bubble. Her excitement was infectious too and as we wandered through the stalls, I began to feel the adrenaline pumping through my veins again. What did the cost matter? It was only money and given a bit of imagination, surely we could somehow adjust to the extra expenditure?

It was then I bumped into Fred. After the spectacle of the race, I knew he must know a thing or two about horses. I explained my plans and to my surprise, the man who would – and could – ride the fastest of ponies when too drunk to walk, visibly shuddered.

"You say you know nothing about horses, but still want to buy a colt to ride?" He spluttered. "You're mad – I'll sort you out with something – but not now. What you want is something 'bomb-proof', something that's getting on a bit, but which can be trusted totally."

This was not what I wanted to hear, particularly not after I'd done so much to prepare the ground with Miranda. Indeed, even now I could see her over Fred's shoulder, bouncing with excitement at the sight of all the wonderful ponies, foals and horses crowding the pens of the auction shed.

"But foals are cheap," I explained. "If we could pick up a pair for, say, fifty quid, then we can feed them for free for two or three years until they're old enough to be broken."

"Well, it's true you might be able to pick up a couple for that sort of price, but then again you might not. Besides, why do you think they come so cheap? It's because the next three years will be expensive – you've got to feed them during the winter, pay vet's bills, put up some kind of a shelter – possibly even give them heated stables in really bad weather. Later on, they'll need breaking and unless you know how to do it yourself, that's another costly expense. At any rate, it all mounts up and an older animal will probably work out much cheaper in the long run."

I could feel my heart sinking. "How much would we have to fork out for one of these?" I asked tentatively.

"Oh, they're not that expensive – maybe £1,000 would do the trick – but this isn't the place to buy a horse. Not, that is, unless you really know what you're doing. You probably know much more than you're letting on, but I'd be careful if I were you."

By now the auction was about to get under way and Miranda was waving frantically at me from across the ring. I went to join her with a heavy heart. My initial instinct was to ignore the unwelcome advice and proceed with our plan regardless (after all, if I could tame the belligerent wildness of a hawk, surely I could manage to train a domesticated herbivore?) But Fred's words continued to weigh heavily with me and within a few minutes I knew deep down that we would not be going home with a horse. Furthermore, as the auctioneer cajoled the crowd to part with ever-increasing sums, I was strongly reminded of the Hereford market fiasco. A livestock auction is a dangerous place for all but the very crafty and when it came to horses, we simply weren't knowledgeable enough for the task in hand.

I didn't know quite how I was going to convey this to Miranda who by now was beginning to nudge me every time a new lot came into the ring, accompanying her elbow jabs with loud whispers about how much she did – or didn't – like the look of each. Somehow I managed to convey my doubts and to my surprise found her much less disappointed than I'd expected. Apparently she too had been doing some costings and worked out that a horse was far more than they could afford. Of course by the time she'd made this discovery, I was fully fired up and she didn't want to be responsible for curtailing my tide of enthusiasm. As a result, she'd carried on providing encouragement to dreams which she realised were increasingly unrealistic while not knowing how to break the news. With a jolt we realised quite how close we had come to lumbering ourselves with two costly animals simply because we were trying to avoid hurting each other's feelings.

I accepted that at least one of my pipe dreams would have to remain just that, and it struck me how much I'd changed over the previous eight months. I was far more pragmatic than before and my new-found maturity was the direct result of our more 'natural' lifestyle. In London, I'd dreamed of an idyllic existence where spontaneity was all: where one wandered into the garden to pick food as and when it was wanted, where one lay in the grass when the weather was fine, read books when it was wet and lived each day and each moment in a different way.

The reality, of course, was that we lived in just as regimented and ordered a fashion as all those millions of 'rat-racers' that we'd left behind – in many ways more so. All our basic needs had to be planned for months in advance. Crops were planted in spring for an autumn harvest; winter fuel was chopped and stacked in the height of summer and it took months to rear meat just for a few brief seconds of gastronomic pleasure. Our daylight hours were almost as regimented as those of any office worker, with both mornings and afternoons punctuated by minor farming chores. Moreover, unlike the friends we'd left behind in London, we worked a seven-day week, so spur-of-the moment 'away breaks' were out of the question.

The realisation of all this was disquieting. It was not that I had any regrets about moving to Allt-y-Gwalch, but somehow it was unsettling to realise that the change of situation had wrought a very different effect on me than I'd predicted.

Barbecued 'Wild Boar' with Aubergine Parcels

'Wild Boar'
2 lbs pork belly strips
2 tbsps crushed juniper berries
½ pint red wine
Sprig fresh thyme
Sprig fresh rosemary
Fresh sage leaves
2 bay leaves
3 cloves garlic
1 medium onion (finely chopped)

Aubergine Parcels
2 aubergines
3 large tomatoes
2 small soft Welsh goat's cheeses
1 handful fresh basil

For the 'Wild Boar': Mix all the wild boar ingredients together and marinate pork at least overnight (preferably for a couple of days). Drain and grill on barbecue until cooked through (probably after about 10 minutes on each side).

For the Aubergine Parcels: Thinly slice the aubergines lengthways. Fry in batches in olive oil until soft (be warned, they soak up a lot of oil). Place a slice of goat's cheese on one end, top with a chunk of tomato, a pinch of sugar and a basil leaf. Roll up into a parcel and secure with a matchstick skewer. Cook on the barbecue for a couple of minutes.

October: Bel

As the first minor frosts tinged the remaining vegetables with a white coating of flaky ice, the squashes turned brown and sank back into the earth in a soft mush. The trough of basil in the greenhouse was transformed into a scene of leafless brown sticks. The tomato and cucumber tendrils died clinging to their bamboo supports and, except for a few mouldy green fruits on the floor, identification would have been near impossible. Signs of life seemed rather pathetic, apart from a handful of red chillies still left on the Jalapeno plants. We had bunches of these hot little fingers in the house tied in groups with thread and dried over the wood burner. Most of the produce that had not been consumed had been packed into kilner jars as some sort of preserve. The garage housed sacks of potatoes packed in straw, nets hanging full of shallots or pumpkins, vegetable spaghetti or butternuts.

You might have thought that all this bounty would have filled me with pride, but after the enjoyment of the summer with all its horticultural demands, October threatened to be an enormous anti-climax. The month signalled the coming of winter and once more I began to feel myself filling up with horror at the cold, wind and rain. I felt a huge depression looming over – it was going to be like the first three months of living here all over again: the shivering, the short dark days and the endless rain. Over the summer I had lulled myself into believing that perhaps living up a Welsh hill in the middle of nowhere with only plants and animals for conversation was indeed the 'good life'. With the excitement of the growing season and all our edible successes and failures I had forgotten that the earth rotated around the sun and we would be plunged into darkness for five months with only an electric blanket and a television for comfort.

Dan, however, was positively looking forward to the winter as this was the beginning of his hunting season. His hawk had finished her moult and he was preparing himself to resume training. He built himself a large 'A'- shaped perch which he placed in the study and had the bird sitting there while he worked. He claimed this was an effective method of 'manning' the hawk, while not appearing actually to do anything. Every now and again a loud squawk would resound around the house followed by a 'splat' sound. I went into the study where Dan was flicking through yet another falconry manual while his hawk was sitting on the perch with the look of a psychopath. There was bird shit sprayed in all directions. When I looked at him quizzically, Dan said he had been about to put down newspaper when he had become momentarily distracted.

I had noticed since Dan's return to falconry that his hygiene had slipped to an all-time low. I am not sure when the high was, but I began to notice his indifferent attitude to bacteria had matured to a total disregard. Before we moved to Wales his friends told me tales of his relaxation towards anything resembling sanitary conditions. One friend told me a story once of staying with Dan and putting her foot inside the guest bed to find her toe resting on a freshly licked marrow bone. I heard other tales of opening an oven door and finding a chicken encrusted with maggots. I foolishly assumed they were exaggerating for effect, but I think they were actually breaking me in gradually. It was bad enough that we had to share our freezer space with several thousand chicks, not to mention the odd lab rat, but now I found that I regularly had to move limp day-old chicks sitting on blood-encrusted saucers from the kitchen to the garage. I once found him cleaning his falconry glove over the kitchen sink with a wire brush and splattering large dollops of botulism on the work surfaces. He appeared to have no sense that rotting flesh might possibly be a health hazard. I felt despondent, perhaps he was doing us a favour by killing us all from some unimaginably awful illness instead of dying from hypothermia this winter.

I felt Jack was picking up on my vibrations of doom. Being, as I perceived it, a very sensitive child, he was moaning a fair bit and looked red in the face. Dan pointed out that a far more likely scenario was that he was teething. He did have two little spiky teeth in his upper gum which sort of clinched Dan's argument, but I still felt that the baby was picking up on something in the air, so one night, to distract both him and me from our melancholy, I read him a story. I picked *The fox went out on a chilly night*, a colourful tale of a hungry fox who grabs a goose and drags it miles through some American backwater town to his lair where he has a barrow load of little cubs. The whole story seemed a little far-fetched, would a fox really carry a goose so far? Would he really carry it alive in his mouth? Jack, by now stoned on Calpol, was laughing away at the fact that he could hit the mobile above his bed with his feet.

The next morning I was up and about unusually early and as I went out the front door, I actually did see a fox carrying one of our geese alive by the neck. The thief stopped to stare at me: I stared back. It was unclear who was more afraid to make the first move. Then the goose began to flap its wings feebly and, stung into action by the realisation that it was still alive, I started waving at the fox. I thought I detected the intruder give a long sigh and shake its head, before it sauntered off down the track with our Christmas dinner. When I told Dan he admitted that he had forgotten to lock the geese away the night before, therefore making the snatch pretty straightforward for the fox. This explained the resigned look on the thief's face: a look of near despair at our incompetence and irritation at how easy his prize had been.

My depression deepened after this incident. It seemed the local wildlife was laughing at us. I imagined the fox going back to his lair and telling his mates about this crazy farm, where the humans didn't have the first idea how to look after their fowl. I am sure he saw what bad condition our fences were in and how there were too many weeds in the vegetable patch. I told Dan that perhaps we should tidy up a bit or we would have the whole mountainside laughing at us. He suggested that perhaps I should get out more and talk to some two-legged creatures.

I took Dan's advice and invited Olek and Miranda over for lunch. Olek was not in a very good temper. He was fresh back from a week in London filming a commercial for a large supermarket. Apparently there were artistic differences with the people playing the fruit.

"Actors. I hate them," he said. "If a banana was alive it would walk upright, does this not make sense to you? You would not see banana wiggle like a snake: this is absurd. Bananas would not wiggle, is stupid. Stupid! They walk, standing up. This is what I make them do and they complain it is not life-like. What is bloody life-like about bananas dancing about to dreadful music? Christ Almighty bollocks."

We walked outside to admire the view with Olek still

muttering about sulky fruit actors, but as we wandered on to the lawn he shouted, "Oh my god! Parasols! I don't believe it – you have bloody parasols on your lawn! Bloody bollocks, these are fantastic!"

I had not even noticed the mushrooms growing up to half a foot tall in the middle of the lawn. They had a tall thin stalk which spread out into a rather beautiful creamy umbrella with irregular brown patterns. I thought they looked distinctly dangerous and like most of the rest of the population, I distrusted all wild fungi. All I knew was that they killed you in horrible ways. I remember reading about one where first you experience acute stomach cramps and vomiting. This lasts for a week, then your veins swell up, but then the physical symptoms subside and you experience a week of intense anxiety followed by a final vomiting attack before cardiac arrest. Mushrooms did not just kill you painfully, they played with your mind.

Olek was jumping up and down. "Quick let's cut them and grill them," he said, pulling out a peculiar type of penknife from his pocket. The knife had a serrated curved blade and there was a small brush at the other end. He cut three mushrooms at their base and rushed inside to cook them immediately. As he pared off the stalks he told us these were woody and not very edible. Then he brushed the mushroom cap with the other end of the penknife and placed them on the grill. Minutes later they were cooked. He cut them in half and ate a slice. "That is fantastic – really this is absolutely delicious: you must try." Miranda saw my look of horror. "Really they are fine," she said. "Olek is Polish and all Poles pick wild mushrooms. It's a national habit."

Dan ate the grilled parasol as I watched and waited, but nothing happened. Of course the symptoms could take twenty-four hours to develop. I queried Olek's expertise.

"Have you been picking wild mushrooms since you were little? How did you learn? Have you ever made a mistake?"

Olek laughed. "It's true that in my country there are many fatalities, but people are careless. I am very very careful. Really, it's easy once you get to know them. The English are funny about mushrooms, they think they will die if they eat anything from the forest. In Poland we live off the forest: everybody goes there to pick wild mushrooms."

Dan was in raptures over their strong, yet subtle, mushroom sweet flavour and took another slice. Concerned that I was looking a bit wimpy and English, I reached out and tentatively chewed the end of a slice. It did taste good: very good actually. This was food for free on our lawn, and really worthwhile food. Why had we not thought of wild mushrooms before?

I will admit that during the course of the evening it crossed my mind once or twice that the sky might turn a ghastly blancmange colour before me and large green moose with luminous horns would come roaring towards us on Harley Davidsons. Occasionally, I was conscious of my heartbeat and wondered whether the toxins were working at that very moment to block all oxygen entering my bloodstream, but of course none of these things happened, and the next day I went down to the local bookshop and ordered some books on fungus identification.

While we were waiting for these to arrive we ate all the parasols on the lawn in various culinary fashions. We stuffed them with breadcrumbs as a side vegetable, we sautéed them in sherry and ate them on toasted brioches. We even had them with cream on fresh pasta. When the books arrived we both sat down and studied the pictures. I preferred the photographic book that just listed about two dozen of the most edible and similarly the most deadly species. The language was fairly scary with words like *Ascomycetes*, *Basidiomycetes*, *Amanita* and volval bag. While I was submerged in these wordy books, trying to understand the process of how the hyphae develop into mycelium and universal veils rupture, Dan was out there with his basket, knife and Jack on his back. He preferred the learn-as-you-go kind of school. This involved him walking with the picture book in front of him and matching a mushroom to the photograph. He had reached the top of the hill when he sent Bracken with a note tied to his collar to find me. It read: 'EDIBLE MUSHROOMS – COME IMMEDIATELY.'

I walked up to Dan and found him standing in the short-cropped grass surrounded by about a dozen neat little rings of small brown mushrooms. He picked one and showed it to me. "I bet this is a fairy ring champignon."

I told him that was ridiculous. There are thousands of species of mushrooms growing in the country and that he should find another of the most edible varieties so quickly was extremely unlikely. I took the fungi and examined the gills, stem and cap. Then I turned to the passage in my book on fairy rings. I looked at the mushroom again. It *was* a fairy ring champignon. We picked a whole basketful and went back home.

The book mentioned that fairy rings could be sometimes mistaken for *Clitocybe Rivulosa*. This was one of the deadly ones, a nasty little mushroom with no friendly name like its edible lookalike, but instead an impersonal Latin label. Although I was certain that we had the correct mushroom, I thought it was better to be careful and I adopted a fail-safe method to avoid any awkward mistakes. This was simply to make Dan eat them first, wait for twenty-four hours, observe him carefully and then tuck in if all seemed normal. This worked a treat and the next day I felt sufficiently comfortable to try this delicate mushroom, which tasted a little like the smell of sweet hay.

This was becoming very exciting. Up until this point I had usually avoided even cultivated mushrooms from the supermarket shelf for fear of poisoning, now I was combing the countryside for these gastronomic trophies which any smart restaurant would pay a fortune for. We showed Olek our fairy rings and he enthusiastically accepted a small basket. As he ate a small selection on toast he stared out the window. "Oh when I think of my childhood rummaging through forests," he sighed. "This makes me very happy. What we really want to find are porcini, they are... Oh! Indescribable! This mushroom is the King and the Queen! The flavour is exquisite: I can smell my mother drying them over the fire."

He breathed in deeply. "You know when you are in the forests – you can smell the fungi growing, especially the porcini."

We went home and looked up porcini: *Boletus edulis* known as cep, porcini or penny bun. These were described as the greatest prize a mushroom hunter can find. Apparently just one could reach as much as a kilo in weight but they take as little as three days to grow. 'A velvet brown top, a white firm sponge underneath and a musty smell of the forest' was how the books described it. By now we were so excited that we vowed to succeed in our quest whatever the cost. I spread out the ordinance survey maps and marked out all the local woodland. Since porcini have a symbiotic relationship with trees, these were obviously the main target. We drove around with the windows open, Dan was sticking his head out to breathe in the air that might be carrying the smell of porcini – which was rather optimistic considering we had yet to smell one. We drove high into the mountain forests, following an old farm lane that I liked the look of. According to my map the bumpy track led the way to some mixed woodland. We parked way off the main road by an abandoned old barn.

There was a small path snaking down to an oak forest. We trampled through heavy clumps of uneven marsh grass till we hit a small stream and then followed its banks down the hill to the wood. The bracken was high and too thick to see the forest floor. We thrashed our way through, taking deep sniffs. I wondered whether we should give up, but Dan was repeating over and over, "I know they're here; I can smell them. They're here, they're here . . . Where are you, my babies? Talk to me . . . where are you, my lovelies? We're getting near."

We came into a clearing and I saw masses of tall red-capped mushrooms with white spots. Without looking at the book, we knew this was the infamous fly agaric. This is the mushroom which is the basis of much of the Father Christmas folk lore. Some say the reason Santa wears red and white is taken from this toadstool. Apparently for recreation the Lapps would feed their reindeer the fly agaric, then they would drink the urine, thus ingesting a refined solution of its hallucinogenic toxin. Then, obviously tripping out of their minds they imagined they saw fat men with white beards flying in airborne sledges.

From our point of view the find was important, as I had read that the fly agaric was an acid-loving fungus which enjoyed the same conditions as the porcini and they were, therefore, often to be found in conjunction. Sure enough, when I looked around a particularly large oak, I saw my first porcini growing at the base of this fine tree.

The mushroom was enormous and had a soft deep brown cap. What a colour! The depth of oven-baked bread. Beneath was a beautiful stalk, pure milky white with delicate light brown streaks. To the touch, it felt very firm and compact, but it was the smell which was really phenomenal: such an aroma of mustiness! A sweet foresty meaty smell with an almost chewy intensity. We were giddy with excitement and lay on the woodland floor studying our incredible prize and taking photos from all angles. Eventually I took a sharp knife and cut the stem at the base, reverentially placing it in the basket before we carried on the search.

Not far away we found half a dozen more porcini in various states of growth, some very small and one very old. The old one had big slug bites and it looked as if a squirrel had attempted to dine on it in the recent past. We picked all the fine specimens and walked further into the forest. This was amazing!

We spent two hours in the wood and it was one of the most exciting afternoons of my life. I had never expected that we would actually find these prized mushrooms, let alone so quickly. It was like the best game of hide and seek that you could ever hope to play. When we got home I weighed our find and it came to 6 lbs in all. I laid the mushrooms out on the terrace table and photographed them repeatedly. We were so pleased with ourselves it was almost embarrassing. Feeling the need to share our exhilaration with someone, we drove round to Olek and Miranda with our treasure. "Oh. Christ Almighty bollocks, this is extraordinary!" Olek was stunned. " Just look at them. I can't believe it. I wish my mother was here."

Then he suddenly grew very serious. His smile disappeared and he stared hard into our eyes as his tone dropped to a conspiratorial whisper. "You can't trust anybody. You must be careful, leave no marks of your presence."

I thought he was being a bit weird. Miranda came in from the garden, with a bunch of roses. As she began to trim them at the sink, I told her what Olek had just said, but she didn't seem at all surprised and she told us of a story she had read. "In Oregon several years ago there was a feud between different factions of chanterelle pickers. There was some dispute over territory and accusations of spying and over a hundred were seriously injured in a violent battle. The FBI were called in, apparently. It was terrible. People are very secretive about their patches."

Olek and Miranda seemed perfectly in earnest, but we laughed. How absurd that sounded: to be so possessive about something which grows wild and belongs to nobody.

We passed the next weeks concentrating solely on fungi. We scrambled down to the valley floors, walked along the streams, riverbeds and lakesides, searching for these amazing fruits in the undergrowth and mossy banks. We clambered up the steep sides of disused railways and followed the former tracks for miles, cutting back the bracken to scour the mossy floor. We drove along hedgerows with our heads out the window looking for signs and trying to catch the smell on the wind. We had become obsessed and our desire turned into addiction. Every day I woke up thinking about them and at night I dreamed endlessly about searching through dead leaves in dark forests for porcini. I even found myself watching some wildlife programme on television, but instead of looking at the cute dormouse in the foreground, I was scouring the background for mushrooms. I marked our large wall-mounted ordinance survey with notes, dates and coloured pins. Every day we spent a minimum of four hours with knives, sticks and baskets trawling the countryside for these extraordinary growths. How bizarre that something which only grows at night in such a relatively short time could be so delicious! There was something magical about them and I suppose that is the very reason they are so mistrusted. Dan developed a theory which was something to do with ancient English history, witchcraft, druids, the Protestant work ethic and the Catholic hijacking of pagan customs, but I was only half listening and I can't remember the crux of his argument. Whatever the reason, we were thrilled that we seemed to have the hillsides to ourselves.

It was not long before we were finding a myriad of different species: horse mushrooms, honey fungi, shaggy ink caps, amethyst deceivers, cauliflower fungus, chanterelles, bay boletes, orange birch boletes and the wonderfully fragrant wood blewits. Although by now my initial phobia had diminished considerably, with any new species I was still insisting that Dan have a twenty-four-hour start on the digestion. I found it disconcerting that many of the best mushrooms were often found in the near vicinity of some particularly unpleasant ones. We saw hundreds of fly agaric, panther caps and too many other poisonous ones for me to feel sufficiently calm just throwing a mushroom into my mouth without precaution. Dan had so much confidence in my identification skills, he was not in the least bit bothered about being my guinea pig.

Our main problem was trying to eat them fast enough and soon we were finding so many that this was simply not possible. The books recommended various ways of preserving fungi, drying being the most practical option. So Dan built a precarious stack of wire mesh trays above the wood burner and we dried our bounty in bulk. In the process they lost their visual appeal completely, shrivelling up to half the size and becoming particularly unappetising to look at. Regardless of this transformation, we stored them in disused sweetie jars in the larder. The smell when you unscrewed the top was overwhelming: the drying process had actually intensified the flavour. It was unbelievably good and Dan was flavouring everything – soups, risottos and stews – with the stock made from our dried mushrooms.

Our greatest culinary achievement – and personally I

believe we should be included in the honours list for this contribution to humanity – was fresh porcini with crème fraîche puréed and stuffed into giant home-made ravioli. This was served with olive oil and shavings of fresh parmesan. I cannot communicate in mere words the excellence of this dish: perhaps Keats might have done it justice.

Our repertoire of productive patches was increasing by the day. We were gaining immense knowledge and understanding of what conditions certain mushrooms seem to respond to. We felt that the boletus family was our chosen specialist mushroom and the porcini most of all. From what we had learned already, we could look at the ordinance survey map and pick likely areas. Mossy banks in mixed woodland which were only exposed to the weaker morning sun seemed to be most productive. One afternoon, when we were on a speculative drive we parked by the river and walked up a large hill, through scrubby birch and into some mature forestry. Not far from the car we came upon the best porcini patch we had found to date.

The place was phenomenal. In one picking we collected 20 lbs of porcini and within two weeks we had harvested over 50 lbs. We began to leave any which were even slightly past their best. By our second visit to the 'forests of ceps' we were beginning to feel ever so slightly proprietorial about the place. We started to park further and further away from the actual site, not wanting to attract attention. Once when we were there we thought we heard voices and hid behind a large mound of earth for half an hour, although no humans ever materialised. When we picked a porcini we would always cover up the cut base and then disguise our own tracks with a stick. By the end of the second week we were going there after dark, wearing khaki clothing and discussing the possibility of leaving mantraps to put off any intruders on to our patch. We even talked seriously about buying the woodland and the feasibility of erecting a large six-foot electric fence, but in the end dismissed the idea as it would only attract unwanted attention.

Dan was more conscious that our attitudes were becoming a tad Draconian than I. He suggested that we take Olek to try to cure our possessiveness. I was not happy: how did we know we could trust him? What was to stop him going there all the time and taking *our* mushrooms? Dan pointed out that we had collected enough dried mushrooms to last us for the year as well as making some pretty unusual Christmas presents for relatives. Besides, he pointed out, it was thanks to Olek that we had discovered mushrooms in the first place and, after all, he and Miranda were our friends. I took a few deep breaths and repeated over and over, "They are wild mushrooms that belong to nobody." I agreed to show the patch to Olek.

Our Polish mushroom guru derived so much enjoyment from visiting our golden porcini patch that it was worth sacrificing our secrecy. He talked of his childhood days in Poland with moist eyes and a smile. There were enough mushrooms for him to pick a healthy 10 lbs and no doubt we would have had more if a hard frost hadn't hit the valleys that night, freezing any remaining porcini and killing off any further growth.

Frost signals a big change in the growth spurts of most fungi and our days began to revert back to the pattern before the great mushroom hunt. The cold, however, was no such deterrent for the hardy wood blewit, which seems to thrive with a couple of good frosts under its belt. This information triggered a memory culled from reading John Seymour. I had forgotten that you can grow winter vegetables in all sorts of inhospitable conditions. We ordered bulbs of a special garlic which, reputedly, would grow to a pound in weight with fifteen or more pink cloves, some young broccoli, assorted cabbages and brussel sprouts seedlings, (even though neither of us really liked any of the brassica family). More worthwhile work involved covering up the existing asparagus with seaweed we collected from the beach at Aberystwyth and Dan concocted an intriguing mulch of various animal excretions for the artichokes.

Even that was not the end of our garden chores, for my mother had unexpectedly sent me a present of a selection of spring bulbs. A sizeable cardboard box arrived by courier, but when we opened it, we found that somehow a mistake had been made during the order and we had been sent double the intended amount. It took us about ten days, working two hours a day, to plant two thousand daffodils, one and a half thousand narcissi, a thousand snowdrops and crocuses, five hundred fritillaries and five hundred tulips. By the end I was almost pleased winter was on the way and I would not have to pick up another spade for months.

During all this, poor Jack had been rather ignored, we shoved him in the old pram with selected brightly coloured plastic while we planted. To alleviate my guilt, I looked for an expedition that might be something special for him. On a trip to the local town I noticed that a travelling circus was announcing its arrival with smart posters of tigers, elephants and seals. Dan was excited – he had romantic memories of a circus back in his childhood days in Oxfordshire: the roaring lions being kept at bay by a whip and an upturned chair; twenty men dressed as Cossacks forming a human pyramid and a woman riding a unicycle high in the air on a thin wire. I asked Miranda if she would come with Rosa and though a little hesitant about the treatment of the animals, both she and Olek agreed.

We arranged to meet at The Mayfly for a drink beforehand and as usual Evan was there propping up by the bar. He gave us a nod. "Hello there. It's a grand day for it, like."

"Grand day for what?" I asked.

"Oh whatever you like – it would be a grand day for it."

Dan bought Evan a drink and enquired what the salmon were up to. Evan took a large gulp of beer. "Well I think they may be on the move, like. If we could get a bit more rain I think that would shift them. But don't you worry, I have never known a year when they didn't run."

Dan reminded him of his promise to take him to the river for a lesson in catching salmon without a fishing rod. Evan slammed his hand on the bar. "Good God man! Do you want to get me in trouble? I don't go down to the river for that sort of thing any more, like. I can't afford to do that. What would a honest man like me do on the river?" Then he laughed and slapped Dan on the back and said he would accept another pint from him.

We finished our drinks and I dragged Dan away before he realised that he would rather stay in the pub with Evan than go to the circus.

We walked to the common where 'The Smiley Circus' had set up the big top. Shortly after we had taken our seats a clown casually entered the arena, a tall lanky man with plus fours, bright red floppy shoes and a large red smile painted on his face. He was holding the reins of three rather wet horses. As people were still milling around before the start of the show, I carried Jack to the clown, who had a badge saying 'Co-Co' on his lapel.

"Hello, Co-Co", I said, expecting him to squirt me with water and pull a bunch of flowers out of his pocket.

Instead he wiped his nose and grunted, "Pound a ride, twice round the tent."

Up close I could see that the painted smile was only just managing to hide a permanent scowl. I explained haughtily that we were just looking and I went back to rejoin the others.

Eventually a large fat man entered the ring, introduced himself as Mr Smiley and brought on his wife, Mrs Smiley, who tripped over a guyrope as she pirouetted in. They took a big bow, then he proudly announced the rest of the team as 'Master Smiley and the Smiley sisters!' They ran in looking shabby and slightly hung over as the spotlight jerked back to 'our resident king of comedy: Co-Co the clown!'

Co-Co was leaning against a side pole dourly rolling a cigarette, and in recognition of the stifled claps he just about managed to raise a hand. Mr Smiley, apparently unperturbed, beamed, as he announced the first act as the 'incredible, fantastic Smiley sisters and their act of a thousand hoops!'. This consisted of the three girls doing the hula-hoop in unison.

Acts of a similar calibre followed. First was Mrs Smiley (who looked like Miss Jones from *Rising Damp*) pushing pigeons up and down a long horizontal pole with her finger; then one of the Smiley sisters did a 'daredevil' high-wire act, barely four feet off the ground (which was just as well because she kept falling off). Finally Master Smiley supervised six horses as they ran clockwise around the tent and then, for variation, anti-clockwise.

The finale was a knife throwing act by Mr Smiley. He ran on dressed in a brilliant white satin cowboy suit brandishing six large blades. Co-Co grudgingly brought on a large board and Mrs Smiley followed wearing a flashy gold outfit. She posed theatrically as her husband walked around the tent in a ridiculously dramatic fashion. There was an embarrassing pause before a muffled drum roll blared out over the loud speaker, whereupon Mr Smiley began walking towards his wife with one knife ominously raised. But rather than stop at an impressive distance, he kept going until he was only a few feet away, at which point he practically pushed the knife into the cork next to his wife. He bowed as if expecting applause before repeating the performance six times.

The lights came up on a rather stunned audience. Co-Co began to walk around the crowd with a bucket for contributions to top up the entry price we had already paid. He took umbrage when people refused the invitation and began to squirt them with the plastic flower on his lapel, to date the nearest to a joke he had performed. In practice this merely provoked one of the farmers who responded by grabbing the clown. Slipping out of his grasp, Co-Co ran towards the arena. The farmer leaped over the barrier and made a dive for the clown, catching him by his large red feet. At this, the tent ruptured into spontaneous applause, cheering and clapping in the first genuine display of approval.

The climax came when Dan, unable to restrain himself any longer, jumped into the arena with a bucket of water and drenched the grumpy clown. After a standing ovation, the farmers let their sodden captive go. He slumped off shouting and swearing while the audience repaired to The Mayfly for a celebratory drink.

Dan's action made quite an impact on our standing in the community and from then on we were always greeted in town with many more smiles and nods of recognition.

Porcini Ravioli

Pasta:
1 lb durum wheat flour; 2 large eggs;
cold water

Filling:
½ cup of dried porcini, 2 shallots
4 fl ozs of crème fraîche
2ozs cultivated mushrooms
Knob of butter, a little flour
pepper and salt, parmesan

For the Pasta: Sift the flour into a large bowl and slowly add the eggs, kneading the mixture with your hands until it forms a firm dough. If necessary add a little more flour or cold water. Wrap in cling film and put in the fridge for half an hour.

For the Filling: To make the filling pour just enough near boiling water to cover the porcini. Leave for 15 minutes. Fry the shallots in butter with the cultivated mushrooms until soft. Add the flour and cook for a moment, then add the crème fraîche. You should end up with a reasonably thick mixture – if too wet, remove from the pan and (without washing it) melt a tablespoon of butter and add a little flour, stirring to make a thick paste. Add the porcini/crème fraîche mixture and then liquidise.

To make the ravioli roll the dough out thinly several times, folding and turning it each time. Then, using a wine glass as a cutter, cut circles and dab a teaspoon of the mushroom mix in the centre of each. Fold in half, sealing the edge with a little cold water. Cook in boiling salted water for 3 minutes and serve with shavings of fresh parmesan and black pepper.

November: Dan

Although by now it seemed as if we'd spent most of the past three months preserving food and we'd quietly promised each other that we'd do no more until next year, nature found delight in throwing us one last challenge – apples. An old friend of my parents rang. She'd recently moved to a Herefordshire farm some thirty miles to the east, and along with the property had inherited an ageing orchard. "Would you like the windfalls?" she asked.

By now Bel was really on the ball: there was something about free food which had captured her imagination and she positively insisted we collect them to finish fattening the pigs for Christmas. As a result, I accepted the offer and within the hour we were chugging off in the Landrover to collect what we confidently expected to be a trailer load of half-rotten fruit.

In the event we were shocked to discover the apples were in much better condition than we had anticipated – and there were far more of them too. Soon, both the trailer and the car's vast canvas-covered rear were full and even though we'd taken almost a tonne of green, gold and red spheres, we'd barely cleared a quarter of the fallen fruit. As we pulled out of the orchard and looked back at the grass beneath the trees, still dotted with spoils, the sight acted on us like thousands of proverbial rags to a bull: no sooner had we unloaded the car and trailer out on to the front lawn at home, than we were turning around for the next load.

It took four trips in all to clear the orchard, by which time we had a veritable apple mountain back at Allt-y-Gwalch. Now, while Pork and Bacon undoubtedly loved fruit, not even their combined appetites could make much impression on this pile before it would melt into a sodden brown heap.

To our now deviously self-sufficient minds, the solution, of course, was stunningly simple. If only we could convert it into juice then we could bottle the best part for human consumption, while still fattening the pigs on the pulp. Unfortunately the one-gallon press and the juice extractor we had inherited from our past urban lives would not be up to the mark. Their combined efforts would make little impression on our six-foot mound.

It was the Major who provided the first breakthrough. As I outlined the problem, he remembered an ancient mill buried in his barn, once used to crush oil cake for dairy cattle. This turned out to be a rusting lump of iron which was, in effect, a clothes mangle with spiked rollers. With the first stage potentially conquered, I returned home to try to construct a serviceable press which would be able to deal with a large quantity of pulp in one go.

After reflecting on the design of the numerous antique cider presses which decorate front lawns and roundabouts along the border, I bolted together some stout beams and powered my home-made apparatus with the Landrover jack.

The next morning Bel and I were out there, she feeding apples into the cake crusher as I spun the huge flywheel with gusto and Jack gurgled approvingly from the pram. The roughly chopped fruit poured into a dustbin and we were in business as I tipped the already dripping pulp on to a sheet of muslin lining the press. When the fruit reached a depth of six inches, Bel turned in the corners of the cloth to produce what cider makers call a 'cheese' and we began the next layer. After a couple of hours of this we had created a huge pile of sopping pulverised fruit, ready to be compressed.

I began to work the jack's lever and we watched in fascination as the mound of pulp gradually shrank. For what seemed an age, nothing happened but then, slowly, the side of the cheeses began to gleam perceptibly. Encouraged, I pumped faster and the flow became a trickle, oozing down the pile of glistening muslin into the trough below. In no time we had five gallons of delicious juice bottled up and sitting in a huge pan on the stove, ready to be sealed – and hopefully sufficiently sterilised to remain in the larder for several months before consumption.

We slaved away for the rest of the day and by nightfall there were 30 gallons sitting in every available container, from Tupperware to plastic jerry cans. Then Bel suggested a rain butt while we located more vessels, but within a couple of hours this was also full of juice and we were growing desperate.

It was then that the lateral-thinking Bel had the brainwave of a visit to the bottle bank. She reasoned that this was one place which would be full of useful containers and we could take our pick of free bottles. It seemed a brilliant solution, but as she was strapping Jack into his car seat for the raid, I noticed tiny bubbles of gas rising to the surface of the juice. Taking Providence's hint, in a flash of inspiration, I declared we would turn it into cider instead.

Treating the natural process of decay that was beginning in the butts as a friend rather than foe, we set to work afresh on the huge pile of fruit on the lawn. By the time the crushing and pressing process was finished, we had two juice-filled butts – 110 gallons in all. Then we sat down to wait. At first, little happened. The bubbles trickled up to the surface, but very slowly. On the third day, however, fermentation began in earnest – and how! In spite of my teenage experience, the sheer violence of it all came as something of a shock. Without warning a vigorous froth developed on the surface and soon it had bubbled up over the top and was cascading down the sides of the butt, drying stickily on the floor so that walking across the garage became akin to a stroll across flypaper.

For a fortnight the activity continued unabated and then, gradually, it subsided, allowing us to decant it into a motley collection of demijohns and two specially bought home-brew barrels. It was all very satisfying, but as with so many of our projects, what had set out as a simple task had ended up consuming far more time and effort than we could ever have bargained for.

It was at about this time that we heard the first hints of our unwanted lodgers. The squatters, keen to avoid the vicissitudes of a Welsh winter, at first went almost unremarked, but one evening Bel pointed out a rumbling sound issuing from above her head, as she began the washing up. I tried to explain that this must just be a mouse or vole, and that its scampering footsteps sounding like a herd of elephants was due to the fibreboard ceiling, which amplified the noise along the same principles as a kettle drum.

She said nothing, but cocked a quizzical eyebrow at me and as the thundering steps scuttled back above our heads, drowning out the murmur of the radio, I had to concede my explanation was a trifle unconvincing. I stuck to my guns, however, not least because I couldn't think of a more credible – or acceptable – alternative. I pointed out that no bird was going to move around like that (certainly not after dark) and that therefore this could only mean mice.

Bel continued to look sceptical, so in the end I mounted a reconnaissance trip upstairs.

I didn't really expect to see anything – after all, by the time I'd unbolted the wooden hatch, lifted it on to the landing and peered inside, any self-respecting wild animal would long since have disappeared – but my conviction was horribly misplaced. I only saw it for a split second because I dropped the torch in shock, but in that brief instant I caught the unmistakable profile of a rat scuttling along the far wall.

It is at this point that I should confess to a mild phobia of rats. I hate them, loathe them, with an unreasonable fear out of all proportion to their size or – until this moment at least – impact on my life. Maybe it was the torture scene in *1984*, or the descriptions of rat-borne diseases in various ferreting tomes I used to read as a teenager, but the mere sight of a rat sends a slight shiver down my spine. Here I was looking at one, inside our house and worst of all, just a few inches from the head of our bed.

After that, everything moved very fast. Before the torch hit the floor, I had grabbed the trap door, shoved it into the gap and was fumbling with the catches. I rushed back downstairs and grabbing the air gun, loaded it with trembling fingers. Then I charged back upstairs and gingerly opened the trap door to crouch, trembling slightly, with weapon and torch at the ready. Naturally there was no sign of the creature, but now I knew it was there, I felt I could not rest until it had breathed its last.

I was still crouched, gun at the ready, when Bel came upstairs to investigate. My first instinct was to tell her nothing – after all, if I was reduced to this gibbering state, what would be the effect on her urban sensibilities? In retrospect, my determination was laughable given the sight that greeted her. In spite of my earlier confidence, she had known it must be something rather larger than a mouse and once she caught sight of my ashen face, she guessed immediately what had happened.

For the second time that evening, I was caught out completely. Bel's reaction was truly remarkable – and unthinkable only a few months before. Instead of announcing that she was leaving for London with Jack, there to stay until I had dealt with the problem, she calmly took the gun from me, muttering that I was trembling far too much to have a hope in hell of hitting anything. Then she told me to return downstairs to look after Jack who had begun to cry, picking up no doubt on the tidal waves of tension emanating from his father.

A few moments later I heard a muffled crack from upstairs and a distinct squeak and a small thud. Bel reappeared, gun cocked over her arm and a slight smile on her face.

"Got him," she said simply. "He's at the end – you'd better fetch him."

My sense of relief disappeared almost as soon as it had arrived. The corpse was at the far end of the roof space, a good twenty-foot crawl from the tiny door, along a cobweb-strewn, three-foot-high passage. That was the best part of the scenario – the worst was that the rat was only wounded. This realisation sent my pulse racing and my stomach churning – I couldn't help remembering tales of big game hunters about the dangers of tracking a wounded tiger through thick jungle. Indeed, buffalo become the 'most dangerous creature in Africa' when injured – if that was true for an overgrown cow, what would it do to something as terrifying as a rat?

Anyway, even if it were dead, rats are the sort of creatures who have big brothers – you know, ones who wear Doc Martens and beat up people who bully their little brothers. There was no way on earth that I was going to crawl along the rafters to peer behind a distant beam. My refusal to enter the loft was justified almost immediately as we heard another scuffle overhead, and then another, a good ten feet from the first. Clearly we had a colony of the creatures living just inches from our bed, separated from our sleeping heads by only the flimsiest of lathe and plaster ceilings. The suspicion became conviction when an hour later I peered into the loft and saw a baby running into a hole in the end wall.

I have had to deal with rats once before. That was when they invaded the compost heap at my parents' Oxfordshire cottage. Then I had been told that short of poison, there was no way I could get rid of the creatures, but I had vetoed the idea, concerned lest a Warfarin-laden rat wandered into the hawk's enclosure. I still hated the thought of poison, but as I contemplated the thought of sleeping with live rats scuttling within inches of my head, any scruples evaporated. My stomach knotted at the mere thought of the night to come and I considered a temporary shift of sleeping accommodation to the front guest room – the one furthest from our latest squatters – but in the end abandoned the idea after studying Bel's remarkably calm air. If she could cope with rats near the end of our bed, my male pride forbade me from appearing too grossly 'chicken'.

Instead I tried to work out what we had done to deserve the attentions of our new visitors. How had they got in? How long had they been there? What were they eating? I had no idea about the first – presumably there was some sort of hole in the end wall of the house, but the same reasons which prevented me from retrieving the dead rat, ruled out any detailed investigation. Nor could I answer the second question, although thinking back, I began to remember other evenings when loud noises had been remarked upon: not a comforting train of thought.

I moved on quickly to the final puzzle and here I

thought I had the answer. We usually stacked our rubbish outside the kitchen door, not ten feet from where our unwanted guest was (hopefully) stiffening in the dust between the rafters. For several weeks now these had been opened by some animal or other. I had assumed the culprit to be a badger or fox, but now it became obvious that the lack of mess and small scale of the problem was the result of a much smaller thief. I vowed instantly to purchase half a dozen galvanised metal bins in which to put sacks awaiting disposal and to store these in the barn across the lane. I was feeling quite giddy with the horror of it all and poured myself a large tumbler of wine, which I downed in two large gulps.

Over the course of the next few hours, we crept back to the trap door at least half a dozen times, gun at the ready. By mutual agreement, Bel took on the role of sniper while I unbolted the door and tried to hold the torch beam steady enough for 'Calamity' to get off a shot. Although the method was at first reasonably effective – we thought we might have bagged another couple – the continuing sporadic rumbling sounds from the loft showed that it was far from a total solution to the problem. Moreover, rats are cunning creatures, and after the first few raids it became increasingly difficult to do anything more than catch the briefest of glimpses. Obviously the gun alone could never be the answer to our problems and it certainly would not rid us of our unwanted guests that evening.

My panic at the thought of the night ahead grew, but Bel continued to remain remarkably calm. The only sign that she was in the least bit perturbed came as we went to bed and she suggested that, for the first time in a year, it might be a good idea if the dogs were to sleep next to the bed. I readily concurred and went further, insisting that Jack should lie between us – just in case. So, that night there were five of us in the bedroom. Dill was at the end of the bed while Bracken reassured me by curling up next to me.

Apart from the baby none of us slept well and at crack of dawn on the next day the three of us humans were on our way to buy traps and poison from an agricultural warehouse, reasoning that the sort of industrial-strength toxins that farmers would use were what we wanted. I bought a large tub of bait, garishly plastered with evil-looking rats and the legend that this was 'effective against super-rats'.

To my mind it seemed self-evident that all rats should be treated with extreme caution. I had no idea whether ours were capable of outstripping jet fighters or stopping speeding trains with one twitch of a whisker, but whatever the case, the rodent equivalent of kryptonite certainly seemed called for. Mind you, in spite of my phobia, I was still concerned for the hawk, dogs and surrounding wildlife. The last thing I wanted was for a highly toxic dead rat to do away with my hounds or bird. I checked the packet and although no chemist, it seemed that this was a Warfarin-type poison. In other words, it was cumulative and in effect turned its victims into haemophiliacs who would eventually die from internal bleeding following the slightest knock.

The first shuffling rustle of a rat overhead that afternoon brushed aside any residual qualms. As I traced the progress of the fast-moving rodent across the fibreboard above my head, I found I no longer cared about environmental side effects. In fact, if someone had recommended scattering nuclear waste around the homestead at that precise moment, I would have been on the train to Sellafield like a shot. They did not, so instead I leaped for the best alternative – the 'super rodenticide' – only to recoil against the psychological barrier of re-entering the rat-infested loft.

To get the poison to the rats meant entering the little attic on all fours. I was not happy at the thought, not happy at all, but in spite of Bel's fortitude when it came to rodents, there was no way I could ask her to do the honours. To her mind rats are one thing, but spiders quite another and the lack of light only enhanced the problem.

After several hours of procrastination I knew I had to act soon or I would have to perform the task after sunset and as rats are nocturnal, this was too much like adding insult to injury. With heart in mouth, I began to crawl into the roof space, clutching the tub of bait in my hand. I was aiming for the plastic containers littering the floor and whose significance I had only just begun to realise. These were old poison trays, put down by our predecessors. Until now I had assumed that rats would never enter an occupied house – at least not unless they were at plague levels – and that the trays were meant for mice. Now I knew better and I couldn't help noticing the ominous holes gnawed in those nearest to me.

I only managed to get three yards into the loft – barely a quarter of its length – before my courage caved in. My mind filled yet again with visions of the torture scene in *1984* where a starving rat is held to Wilbur's face. The cobwebs brushing my face were just the last straw. I hurriedly opened the tub and poured the bait into the two closest trays. Outside and filled with relief, I looked at the poison. It was wheat, obviously laced with the drug and coloured blue – the theory I suppose being that humans have a reluctance to eat bright blue food and not only are rats colour blind, but being nocturnal can't see their grub anyway. We retreated downstairs for yet another fortifying drink – or rather I did, but then I remained far more upset about the whole incident than the remarkably phlegmatic Bel.

The next morning there was a small rat in the catch 'em

alive trap where the rubbish bags had been. It was barely bigger than a vole, but in my eyes it might just as well have been a giant mutant the size of a dog. Like the fusillade of shots on that first dreadful evening, its capture made little impact on the noise levels from the attic and that night was worse than ever.

The following evening was the worst of all. By now the whole colony had discovered the blue-dyed wheat and was running back and forth to the piles, stuffing their mouths with the grain before retreating to the safety of their warren at the end of the attic. The noise hit a crescendo at five in the morning when Bel heard two or three fighting a pitched battle – presumably over the poison – squealing and chattering in rage at each other.

I tried to sound convincing as I explained to Bel that the increase in noise was a good sign, that the poison was cumulative and it would take a few days before it took effect. By now even she was beginning to look a trifle tense at the thought of all these four-legged distributors of disease so close to the three of us and her faith in my rat-expertise had become distinctly jaded.

Fortunately, on this occasion, I was proved right. After five days there was silence from upstairs, a silence which deepened over the following week. It appeared that the poison was everything its advocates claimed – quick and extremely effective. A fortnight after Bel had shot the first rat, we could look at each other with a smile and conclude we were now genuinely rat-less. There was just one lingering worry – a funny musty smell began to pervade the house and it didn't take a genius to work out that one of our deceased visitors had returned to haunt us.

With a shock I remembered that I had yet to retrieve Calamity Bel's victim and that this must be the source of the odour (while poisoned rats are apparently more thoughtful, by becoming terribly thirsty and wandering off to perish near running water). As I tried to screw up my courage for the role ahead, I was saved by the arrival of Evan and his two sons. Catching sight of Maldwyn, I realised this was the perfect opportunity to pass the buck. In return for the promise of a pound for every corpse, he readily scampered into the loft, to return with two half-grown carcasses both of which were definitely on the whiffy side.

Once the two rats had been carefully shrouded in multiple plastic bags and consigned to the new bins in the barn opposite, we returned inside to find out the purpose of Evan's trip. To my delight, it turned out he had come to announce that the salmon were running and that if we had time, tonight would be the perfect opportunity to do some illicit fishing. It seemed that a friend of his had tipped him off that all the Wye bailiffs were on duty way down river at Monmouth that night and thus the coast was clear.

Naturally both Bel and I jumped at the idea and said wild horses wouldn't keep us from joining him. This was not quite what Evan had envisaged. Notwithstanding the absent bailiffs, he had an instinctive resistance to involving women in his business activities, particularly when the woman in question was encumbered with a six-month-old child. He pointed out that his own children were to be left at home – an argument which would have carried more weight had I not known of their mother's antipathy to the activity. All the same, it took some time for me to persuade him to allow Bel to participate and when he relented, it was on condition that she act as chauffeur and didn't participate in any actual fishing.

In fact, he wanted Bel and Jack to remain in the car full stop, but we hung on and in the end he agreed she could at least participate in the reconnaissance. With the bare bones of the campaign settled, we agreed to meet at a local bridge at eleven p.m. It was raining as we arrived, but Evan was already there sheltering under an overgrown hedge, collar buttoned up against the wind and a greasy woollen hat pulled down tight on his head.

The three of us slithered across the short turf, sodden from the recent rain towards the sound of the river roaring at the bottom of the steep-sloping, bracken-covered hillsides. Opposite lay a hill whose sides were so steep they almost constituted cliffs – rising 700 feet in less than a couple of hundred yards. As we scrambled down the slope, Evan was explaining to Bel that this sheer hillside was the best way to escape pursuing bailiffs.

"They're just as human as the rest of us," he panted, pausing to catch his breath on an overhanging hazel. "You've got to be fit to run up that thing and halfway up they begin to think that it would be easier to circle the hill by car, waiting for you to come down. Then, as long as you're sensible, you're away."

The little valley we were in was, according to Evan, both the best and worst place to poach. On the one hand the river was narrow and full of fish, but on the other the bailiffs knew this too and with just one road leading in and out, it was all too easy to stake out. The little stream which snaked along the valley bottom was a tributary of the Wye and one of the spawning grounds of the salmon which had spent their last three or four years out in the Atlantic, off the north-west coast of Ireland. In early autumn something stirs in the souls of the mature fish, driving them to return to the place of their birth. By late September they are entering the Bristol Channel and nosing their way upstream towards the Welsh hills. They slice their way confidently up the Channel and flicker into the faster flow of the Wye, but have to work harder as they gain altitude. By the time they reach Hay-on-Wye they are tired and stop to rest for a few days or even weeks. It then takes rain to move them – a heavy shower in the mountains upstream, to swell the river, stir their primal instincts and send hormones pulsing through their tired muscles, driving them ever onwards. By the time they reach the upland waters, they are exhausted, with 120 miles of river behind them and nothing to eat since leaving the open sea.

The scent of the gravel beds, which lie up every mountainside, swirls thick in the water and with the next shower the fish make the final effort to reach the place of their birth. How far up the streams they will manage to struggle is now up to the rain – in today's age of improved land drainage and forestry the water is on and off the land in a matter of hours and it takes a steady fall over a matter of a week or two to make a good spawning year. After the rains of the past two months, this autumn had the makings of just that.

The first fish we glimpsed in the light of our heavily shrouded torch was a ten-pounder which flickered out of the white arch of water cascading between the rocks beneath the falls. The sight was fleeting, but exhilarating. Bel and I were ecstatic at the prospect, but Evan dismissed it as a 'river fish' – one which had been in the Wye for several weeks and had thus depleted its energy reserves. The best fish, he explained, were the 'reds' – larger, fitter and ocean fresh.

He then led us up above the falls where a huge overhanging rock shielded us from any observers on the road and where he said he thought there was a good chance of catching a glimpse of a fish. Very cautiously he flashed the torch across the water, extinguishing the beam immediately he had made the sweep. At first neither Bel nor I saw anything, but Evan did and he whispered to us to follow him back to the foot of the falls where, carefully shielding the torch from the road with his body, he pointed the beam down into a hollow beneath a tree root. For a split second Bel and I glimpsed the back of a huge fish before the torch went out again. I was excited, but Bel was positively bouncing up and down with elation at the thought of such a monster, just waiting to be pulled from its watery environment.

"Quick, quick, quick!" She squeaked at Evan. "Gaff it now – it's there for the taking."

"Oh no, I couldn't do that, like," replied the poacher with a note of genuine horror in his voice. "That's a hen, full of eggs – I wouldn't touch her if you paid me. No, what we're after is a cock – there's two of them for every hen and every one can cover a dozen females. No, we can take as many cocks as we like without harming the stocks, but we'll leave the hens to do their thing. That's the way we've always done it up here, and that's the way I like it."

Bel could barely conceal her disappointment, but the poacher was adamant and as if to back him up, Jack began to stir in the rucksack on my back. Evan said firmly that it was time for her and the baby to depart, so I slid off the pack's straps and handed Jack over to his mother. A moment later she had vanished into the night and after another short interval Evan and I caught sight of the headlights slowly winding off up the valley.

We had agreed that the merest whiff of a police or National Rivers Authority vehicle should trigger the alarm signal. I had first suggested a rapid succession of toots on the car horn, but Evan had vetoed this, pointing out it would immediately tell any law enforcement officer that there were others down by the river. Instead he suggested that she drive repeatedly up and down the road. This would be spotted quickly by anyone by the river, but if asked, she could always say she was simply trying to get the baby to sleep. As soon as she judged prudent, she would leave the valley to drive slowly back to town and then return up the main road. At its nearest point this was no more than a mile from our present position and she would continue to trawl up and down this stretch until we flagged her down.

In fact, as Evan explained grimly, whatever might have gone on before, the real danger would come after the fish were loaded. "If they can prove a connection between the car and the crime, then it'll be confiscated, like," he said cheerily to me. "I know a guy who lost his motor because of just a few scales the forensics pulled off the boot trim, like!"

As soon as the tail lights had vanished into the rain we were off, slithering back down the glassy surface of the springy turf to the river. I thought I had come fully water-proofed, but moisture had penetrated every pore in my body and I was shivering, although the cold didn't seem to affect Evan, in spite of his wearing apparently less substantial clothing. Whereas I was wrapped in an oiled stockman's coat (the legacy of a year spent in Australia after University), he had nothing more impermeable than an old felt workman's coat. What little proofing it had ever possessed – the orange plastic coating over the shoulders – had long since been ripped off as far too conspicuous for the task in hand. When I questioned him about this he laughed, saying that this coat had seen so many fish eggs and oil that it was as good as any lifeman's survival suit.

"Anyway, it's a warm night for the time of year," he added cheerfully. "I've fished waist-deep with chunks of ice floating past me!" I was sceptical about this last claim, but before I had a chance to ask him for more details, we were back on the bank and Evan was signalling for total silence.

He crept closer to the beds where the fish spawned and, after listening intently for a moment, began to take off his boots and socks. He whispered to me to follow his lead and with a jolt I realised that we were to wade into the torrent. Mutely, I obeyed and a few seconds later I found myself cautiously lowering my toes into the water.

Christ it was cold! My worst recollections of compulsory swimming lessons in an outdoor pool just after Easter paled into insignificance. Evan seemed oblivious to the temperature and had plunged deeper into the rushing torrent, heading for the shallower water of the gravel bank in the middle of the stream. I followed him, biting my lip as my toes stubbed against the sharp shale of the riverbed, stumbling as I lurched in and out of the potholes that lurked like mantraps across the river bottom. It was a miracle that I managed to reach the gravel bed in the middle. By the time I had reached the security of its shallower water, I was gasping with the cold, but Evan's voice came calm and collected through the dark. "Here, take the torch – wait for your eyes to get used to the dark, like – then point it upstream and sweep it slowly to your right."

With chattering teeth, I followed his instructions, only to be halted almost immediately as Evan's gaze caught a glimmer of silver. "Keep it there," he hissed, lurching forwards with the gaff outstretched. A moment later and he had pounced, stabbing the pole into the water and immediately hooking it backwards: nothing.

We repeated the procedure and again were greeted with failure. Three more times Evan halted my torch and three more times there was no catch. Then, just as I felt I could take the cold no more and was about to say I'd had enough, he stopped my arcing beam and lunged forwards, to be rewarded with a flash of gleaming scales. "Ha!" He muttered with satisfaction, as he flicked the stick back over his head towards the bank where our boots stood, the socks stuffed clumsily into their open necks. Then he grabbed the torch and was off, splashing at full pace through the foam, seemingly with no thought either of the cold or the potholes. Instead, his gaze followed the torch's beam, fixed on the spot where the fish lay flapping on the turf.

In my excitement I too plunged forwards at breakneck speed, only to be rewarded with the fate that I'd so narrowly avoided on the way over – I tripped and fell headlong into the river. The chill of the water hit me like a blow to the solar plexus, my breath rushing out in a frantic gasp. As I gulped in sharply, my lungs filled with icy water. I floundered to the shore retching, but found Evan was paying me no attention. Instead he was clubbing the fish with a short little truncheon. "My priest!" he laughed. "I always like to give it the last rites with this, like." The task completed, he handed over the stick which I found was weighted at one end with lead.

I was shivering with the shock and cold of my unplanned dip, but at the same time was filled with a wonderfully warm glow. Here at our feet was a king among fish, his silver seawater scales flushed pink with an Atlantic prawn diet, hooked bill arched like an evil pair of dental pliers. Admittedly he was not a monster, as Wye salmon go, but my excitement endowed him with greater stature. As I looked, he swelled in my triumphant mind's eye from his actual fifteen pounds into a fifty-pound giant. I grabbed him by the gills and held him up in the torchlight, exhilarated.

It was at this point that Evan noticed the lights on the road and instantly hushed me into silence. As we watched the car moved slowly up the road, paused, turned around and returned the way it had come. A few moments later the same procedure was repeated, but as the car mounted the slope another pair of headlights appeared, stopping in front of the first.

In an instant Evan was running for his boots and socks. I stumbled after him and together we thrashed back across the river, somehow managing to keep on our feet as we stumbled through the water and into the overhanging willows on the other side. We carried on up the opposite bank, pausing only when a good fifty feet above the water. Through the rain we could see two pairs of headlights up on the road on the other side of the valley.

Cursing softly, Evan stopped to pull on his socks and boots, whispering urgently for me to do the same. I needed no encouragement, but as I followed his lead, found I had lost one of my socks somewhere along the way. This was no time for comfort, however, and I pulled on my boots regardless, lacing them up hurriedly before following Evan further up the bank. We thrashed on through the hanging oak wood – mercifully too closely-cropped by sheep to be covered with brambles, nettles and bracken – and after ten minutes or so, I found myself gasping for breath next to Evan on a piece of flat ground.

"The old railway," he hissed. "It's easy going from here." And with that, he darted off again.

I jogged after him, but was so out of breath, I found I could barely manage a walking pace. Also, it turned out that Evan's dismissive description of the terrain was optimistic to put it mildly. True, the ground was vaguely flat, but the railway had not been used for a very long time and much of it was little more than squelching bog, littered with deep puddles and strewn with fallen rocks from the high cutting on our left.

A few minutes later, just as I had decided to throw in the towel rather than take another step, Evan hissed at me from the darkness on my right. "Come up here – we'll pause a while here, see how the ground lies, like." I felt like replying that if it was anything like as rough as that we had just covered, I'd rather pay the £1,000 fine but, perhaps fortunately, was too out of breath to do anything but make a strange whistling sound.

Evan was intent on the road on the other side of the valley and as I fought to cool down my red-hot throat and aching lungs, I suddenly found myself preoccupied with paranoid thoughts of my missing sock. What if the authorities found it and used it to trace me? Thoughts of all those TV detective dramas flashed before my eyes as I imagined white-coated scientists extracting DNA from my sodden sock.

As I began to regain my breath, a different problem emerged – now I had stopped running, the cold was ripping through my drenched clothing. Evan was still watching the other side of the valley intently, scanning the hillside 200 yards away for torch beams or headlights. He was so intent on his purpose, so determined not to be caught, that I began to fear he would never allow us to begin our journey back home but, fortunately for my pride, before I had to beg him to abandon his natural caution, the sound of my chattering teeth won him over. Later he was to laugh that the racket was so loud he thought the bailiffs would be able to track us down by that alone, but at the time he merely grunted that we should descend to the side of the main road as a first step. As we approached the tarmac, he paused once more by a clump of bracken, pulling back the ferns to shove both fish and gaff into the foliage. He carefully rearranged the fronds so there was no sign of disturbance and then – for the first time since we had left the gravel beds – he flicked on the torch to check all looked natural. He took in everything in an instant and switched the light off immediately. There was another brief rustle of leaves as he made his final adjustments and we descended to the road where we hid once more.

The next few minutes seemed to take hours as we watched headlights move rapidly up and down the main road. Eventually I saw him stiffen. A car came slowly up the main road heading northwards, indicated and turned up the valley we had just left. It pulled into the lay-by nearest the main road and waited, lights still blazing. Then the headlights went off and the internal light went on. Although separated by 150 yards and a river, I could clearly make out Bel reaching into the back seat to pick up Jack. As we watched she lifted him into her arms and began to breast-feed.

I could have cried for joy. Without waiting for Evan's approval I was off, bounding down the hillside, running fit to burst as if convinced she would drive off without us. I could hear my partner's footsteps behind me – evidently he was equally sure the coast was clear – and a moment later we were tapping on the car window.

Bel showed no surprise at the sudden sound in the dark, but quickly got out of the driver's door and moved around to the passenger side, the baby still clamped to her chest. As I turned the car around, she explained what had happened.

"I was in the lay-by, waiting for you, when I saw headlights coming up the road ahead. As they got nearer, I was sure it was the police, but decided I was being paranoid. I stayed put, hoping it was a farmer, but of course it pulled up and a policeman came over to ask if everything was all right.

"Fortunately, at that point Jack began to cry, so I said the baby had been screaming all evening and in desperation I'd taken him for a drive. I'd stopped here to check he was really asleep and their interruption had spoiled everything and would he really mind if I got going before I lost my marbles completely! Of course with that he melted and went back to his car. As soon as he was well past, I gave a few hoots on the horn and began the circuit back to town. I reckoned it would take you a while to make it up on to the main road. All the same, you had me worried: this is the second time I've done the rounds."

The next morning we were back to pick up the fish, and after a careful reconnaissance to check the coast was clear, soon had it safely stored in the carrycot in the car's boot, hidden under a couple of blankets. We weighed it when we got home – it was a splendid 14 lb 5 oz cock fish, still flushed red with his seafood diet.

There was only one possible fate for a monster such as this – he would have to be smoked and I hurried down to see Bill for advice. He gave me a fertiliser sack full of fresh oak chips from his latest sculpture and a fistful of rudimentary smokehouse designs. This process, it turns out, is far simpler than one might think, the basic principle being to immerse whatever one wants to treat in as much cold smoke as possible. All I had to do was pipe smoke from a smouldering fire into a largish box where I'd hang the fish.

I returned home and, after some thought, began to hammer and saw. If I say so myself, I came up with a pretty good prototype. The oak-chip fire was housed in an old oil drum and a piece of discarded drainpipe led from this to a huge wooden box constructed from recycled wooden pallets. It looked ghastly and when fired up smoke billowed from the thousands of cracks which peppered its surface, but the important thing was that the smoke was cold and – in theory at least – the contraption seemed serviceable.

Certainly, when Bill came up to cast his eye over my handiwork he nodded sagely in approval. "It'll work," came his curt blessing as he helped me hook the fish on to the broom handle stretched across the top of the chamber.

It looked good enough to me and as we lowered the top on to the box, I swore that when our hard-earned catch emerged, it would form the basis of a meal to remember.

I hardly need add that I was in seventh heaven. My interest in poaching was one of my oldest romantic obsessions, predating even falconry and self-sufficiency. I had always admired the men who pitted their wits and ancient skills against the system – and now I was one of them.

Better still, I had an impressive trophy to prove it. As I lay down to sleep that night next to the already dormant bodies of Jack and Bel, I felt like one of the happiest, richest people in Britain. As far as quality of life was concerned, I was now a millionaire.

GRAVADLAX

1 filleted salmon
4 ozs castor sugar
4 ozs fine sea salt
1 bunch fresh dill

For the sauce
1 tbsp Dijon mustard
1 tsp sugar
1 lemon
Salt and pepper
2–4 fl ozs olive oil

For the salmon: Chop the dill finely, reserving a little for the sauce. Mix the sugar and salt well and spread a thin layer on the bottom of a high-sided dish. Scatter a little chopped dill on top and then lay a salmon fillet on top of this, skin side down (if necessary, cut the fillet in half or thirds to fit the dish). Scatter another layer of salt/sugar on top, add a salmon fillet skin side down, then a layer of dill on the exposed flesh, repeat process, building it up in layers. When finished, place a plate on top of the pile and weight lightly. Place in the fridge overnight.

For the sause: Cream the mustard, sugar, lemon juice, salt and pepper in a small bowl. Then slowly dribble in oil as if making mayonnaise. Finally stir in a little chopped dill.

Serve like smoked salmon – on brown toast or rye bread.

December: Bel

On December the first, Jack mastered the ability to crawl.
Within a week he was shifting at near breakneck speed.
We were totally unprepared. Until now we had been able
to place him in one spot and be assured that he was free
from harm in the safety bubble we had created around
him. A crawling baby, however, wants to boldly go and
seek out new worlds beyond his boring bubble. Jack
needed to know what was in those cupboards, what was
behind the rubbish bin, what it felt like to climb stairs on
his own, how many objects he could stuff into the video
recorder. Our house resumed the mantle of 'deathtrap'.
From the moment he first crossed the room, our days
were consumed with following him around the house and
foiling all his best plans.

One of his greatest wishes was to try to suck the oozing
home-made cider out of the demijohns in the larder. Dan
settled this battle by announcing the time had come to
bottle and drink this strange-smelling concoction. The
murky liquid had cleared enough to embark on a tasting
session and Dan invited Evan and Bill over to put their
expert palates to the test. Olek declined as he was off to
London to make a commercial about pork pies.

To soak up this experimental drink, we retrieved the

salmon from the smoker. The result was very different in colour from the shop-bought product we were used to. It had a sort of grey sheen and a much darker hue. It tasted absolutely wonderful, particularly on home-made granary bread, though it looked rather unappetising. Dan cracked open the cider and filled our glasses. I stuck my nose in the glass and took a deep breath. I came up with a head rush from the alcoholic fumes and the intensity of the apple aroma lurking in this thick, cloying, astringent liquid. I took a sip and the burning alcohol fought all the way down my throat till it laid siege in my stomach, leaving a trail of throbbing tissue. For a minute I was speechless while my body went into shock. I was left with a dry prickly feeling at the back of the throat.

Evan was banging the table. "That's damn fine brew you have there, like. It's got a lively little character I would say, perhaps a little heavy, like, but very... very... *sure* of itself." He spoke in a hoarse whisper. Bill had gone a little red in the face, but agreed he thought it had potential, although it seemed to have taken the fermentation process rather seriously. Dan was pleased with his efforts and they got stuck into another glass for a second opinion. I bowed out, telling them that if I wanted to feel that awful it would be easier to drink lighter fuel.

By about eleven I could no longer understand what they were saying and went to bed. Through the thin floor-boards of our bedroom, I could hear them singing James Bond theme tunes extremely loudly. Bill was taking the main vocal and Evan and Dan were the backing. The only reason I know it was James Bond was because, through the general unintelligible incoherency, there were sporadic grand crescendos of 'Live and Let Die'. Then they all tried their hand at Sean Connery impersonations and muffled sounds of 'Yesh Miss Moneypenny' ricocheted around the house. Unable to sleep because of the din, I went downstairs to find them still sitting in the same chairs they had occupied at the beginning of the tasting.

Dan said he had tried to move, but had temporarily lost the power of his legs owing to the cider's powerful anaesthetic effect. Bill said it was time for him to weave home and stood up. Steadying his balance, he gave a salute, opened the door to the larder and disappeared. He reappeared a moment later from the small cul-de-sac and complimented us on our choice of condiments before choosing the correct door. Evan then said he might just have a quick rest on the sofa before wending his own way home, as Dan stumbled from his chair and walked towards the stairs. Until I saw Dan trip, tumble and crawl his way to the bedroom, I did not realise it was possible to fall upstairs.

The next day I suggested that we should donate the cider to the army for research into chemical warfare. Dan wouldn't hear a word against his drink, but this was more due to the fact that any noise was like torture to his head, which was clearly horribly poisoned by the abuse of the night before, rather than a result of any genuine liking for the potion. He might have been tempted to tip the remainder down the drain if a procession of friends and neighbours hadn't begun to arrive at the door over the next few days. It seemed Evan had been talking and now every home-brew fan in Powys wanted to test our cider on their thick heads. Dan's vows never to touch the stuff again were drowned by the obligations of rural hospitality.

During one of these scenes of indulgence the revelry was disturbed by the arrival of Fred Hir-Rhiw with a sombre face and a dead sheep. He pulled the carcass from the back of his Landrover on to the lane and pointed out various wounds. "You see these bites here? Well that's badger or dog, I reckon, and my money's on the dog. It would have to have been a big dog." The farmer shuffled his feet and avoided our eye as he continued. "I have to ask – has your big brown dog been wandering on his own much?"

We looked behind us to find most of our cider-drinking guests standing subdued on the terrace looking blearily down at the sheep. They were nodding and mumbling. I noticed Bracken had crawled under our car.

We had lived in sheep-farming country long enough to realise the severity of the crime. Anything responsible for the death of a sheep had, by unwritten law, to pay for it with their own life. I might have thought that Bracken was innocent, but two days earlier I had seen him out of the window with his teeth wrapped around the back legs of a ewe. I shouted to Dan who instantly dropped everything, leaving Jack perched on top of the ferret cage, to retrieve the wayward dog. He gave him an almighty rebuke and then we forgot about the incident, hoping that it was a one-off.

Dan admitted that it could have been our dog. I expected the farmer to get out his shotgun and start shooting, but instead he was rather saddened. "There is nothing worse than when your dog finds the wolf in 'im," he said. "You'll never cure a dog that has the taste of blood. Your best bet is to put him down, the quicker the better in my opinion – I'll do it if you want."

Thanking him for his understanding, Dan offered to pay whatever compensation was needed and promised to deal with the dog. Later when we were alone, he asked what I thought we should do. Once, I might have grabbed this opportunity to rid ourselves of yet another turbulent canine, but not even I could face sentencing Bracken to death for following his natural instincts. Dan thought it was our only avenue, but I totally surprised myself, convincing him that perhaps we could find an alternative home free from fields of tempting sheep? I took on this task and rang every friend who might have the space and possibly the inclination to adopt a sheep murderer. I tried hard to sell the dog's positive qualities.

"He is a very... long dog, with brown eyes. He doesn't eat much and he can run fast," was my main sales pitch.

I met with stony responses from our entire address book. Then I tried the RSPCA, who were too busy even to talk to me and the lurcher rescue centre advised me to move to a more suitable area for the breed. The local rescue kennels told me to be kind to the dog and put him down. Another told me of a revolutionary dog training tool: an electric-shock collar which you could operate from a remote control. I argued with Dan that this sounded absolutely excellent and it would be worth investing in such a contraption to save poor Bracken's life. "Who knows, maybe Dill would benefit too?" Unfortunately it cost hundreds of pounds and my arguments fell flat.

Dan went to see Fred Hir-Rhiw to explain the situation. He expected him to be anxious to hear of Bracken's demise as was his right, but the farmer seemed positively relieved. "I once had to shoot one of my own dogs and I swore I'd never do it again," he said. "No one likes to see a dog killed. You're doing something about it, that's the main thing."

The whole episode plunged Dan into a depression. I would find him late at night drinking the explosive cider, while patting Bracken who lay asleep at his feet. I began to be seriously concerned about his mental state, but fortunately the flow of curious drinkers was such that the stash of cider soon ran dry and Dan was saved from a permanent alcohol-inflicted vegetative state.

His return to sobriety was timely as the moment had arrived when our two enormous pigs, Pork and Bacon, were due to live up to their fateful names. They had reached the required weight and we needed to leave enough time for the preserving process for us to be able to eat home-made Parma ham for Christmas.

As usual Dan was over-confident that he understood the necessary techniques to cure pork. He dismissed the actual slaughter as quite easy in principle: all you needed was a long sharp knife, a large vessel of boiling water and lots of buckets. I flicked through our battered copy of John Seymour, which had diagrams of a suspicious-looking man carving up a pig with a large hacksaw. The pig was winched up on a pulley and the man was sawing the pig's head off, collecting blood and pulling the guts out of its gaping stomach. Apart from the fact that my mental condition was not up to witnessing this gruesome process, as novices, for us to attempt this operation was verging on the irresponsible. After I had reminded him of these diagrams, he agreed that perhaps it was rather a big operation to tackle on our own. I rang around some local butchers to see if we could employ a professional to perform the deed and spoke to several potential pig-killers, all of whom expressed problems with the proposal.

"You have to scald 'em with boiling water," said one. "Have you got anything big enough? It makes one hell of a mess, you know." It all sounded so disgusting that I wondered if we should drive to the forest and set them free. Dan was still keen to do the dastardly deed at home, but he agreed it presented insurmountable problems and instead we plumped for the local abattoir and booked them in for a frosty December morning.

To mark such an auspicious occasion, I decided to make a short film with the video camera that I had borrowed from my mother. I made a title board and called it: *Bring Me the Heads of Pork & Bacon Garcia.* I had filmed the pigs the day before as they scampered about their field without a care in the world. The abattoir wanted the pigs early and since it was a forty-minute drive, we had to get up before first light. This was far earlier than I was comfortable with, but I needed to be there to include the next shot of my film of Dan coaxing them with a bucket of sow nuts into the borrowed trailer. I sensed a tension in his voice as he patted them and talked gently of green fields and rotten vegetables. I felt my cinematic project was showing all the signs of being a classic, if unbelievably tasteless.

Eventually we were on the road in our 1955 Landrover. We were both feeling a little guilty about the fact we were taking Jack on a trip to an abattoir before he'd even been to a museum or zoo. The car was shaky and noisy, but this was an important scene for my film and as we rolled along I asked Dan subtle probing questions.

"So how do you feel about the fact that the animals you have formed a close relationship with, taken for walks, fed and cared for these last ten months, are hours away from being shot in the head and chopped up into small pieces so you can have sausages for breakfast?" I asked.

Dan looked a little peaky. "It is going to be fine," he said, quickly. "I don't feel too bad." I could sense he might break and thought this would add the drama my film needed.

"Although the escapes were frustrating, won't you miss their curly tails skipping across the lawn towards freedom?" I persisted. "Their expectant piggy faces as you go to feed them in the morning? How much they clearly enjoy it when you scratch behind their ears? I know I will. And the next time you see them you'll be pushing bits of them through the mincer."

Dan was running his hands through his hair. I had him on the ropes and I think he might have cracked had we not arrived in the nick of time at the abattoir. A man asked us to back the trailer up against the entrance and Dan recovered his composure as he concentrated on attempting to steer into the desired space. But, every time he turned the wheel the loose box turned in the opposite direction. Unused to backing trailers, he found it impossible to guide the pigs to the right place. I got out of the car to pan a wide-angle shot and then zoomed in on the abattoir men laughing. At Dan's sixth attempt I began to worry that he might be feeling a little stressed and suggested that it might be an idea to let someone else have a go. Dan scraped his self-respect off the car floor and slumped to the gate. I followed with my camera, not wanting to miss any expressions.

The abattoir man backed the Landrover to the gate in a single smooth movement. Two other men opened the trailer door and the gates to the holding pens. I positioned myself so I could film Pork and Bacon bouncing out of the trailer, scampering down the ramp and down a passage which led to the holding pens inside a large redbrick building. These were clean and roomy with an interesting mosaic effect on the walls. The most extraordinary feature was the PA system which was softly playing Chopin's *Nocturnes*.

Dan, with Jack on his shoulders, leaned on the gate to the pen containing Pork and Bacon. The pigs seemed remarkably nonchalant considering their impending fate. I shoved the camera in Dan's face and asked if he would like to say goodbye now? He obliged by giving them a final pat. Just then one of the men came up.

"So how would you like the meat cut?"

Dan stumbled slightly and leaned against the pen. Obviously not wanting to appear too sentimental, he tried to look as if he was thinking hard. I think the camera captured his dilemma as I focused on his hand gripped tightly around the lock. I told the man that we needed four hams, two sides for bacon, some fillets, loins, belly and the four hands and shoulders which we would process for sausages. As he nodded and made some notes in his pad, I asked what would happen to the pigs next.

"Oh they will lay up here for an hour or two – I should think we will kill them in the afternoon and chop them up tomorrow. You can pick them up Wednesday."

"How do you kill them?" I asked.

"Oh we use the stun gun, it's very quick and they don't have time to squeal – much."

We took a last look at our piggies and climbed back into the Landrover. Dan was quiet and I resumed my task as documentary film maker. I put on my most understanding and sensitive voice. "I guess they are being prepared for the slaughter room now, do you feel guilty at all?" I said.

He gulped. "I shouldn't, they lived twice as long as they could have hoped for with a commercial farmer," he said weakly. "They've eaten well, had a varied diet, a good-sized run, plenty of sun, mud to roll in and each other to frolic with." His voice tailed off.

We had a quiet drive home as Dan reasoned with himself and he seemed to have resolved his guilt until we arrived home and he turned to put a tea bag in the pig bucket. He became despondent and stood looking at the poignantly half-full bucket. "What's the point of keeping a bucket, now," he said. "What are we going to do with all this waste?"

The day came to pick up the chopped-up pigs and to begin processing. I let Dan go alone as I didn't think another trip to the abattoir would lend much to my promising home-documentary. However, I was ready with the camera as Dan pulled up in the car with the six large boxes of meat chunks. He laid out all the meat on the worktop in the garage. We stood there looking at the mountain of protein. Dan admitted that he now found it rather easy to divorce himself from where the meat had come from. I knew what he meant, Pork and Bacon had been reduced to pork and bacon, the kind of meat you might buy at the butcher's. The abattoir had removed the trotters, curly tails and heads. There was nothing to link the meat with our poor late lamented pigs.

Processing the meat took an inordinate amount of time. We froze the chops as they were and buried the sides in salt to make bacon while the hams went into an old bath filled with some bizarre concoction pinched from an old French charcuterie book. This left the sausages. For these we had borrowed a mincer and sausage-filling attachment for our old Kenwood. Dan took a couple of hours to chop the shoulders and hands into ready-to-mince pieces, while Jack and I went to town to buy all manner of ingredients that could conceivably be mixed with the meat and shoved into a sausage casing.

For health reasons the abattoir would not supply us with Pork and Bacon's own guts, traditionally used to encase sausage meat. This seemed extremely sensible to me, but Dan was disappointed, he seemed to have completely recovered from his period of mourning and his love of good food had taken over as he busied himself making up recipes and marinades. We drove down to the town to buy something suitable, to be told by the butcher, "You'll be needing a lot of gut. I'll give you three tubs of sheep gut: that's about 600 feet."

He gave us the casings in polystyrene take-away coffee cups: they looked absolutely foul, but by now Dan was excited and suggested a slap-up tea in The Valley Cake Shop to prepare ourselves for our long night of sausage-making. Jack sat in a high chair and worked his way through a selection of muffins, while Dan and I worked out what ingredients we might marry to create the perfect sausage. As we talked I was vaguely aware that there seemed to be some commotion in the kitchen of this small friendly establishment.

The proprietess, Angela, was speaking in a tense whisper to Dr McBain who was busy filling out some sort of form. The Doctor left and Angela went to speak to the waitress who was standing in front of the loo door. Suddenly the front door opened and four formally dressed undertakers entered, each carrying a corner of a coffin. They walked past our table and I recognised one man as the butcher we had just been talking to and another as the owner of the local newsagent's. The former nodded at us sombrely.

With the arrival of the coffin, the waitresses left their posts. As the head undertaker opened the door, I could see an elderly lady sitting on the loo with her head slumped forward resting on the washbasin through the gap. A large lady was at the counter talking to Angela. "I just left her here while I did some shopping, she said she was dying for a cup of tea," she was saying tearfully. "We were off to the car boot this afternoon – she wanted to find a new doily for her tea table. You can find some very good bargains at the leisure centre car boot. Have you been? It's very good."

The undertakers were finding it impossible to manoeuvre the coffin within the cramped layout of the loo and in the end they had to lay the box in front of our table. Then they lifted the body with a 'one two three lift' and shuffled out with the old lady. They placed the corpse in the box, sealed the lid and carried it out of the coffee shop. As the butcher passed he turned to Dan. "You'll be wanting to keep that gut moist and I wouldn't leave it lying around for too long." The newsagent gave us a wave and told Dan that his copy of *Cage and Aviary Birds* had arrived if he wanted to pick it up. And with that they left, disappearing around the corner to where the hearse was parked.

We returned home to prepare for our night of sausage-making and I began to wonder if the bizarre events were a bit much for my soft middle-class upbringing. So we opened a bottle of cold white wine and, thus fortified, I felt better equipped to tackle the task. As soon as Jack had fallen asleep on the sofa we began. Dan showed a particular talent for the mincing while my expertise was best employed shoving the resultant purée into the casing without splitting the gut.

The sensation of squeezing meat into gossamer-thin small intestine ranks as one of the most peculiar tactile experiences I have endured. Needless to say, throughout the process I had the camera fixed on a tripod and by using the remote control I could film the best moments of the two of us elbow-deep in pig meat. By midnight and a few bottles of wine later we were becoming very inventive with our sausage filling. Having started out with traditional recipes of leek, chilli, spinach and nutmeg, we graduated to the more bizarre combinations of orange and walnut, apple and port, peas and whisky, Madeira and cep and sherry and fennel.

We finished at three a.m. with 80 lbs of assorted sausages in the freezer. Dan had also made some herb salami which apparently is just raw pork stuffed in a casing and hung for three months where it ferments anaerobically. Whatever the theory, Dan's creation looked disgusting and I suggested a nice place in the garage where it could hang quietly and grow its mould away from delicate baby lungs.

I now had time to return to my Pekinpah role. I was pleased with the material I had so far, but I felt it needed a grand finale. I decided the last frame should be Sunday lunch with a large pork loin on the table accompanied by our garden vegetables. Olek and Miranda came, which might not have been the best plan considering her sensitive nature towards animals. She was rather shocked to discover the origin of her meal. Olek dismissed her vegetarianism as 'namby-pamby' and an explosive discussion ensued which, of course, I duly captured on camera. After some careful editing and the addition of suitable subtitles, I made copies and sent them to friends. They wrote back quickly saying it was one of the most disturbing home movies they had ever heard about let alone seen, and suggested I seek psychiatric help.

The mixed reviews of my brilliant film made me reassess whether it was appropriate as a Christmas present for assorted relatives. The festive period was to be split between Dan's parents in Oxford and mine in London. The trip to the two cities would be the longest time I had spent in urban surroundings since our defection to Wales and I was especially looking forward to spending quality time in large retail stores. We had offered to provide a large portion of the food for both families from our own resources. Four geese had been saved for the main meal, accompanied – naturally – by some of our now infamous sausages.

Although Dan seemed to have forgotten about Pork and Bacon, I knew that really he missed having them about the farm. He had loved the way that 'they had instantly recycled all our kitchen waste, but I think he also just liked them for being pigs. So I decided to buy him another one for Christmas, but this time a big sow whom he could breed from and he would only have to bid good-bye when her natural life came to a close. After some rooting around I found a two-year-old Oxford Sandy and Black called Phoebe, who lived with some chickens in a hut owned by a schoolmistress on the other side of town. Obviously I could not disguise the pig sufficiently to hide her in our luggage for Dan to unwrap on Christmas Day, but I could pack a photo. I tied some tinsel around her neck and took a close-up colour picture.

A few days before we were supposed to leave, the skies went a dark thick grey and it began to snow heavily, with hard frosts at night. The day of departure came and there was no let up in the weather. Dan didn't think this presented a problem because we could use the car as a giant sledge to get down the hill, but he did concede that getting back up would be a little more taxing. Because his sliding idea was clearly insane, I let him test it on his own while Jack and I travelled behind in the Landrover, but as I watched him skid and slide the four hundred feet down to the main road it looked rather fun and I wished I had gone with him. We left the Landrover out of the way with some tow rope in the back for our return journey.

The first part of our holiday in Oxford was relaxing, especially since Dan's parents lived within spitting distance of some major department stores. As soon as we arrived he went off shopping on his own and I hoped that he was concentrating hard on picking out the perfect present for me. On Christmas Eve, he totally surprised me with the gift of an old wooden mushroom knife and a beautiful antique wicker collecting basket. In return I gave him the picture of Audrey the pig. At first he was under the impression that I had simply given him an unimpressive photo of a pig. When I explained that his present was the two-hundred-and-fifty-pound pig he could not quite believe that I had actually bought him a live pig. I had to repeat it several times before he accepted the reality.

On Christmas morning we left Oxford for my mother's house in London. Once there, I left Dan with my Mother and Jack while I went to walk around the streets where I had lived for the first twenty-nine years of my life. The neighbourhood felt as familiar as if I'd never left and I enjoyed walking past shops I had known since I was a child. I thought of all the changes to the area that I had witnessed over my lifetime: the terrible bands that used to play upstairs in the Wimpy, which then became a supermarket and was now a kitchenware store. Then there was the Queensway cinema where I saw my first X-rated film, which later became a health food bar and then a hairdresser's. I remembered wandering through the market, picking up junk which I never used and the late-night film shows at the Electric cinema (always *Eraserhead*, I seem to remember). Then I walked past the house where I had lived in the street where I had played for endless hours, past friends' homes where I had watched videos, talked and drank tea. I thought of all the parties I had been to in flats, disused churches and in musty reception rooms above pubs. As I looked at the deserted delicatessens; the bars where I had spent evening upon evening; the empty restaurants where I had eaten hundreds of meals; my favourite bookshops and cafes; I realised how much I had missed them. For a few hours I felt very comfortable as I walked around and I began to wonder if I belonged back here with what I knew best.

The day after Boxing Day the city came back to life and the shops were open for the sales. Everybody poured out of their houses and into their cars to shop or return to work. Jack grew restless indoors and I put him in the pushchair to wander the streets again, but this time it felt very different. On Christmas Day the city had been empty, but now I had to share it. Everyone was jostling to achieve their individual objectives and the sheer volume of people and cars seemed to have doubled in the long year I had been away – or maybe I had just forgotten the incredible crowds. I felt unused to sharing my space with so many others and Jack looked alarmed by the noise and continual movement around him. By the time we returned to my Mother's house I actually felt ill from the exhaust fumes.

The holiday came to a close and we were back in the car heading for Wales where the frozen snow had melted sufficiently for the car to make it up the hill to our own secluded home.

New Year's Eve would mark the end of our first year in Wales and we had invited friends and family down for the occasion. Surprisingly, more than we had anticipated accepted the offer, which presented problems considering the size of our dining table. We decided that, with a little imagination, we could use the adjoining barn for our party. It was as old as the house and in a terrible condition, but it did have electricity, a roof and walls, of sorts.

To make it more comfortable, Dan built a crude fireplace from some old bricks (there was no need for a chimney – the smoke would have no problem filtering out of the holes in the slates and walls). I decorated the interior with the abundant local holly and mistletoe and put shades on all the naked bulbs. Then we fixed up a long trestle table and found some old folding chairs in another of the outhouses along with a box of old church candles and some tall cast-iron candlesticks (a previous resident of our house had been a Church warden). Our only problem was going to be the cold west wind blowing incessantly through the holes in the masonry and slate, but at least we had two gas heaters which could kick out serious amounts of energy and, together with the fire, should be enough to keep us thawed.

Dan and I had spent some time discussing the food for the evening. Eventually we decided to cook three large geese, dig up some new potatoes from the cold frame and uproot some celeriac, parsnips and leaf beet. The parsnips were baked with parmesan and the celeriac chipped and fried in goose fat with breadcrumbs. It took hours to prepare. Our city friends and family arrived looking slightly apprehensive and distinctly chilly. Fortunately the wood-burning stove was working at full blast, fuelled by some particularly dry ash which was burning a treat. The house felt warm and dry and the dreadful draughts which had plagued us the previous winter had been fixed and sealed. We managed to squeeze most people in and the overflow were happy to sleep in the village pub.

We had invited everybody we had met locally over the last year to the party. Olek brought some special vodka he had been saving for such an occasion; Evan arrived with a hare and a large sea trout and Bill presented Dan with the wood carving of the hawk that he had so admired for the last six months.

Lit by candles and storm lanterns, the barn looked stunning with its thick stone walls, small oak-framed windows and beautiful roof constructed from enormous wooden beams and trusses. Olek was the first to point out that the barn would be wonderful if it were to be converted. Then everybody seem to notice and comment on what a beautiful extension to our house it would be. Dan was electrified by the thought.

"The potential is incredible, it would make our house twice as big," he said filled, as ever, with enthusiasm. He spent the next hour tapping the walls and measuring the floor with his feet. I could see that this was an idea he would not relinquish easily. We discussed the various different ways of converting the space, as we sat on the hay bales arranged in a semi-circle around the brick fireplace. Thinking seriously about it, I could see that it would be fantastic, but that it would also tie us to staying there for at least five years, maybe more.

I don't really like New Year's Eve with all the attendant pressure to enjoy yourself, but our party was wonderful. The food was spectacular, and we were all bonded by the beauty of the setting and the freezing weather blowing outside. Bill brought out his guitar, an occurrence which would usually send me running for cover under the table, lest somebody break into a rendition of 'Cum-bi-ya', but not this time. He played some local folk songs which Evan accompanied with the most wonderful singing voice. Some of the best were in Welsh and for each of these Evan gave a summary explanation. "This is old local Welsh song, like. It's about a lake very near where we are sitting tonight: an enchanted lake, like. It describes how beautiful the lake is, with its purple waters, silver shores and pearl-coloured fish. Around it, a thick green forest is filled with fairies who only come to drink in the dead of night. The song says that if you sit there for long enough you can hear a maiden's voice carried on the wind, singing a song so lovely that you are frozen to the spot, unable to move for its bewitching powers, like. This is the lake of truth and anyone who can stay there all night will know the truth of their hearts. When I was a child, like, folk around here still believed the story of enchantment and some were afraid to go down there lest they discovered something they would rather not know."

Evan then sang the song. It was hauntingly beautiful.

Dan's imagination had been so captured by Evan's song, he wanted to visit this mysterious enchanted lake. I was similarly intrigued by this local legend that was apparently on our doorstep. Evan declined to accompany us on account of his leg playing up and described the quickest route to find the lake. The rest of the party were too warm and comfortable to move, except for Olek and Miranda who were equally interested. We packed on layers of clothing and walked with a torch the two miles down to the lake.

After half an hour of downhill trudging, we reached the final approach. A nearly full moon flooded the countryside and we had little need for the torch. The forest was full of mature oaks surrounded by a bedding of sphagnum moss. It *was* the wild wood from *The Wind in the Willows* and around every large tree I looked for a weasel or stoat who might be ready to ambush us.

Eventually the trees cleared and we entered an enclosure, centred around a glistening lake. The moon gleamed off the smooth surface and it was immediately obvious why stories had developed about such a place. Olek and Miranda sat on a bank to wait for the maiden's voice. Dan and I climbed some rocks by the side of the water. From the top we could see the lights of our house and the vague outline of our buildings in the bright moonlight. As we stood on the highest outcrop staring at the view, I had to admit this was an incredible place. Dan listened, entranced, to the tawny owls who were calling to each other, warming up for next spring's breeding season.

I looked up the valley at our home glowing dimly through the dark and thought of our son fast asleep in his bed. I still had some reservations about living in such isolation, but at that moment I knew at last that I could be really happy here.

STUFFED GOOSE

For the Goose:
10 lbs free-range goose
2 lbs prunes
(or dried mixed fruit)
2 lemons
10 ozs Brandy

For the gravy:

Goose giblets
1 oz duck fat
4 rashers bacon
1 onion, 1 carrot
3 sticks celery
1 tbsp flour
2 pts chicken stock
½ pt dry white wine
1 tbsp redcurrant jelly
Salt and pepper

For the goose: Soak the prunes and zest of the lemon in the brandy and lemon juice overnight. Next morning, prick the skin of the goose thoroughly and pour two kettles of boiling water over it (this lifts the skin off the flesh and helps it crisp properly). Leave to dry by an open window for two hours. Then rub the skin with salt, stuff with the brandied prunes and put in a hot oven (425°F/220°C/gas 7) on a wire rack. After 30 minutes reduce the heat to (350°F/180°C/gas 4) for another 2½ hours. Do not baste, but drain off fat carefully for roasting potatoes. Remove from heat and allow to stand for 15 minutes before carving.

For the gravy: Meanwhile, brown the bacon in a little goose fat. When crispy, add the giblets and chopped vegetables, brown and stir in flour. After a moment, add stock, wine and jelly. Simmer and add any juices (but not fat) from the roasting tray. Strain and serve.

Epilogue

It is four years since we arrived at Allt-y-Gwalch and Bel's last doubts have vanished. With work about to start on the barn conversion and Jack enrolled in the village school, we are firmly committed.

Of course there are still problems – nothing has changed to alter the weather – but Bel now recognises rain is necessary for her beloved mushrooms. For all her initial suspicion, she has become a skilled mycologist and this autumn we gathered over a hundredweight of perfect porcini. This is far more than we could ever consume in a year, but fortunately Olek and Miranda are only too willing to help out during our frequent communal meals. We've even introduced Bill and Evan to the experience, although admittedly the lure of home-made beer is even more powerful than any culinary creation.

We have also learned from our mistakes. The garden has been transformed since our first clumsy efforts with rotovator and muck. Bel always takes visitors to the asparagus beds and soft fruit, but I maintain that the compost bins are the main attraction. We're also justly proud of the orchard we planted after our cider experiences, not to mention three hundred yards of hedging (the excessive length was thanks to my miscalculation in the nursery).

Instead of expensive visits to Hereford market, I now buy duck and goose eggs locally to hatch under bantams. These range free in the meadow, thus keeping food bills and horticultural damage to a minimum. Audrey, successor to Pork and Bacon, has just given birth to eight piglets which she is nursing contentedly in the sty, while Gwen is paired up in the aviary – although so far without results.

In April 1997 a daughter, Molly Megan, was born in Hereford and is a model of good humour and health.

November 1997